THE LIFE OF
SIR ALEXANDER FLEMING

Some other books by André Maurois

BERNARD QUESNAY
THE ISLAND OF THE ARTICOLES
BYRON
COLONEL BRAMBLE
A HISTORY OF ENGLAND
THE THOUGHT-READING MACHINE
CHATEAUBRIAND
CALL NO MAN HAPPY
A HISTORY OF FRANCE
THE QUEST FOR PROUST
LÉLIA: THE LIFE OF GEORGE SAND
VICTOR HUGO
THREE MUSKETEERS

Sir Alexander Fleming: a portrait by Karsh

ANDRÉ MAUROIS

THE LIFE OF
SIR ALEXANDER
FLEMING

DISCOVERER OF PENICILLIN

Translated from the French by
GERARD HOPKINS

and with an Introduction by
PROFESSOR ROBERT CRUICKSHANK
formerly Principal of the Wright-Fleming Institute

JONATHAN CAPE
THIRTY BEDFORD SQUARE · LONDON

FIRST PUBLISHED IN GREAT BRITAIN MAY 1959
SECOND IMPRESSION, MAY 1959

★

Translated from the French:
La Vie de Sir Alexander Fleming
© 1959 by André Maurois
English version © Jonathan Cape Ltd, 1959

PRINTED IN GREAT BRITAIN IN THE CITY OF OXFORD
AT THE ALDEN PRESS
ON PAPER MADE BY JOHN DICKINSON & CO.
BOUND BY A. W. BAIN & CO. LTD, LONDON

CONTENTS

	INTRODUCTION	9
	FOREWORD	11
I	IN THE BEGINNING WAS SCOTLAND	17
II	THE TWISTS IN THE PATH	30
III	THE NATURE OF WRIGHT	39
IV	FLEMING AND WRIGHT	54
V	THE PRENTICE YEARS	66
VI	THE WAR OF 1914-18	83
VII	CHILDREN AND MEN	98
VIII	FIRST HOPE: THE LYSOZYME	109
IX	THE MOULD JUICE	123
X	PENICILLIN	131
XI	A NEW MAGIC BULLET: THE SULPHONAMIDES	143
XII	THE OXFORD TEAM	159
XIII	WAR AND GLORY	176
XIV	SIR ALEXANDER FLEMING	193
XV	THE NOBEL PRIZE	206
XVI	ENVOY EXTRAORDINARY	221
XVII	THE SILENCES OF PROFESSOR FLEMING	241
XVIII	THE DELPHIC ORACLE	246
XIX	TOO SHORT A HAPPINESS	260
	EPILOGUE	274
	BIBLIOGRAPHY	281
	INDEX	287

ILLUSTRATIONS

Sir Alexander Fleming. A portrait by Karsh   *Frontispiece*

Fleming at the door of the little school-house of Loudoun; as a young clerk in the City about 1900; and at work at 29 York Street   *facing page* 32

Fleming as 'Private 606': a cartoon by Ronald Gray, 1910; and in the hospital laboratory where the discovery of penicillin was made, about 1925   33

Captain Fleming in the laboratory at Boulogne   112

Tears embedded in the form of a T in agar which was then flooded with a coccus   112

Lady (Sareen) Fleming (died 1949), and Robert; and one of Sir Alexander's own paintings done at Barton Mills   113

Fleming's drawings of the inhibitory effects of lysozyme and egg white on the growth of bacteria   128

Fleming's original laboratory notes on the first use of penicillin to cure bacterial infection in man; a colony of the mould *penicillium notatum* on solid medium; and the mould as seen under a microscope   129

The original mould growth of *penicillium notatum*, and Fleming's drawing and notes on its anti-bacterial action on staphylococci   192

Fleming printing photographs of bacterial plates in the darkroom of the Wright-Fleming Institute; and a typical photograph of a colony of penicillium showing its inhibiting effect on the growth of various micro-organisms   193

Florey, Chain and Fleming at the presentation of the Nobel Prize by the King of Sweden   208

Fleming and Sir Almroth Wright   208

ILLUSTRATIONS

The little lab. at The Dhoon; and the photograph of it which Sir Alexander inscribed for Amalia Voureka   209

Lady (Amalia) Fleming; and with Sir Alexander in Rome, September 1953   264

Alexander Fleming as a young laboratory worker; and in his last years   *between pages 264 and 265*

Sir Alexander Fleming in 1954 in his last laboratory at the Wright-Fleming Institute. A photograph by Douglas Glass   *facing page 265*

On the endpapers are reproduced some of the paintings Fleming made with bacterial pigments (see page 153)

INTRODUCTION

THE biography of a great and famous man requires much research and study by the biographer, not only regarding the subject of his portrait but also about the environment in which his hero has grown up and lived. We are today increasingly conscious, both in health and illness, of the important influences which heredity, on the one hand, and environmental factors, on the other, have upon our lives and destinies. M. André Maurois has painted this picture of Sir Alexander Fleming against the backgrounds of boyhood on a Scottish hill farm and manhood in the bacteriological laboratories of a London medical school. It would be idle to deny the effects of early experiences on the Ayrshire farm or of Sir Almroth Wright and others in the Inoculation Department at St. Mary's Hospital in moulding the life and shaping the destiny of the discoverer of penicillin, while he, himself, and others have been impressed by the curious concatenation of circumstances which seemed to direct his footsteps.

But these outside influences and, later, the glittering prizes and the adulation of kings and commoners in many lands could not mask the innate qualities of a man who, through all his trials and triumphs, remained staunchly true to himself and to his ancestry. For Fleming had, to a remarkable degree, those qualities which we attribute to the Scots: a capacity for hard and sustained work, a combative spirit which refuses to admit defeat, a steadfastness and loyalty which creates respect and affection, and a true humility which protects against pretentiousness and pride. He had other great gifts which helped to make him an outstanding scientist: keen curiosity and perceptiveness, an excellent memory, technical inventiveness and skill of a highly artistic order, and the mental and physical toughness that is characteristic of great men in many walks of life.

The picture of the man and the scientist emerges for us from the background of laboratories and test-tubes and pipettes, antiseptics and antibiotics, Paddington and Chelsea and the country house in Suffolk, Greece and Spain and the Americas. The appraisals

9

and letters of friends and colleagues are interspersed with his own terse remarks in his diaries, notebooks and letters; and through it all goes the thread of continuous effort to lay bare the truth about the body's fight with infection, which was Fleming's abiding interest. It is a fascinating story for all of us, and Fleming's part in it, leading up to the discovery of penicillin, will surely never be forgotten. It was left to others to develop penicillin as a lifesaving drug, but Alexander Fleming and penicillin will always be linked together in the public mind and his name will be remembered with those of other great men, like Louis Pasteur and Joseph Lister, who have made major contributions to the conquest of disease.

As his colleague and successor, I salute this fine portrait of a great man.

ROBERT CRUICKSHANK

FOREWORD

My choice of subject may seem surprising. I have written about poets and novelists and men of action; never about research-workers. That in itself was a good reason for doing so. In an age when science is transforming human life for better or for worse, it is natural that we should take an interest in the scientist, in the way his mind works, in the nature of his investigations.

But why Fleming? I might answer, plausibly enough, that the importance of his discovery was sufficiently great to determine my choice. As it turns out, however, the initial decision was not mine at all. In November 1955 I received a letter from Lady Fleming in which she said that she very much wanted me to write a life of her husband, who had died in the early part of that year. The suggestion excited me and I replied that I was prepared to discuss it.

Lady Fleming came to see me in Paris. Being, herself, a doctor and a bacteriologist, she was able to explain very exactly the nature of the problems with which I should have to deal. She promised to make her husband's papers available to me. But, persuasive though she was and tempted though I felt to try my hand on so unfamiliar a subject, I was still uncertain about my ability to do what she wanted and asked for more time in which to think over the proposal.

There were good reasons for my hesitation. For one thing, a scientist, I thought, would produce a far better book than I could hope to and, for another, the character of Fleming, a silent and secretive man, would be difficult to portray. But difficulty is itself a challenge and I felt eager to accept it. Several French friends — Professor Robert Debré and Professor Georges Portmann, who had known Fleming, as well as Dr Albert Delaunay of the Pasteur Institute, who promised to instruct me in such bacteriological knowledge as I should need — were encouraging.

I began my literary career as a young man with *The Silences of Colonel Bramble*, a taciturn Scot. There would, I felt, be a certain satisfying intellectual symmetry about writing, in my old age, *The Silences of Professor Fleming*. The two men had much the same

11

virtues, though in different forms. The mixture of quiet humour, of loyalty and independence, of reserve and intelligence, were precisely what I found attractive. To cut a long story short, I said 'yes'. I do not regret my decision. By studying at close range the methods and the way of life of those who are engaged in scientific research, I have learned a great deal. But there is more to it than that. I very soon realized that there was no lack of human drama in an existence which on the surface appeared to be remarkably uniform. The relationship between Fleming and his master, Almroth Wright, contained a number of dramatic elements. To live in a laboratory is to be one of a group, and this life I have done my best to describe. As to my hero, the better I got to know him, the more attractive did I find him.

I should never have been able to collect the necessary evidence and documentary material but for the unwearying and generous help given to me by Lady Fleming. Thanks to her, I was able, on my visits to London, to meet almost all those — scientists, doctors and friends — who had played a part in Fleming's career. Among them I was surprised and delighted to renew acquaintance with Dr G. W. B. James to whom the 'Dr O'Grady' of my first book owed so many of his paradoxical and brilliant ideas. The threads of which our lives are woven sometimes cross in the most unexpected, strange and helpful manner.

To mention by name all those who have been so kind as to tell me, to write to me, or otherwise to record their memories, would make too long a list. They will be found mentioned in the course of this book wherever I have occasion to quote from them. Let me here express the gratitude I feel. First and foremost I wish to thank Lady Fleming, but for whom this book would never have been written; and, next in order, Mr Robert Fleming, Sir Alexander's brother, who has provided me with many invaluable details of his early life. I am no less beholden to Dr Albert Delaunay who not only undertook, with great patience, my instruction in a field of knowledge which for me was strange and difficult, but also read more than once my manuscript and proofs. Finally I owe a debt to Professor Cruickshank who, as Fleming's successor as Director of the Wright-Fleming Institute, has done me the honour of writing the Introduction to this volume.

A. M.

To
AMALIA FLEMING

ACKNOWLEDGMENTS

Grateful acknowledgment is made to the Society of Authors and to the Public Trustee for permission to quote from *The Doctor's Dilemma* by George Bernard Shaw and from the Preface to that play; to the Editor of the *British Medical Journal* for permission to reprint his editorial on p. 276; to Karsh of Ottawa for permission to reproduce the frontispiece portrait; to the Keystone Press for the photograph of Lady Fleming facing p. 264; and to Douglas Glass for the last photograph facing p. 265.

THE LIFE OF
SIR ALEXANDER FLEMING

CHAPTER ONE

IN THE BEGINNING WAS SCOTLAND

As a good Scot, I was in my youth taught to be cautious. FLEMING

THE Scots are not Englishmen. Far from it. They have often governed England; they have given to Great Britain many of her leading men; they have ranked among her greatest soldiers. But they think of themselves as belonging to a different race, and with good reason. The Scottish nation is a mixture of Celts from Ireland and Wales, of Angles and Scandinavians, of Teutons and men from Flanders. For a long time it had a close connection with France. Scotland, at first Catholic, then Presbyterian, has always refused to adopt the liturgy and hierarchy of the Anglican Church. In the sixteenth century, and again in the seventeenth, in circumstances of the utmost gravity, the Scottish nobles, bourgeoisie and peasants signed a solemn Covenant in which they promised to be faithful to their Church. In the nineteenth century the spirit of the Covenanters was still very much alive. Though Presbyterianism had become less narrow, it was still austere. The Sabbath was strictly observed. Scotland was never touched by the raffish scepticism which had been so prevalent among the English aristocracy of the eighteenth century.

Poverty, combined with severity of manners, produced a race of dour, courageous men. The soil of their country was far from rich, means of communication were largely lacking, the climate was harsh. A Scottish farm could support only a single family. The younger sons left home, first for the University where they lived frugally sometimes off the oatmeal which they took with them in a bag slung over their shoulders, and later for England, where many of them achieved brilliant success by dint of sheer hard work. Their austere and penniless childhood had made them economical. In England their stinginess was a standing joke, as, too, was their language, thick-sown with Celtic words, and r's

B   17

which they rolled with the noise of pebbles in a mountain torrent. The English laughed, too, at the absence of humour with which (so they said) these northern immigrants were afflicted. It took hours of hard work, they maintained, to drive a joke into a Scotsman's head.

This picture was very inaccurate. The Scots have their own sense of humour, which is utterly unlike that of the English, who love long stories full of mockery and sentiment. The Scots, on the other hand, delight in a humour which is laconic, dry, vigorous and expressed with a perfectly straight face. Their reputation for niggardliness, too, is only in part deserved. Careful with their pennies they may be, but they are generous with their millions, when they have made them — often at the expense of the English. In their country, hospitality is a noble tradition. Over against the rigid Covenanters must be set the romantic figures who haunt the pages of Sir Walter Scott, their appeal heightened by their picturesque equipment — kilts of varied and famous tartans; bagpipes; the glengarry and the long-haired sporran. The Scots have always been rash and gallant fighters, from the days of Bannockburn to the two world wars. A fire burns deep within them which they do their best to conceal.

It is customary to distinguish Highlander from Lowlander, though, in fact, the two types have, to a great extent, become merged as the result of migrations and intermarriages. The Lowlander, like the Highlander, is emotional, romantic and passionately Scottish, and more than anything else he dreads giving himself away; whence come his stubborn silences and his dislike of exhibiting his feelings even when — especially when — they are strong. This attitude has, no doubt, been intensified by English mockery. We know from Boswell how that eminent Englishman, Dr Johnson, spoke of the Scots. His sallies were, no doubt, the product of a wish to amuse rather than of malevolence: still, jokes at their expense have had the effect of creating in the Scots a definite inferiority complex. That is why they try to make themselves less vulnerable by maintaining an outward show of unconcern and secretiveness. It accounts, too, for something in them which amounts almost to aggressiveness. The Lowlanders are given to teasing. They do not take easily to praise and are fonder of pointing out faults than acclaiming successes. According to their code, eulogy should be preceded by disparagement. They are mentally stiff-jointed, which to some extent explains their liking for whisky, which is a great loosener.

To sum up — a fine race, brought up in a hard school, richly endowed with strange traditions, secretly romantic and cautiously touchy.

Fleming is a common name in Scotland. It was, no doubt, originally given to the weavers and cultivators who fled overseas from religious persecution in the Low Countries. The grandfather of our Fleming, Hugh, was born on the family farm of 'Low Ploughland' in the County of Lanark in 1773. He married the daughter of a neighbouring farmer, Mary Craig. The Craigs had been settled at 'High Ploughland' from far back, as is clear from the fact that a Craig carried the banner of Avondale at the battle of Drumclog in 1679.

Children came thick and fast, with the result that these farming families 'swarmed', some of their members moving to London, others to the neighbouring counties. Hugh Fleming, Alexander's father, had leased from the Earl of Loudoun a holding of eight hundred acres, called Lochfield. It lay close to the meeting-point of three counties, Lanark, Ayr and Renfrew, though it was actually in Ayrshire of which it formed one of the boundaries. It was on high ground in a remote countryside. The nearest house was a mile distant and, since the public road went no farther, few people passed that way. The climate made the growing of corn impossible, but the cultivation of oats and forage and the grazing of sheep and cattle provided a livelihood for the hard-working family. The house was approached over a chain of green hills interspersed with winding streams. Behind it lay a wide expanse of moorland. Dwarfed by these vast and treeless distances, a man should surely come to have a proper sense of the world's greatness and his own humility.

Hugh Fleming had married twice. His first wife bore him five children, one of whom died in babyhood. The names of the surviving four were Jane, Hugh (the eldest son who would inherit the farm), Tom and Mary. The father married again when he was sixty, this time, Grace Morton, a neighbour's daughter, by whom he had four more children: Grace, John, Alexander (known as Alec) who was born in 1881, and Robert.

All that the younger boys remembered of their father was a kindly old man with grey hair who was always ill and spent his time in a chair by the fire. He had had a stroke and knew that he would not live long. He felt a deep concern about the future of his family. Hugh junior and his stepmother ran the farm and Tom had left home for the University of Glasgow, where he was studying medicine. What was to happen to John, Alec and Robert? Would their elder brothers help them? His knowledge of Scottish tradition reassured him on this point: of course they would. His second wife, a remarkable woman, had succeeded in uniting the children of the two marriages in a common bond of affection.

The young people were physically attractive, with vivid blue eyes, frank and open expressions, and a way of looking their fellows straight in the face. Alec, a sturdily built boy, with fair hair, an unusually high forehead and a sweet smile, was his mother's own son. He spent his days with his two brothers, John, his elder, and Robert, known as Bob, who was his junior by two years. All three of them enjoyed complete liberty. A large farm in the heart of the country makes a world rich in discoveries for lively boys with the gift of curiosity. When they were not at school, they explored the valleys and the moors. Nature, their first and best of teachers, developed their powers of observation.

In the two rivers of their countryside, Glen Water and Loch Burn, they fished for trout and learned to know the habits of that wily fish. Loch Burn was little more than a stream, though fed by a strong head of water. It was the type of river loved by trout because it never dried up completely. On the moors there were hares and rabbits in the glens. The boys had no guns, but set off on their hunting expeditions accompanied by an old dog with a good nose who was adept at locating the dense turfs in which the rabbits hid. They slipped their arms in, Alec from one side, Bob from the other, and it was agreed between them that the one who could first lay hold of the animal's hind-legs should have the right to claim it as his own. This playing at trappers demanded an unusual degree of speed and skill.

They also employed another method which was their own invention. On fine summer days the rabbits left their burrows and sheltered among the bushes. The boys walked slowly over the area which they had decided to beat. When they came upon a motionless rabbit, they pretended not to have seen it and continued to move forward with their heads raised. They had noticed that a rabbit never takes to flight so long as the hunter's eye does not meet its own. Then, just as they were passing the animal, they pounced upon it. No adult could have played that particular game, for his pounce would have been too slow. The boys, however, who at that time were very small, won every time.

There was an abundance of birds on the hills, but partridges and grouse were regarded as sacred. The Earl of Loudoun made as much money out of his shooting rights as he did by farming. Spring brought peewits which nested on the pasture land. The boys had noticed that these birds prefer places where the cows feed to those cropped by the sheep, the reason being that where sheep have fed there are always scraps of wool left on the ground, in which the young birds get their feet caught. The grouse, on the contrary, will venture on to the sheep-runs because their young are stronger.

The taking of a few peewits' eggs was not forbidden, and these the boys could sell for fourpence apiece to the travelling salesmen who sent them to London where they were looked upon as great delicacies. In this way they managed to make a little pocket-money. But this looking for eggs, too, required keen observation and a knowledge of the fact that the mother-bird, when she sees a man or an animal approaching, runs through the grass and goes some distance from her nest before flying off, in order to conceal the actual position of the nest from the intruder. John, Alec and Bob looked for the nests at a point well away from the place at which the hen had taken flight, and usually found the eggs, of which they took only a few so as not to destroy the species.

The winters were hard. The Atlantic gales swept across the hills and covered the roads deep in snow which had to be shovelled away to enable the carts to fetch the necessary food. At night, when the wind was heavy with snow, this could be noted because of a changed note in its whistling. At such times, as soon as it was light, the moors had to be searched for buried sheep. A yellow patch produced by their breathing made it possible for the seekers to find and rescue them. That, too, was one of nature's lessons.

Experiences of this kind taught Alec Fleming how to apply his powers of reasoning to what he observed, and to act in accordance with his observations.

When he grew older, he took part in the annual sheep-shearing day. Seven or eight men did the actual shearing, while another brought the sheep to them and yet another made the wool into bales. Alec helped in the rounding up of the animals. He loved the work. 'The countryman', he once said in later life, 'may have to work harder for his living than a townsman, but he has a man's life. He does not do the same thing day after day.'

He began to go to school when he was five. It was a small place about a mile from Lochfield and served the needs of the children of the surrounding farms. To get there, the boys went down into the valley in all weathers, crossed the river on a wooden bridge without a rail, clambered up the farther bank, and so reached the school. One day, John and Alec, caught in a sudden snow-squall, lost their way. When it was very cold, as Alec later recounted, their mother sometimes gave each of them two piping-hot potatoes to keep their hands warm during the walk and to provide them with a hot meal on their arrival. When it rained, they took a change of boots and stockings slung round their necks. On fine days they went to school barefooted. This caused them no embarrassment, for, out of the twelve or fifteen pupils, nine were Flemings or their friends and neighbours, the Loudouns.

There was only one teacher, a young woman of about twenty. She was in sole charge of a collection of children of all ages. Alec remembered two successive ones, Marion Stirling and Martha Aird. They must have been truly devoted to their calling, for how else would they have been willing to fill the post of teacher in so remote a spot? Discipline was elastic. After the midday meal, when the weather permitted, the teacher took her class down to the river. So long as the children were enjoying themselves, she conveniently forgot the time. But this did not prevent her teaching from being serious and efficient.

Sometimes an inspector would climb the hill to the moorland school, and question the children. His trap could be seen from a long way off and, if it so happened that the party had lingered by the river when they should have been in school, mistress and pupils hurried back by a short cut, entered the class-room by a window at the back, and were all in their places, the children at their desks, the mistress in front of her blackboard, looking very serious, by the time the inspector arrived. Everything went off well and the mistress was all smiles, which meant that she had been complimented. She taught reading, history, geography and arithmetic.

When the two young Flemings were, respectively, eight and ten, they moved on to the school at Darvel, the nearest town. But all through his life Alec maintained that the better part of his education was what he had learned in the little moorland school, especially in the course of his daily walk to and from it. 'I think I was fortunate in being brought up as a member of a large family on a remote farm. We had no money to spend, and there was nothing to spend money on. We had to make our own amusements, but that is easy in such surroundings. We had the farm animals, and the trout in the burns. We unconsciously learned a great deal about nature, much of which is missed by a town-dweller.' Boys who live in towns do their studying from books. The young Flemings had something better — a living book.

Though not top of his form, Alec worked well at the Darvel school, to reach which he had to cover four miles, morning and evening. These long journeys on foot made of him in later years a man who scarcely knew what it was to be tired. It was at this time that an incident occurred which altered his appearance by giving him the flattened nose of a boxer. One day he happened to run round the corner of a wall just as another boy, named Jackson, who was smaller than he was, collided with him. Fleming's nose came into violent contact with the other's forehead. The cartilage was broken. He bled profusely and, when the swelling had subsided, the change in his looks was clearly visible. Since he suffered no more pain, it was not thought necessary to call a doctor. Alec Fleming had a boxer's nose for the rest of his life, but, though it considerably altered him, it did not make him ugly.

When he left the Darvel school at about the age of twelve, plans had to be made for his future. Should he work on the farm or should he continue his education? His mother and his elder brothers decided that he should attend the Academy at Kilmarnock, an important Ayrshire town which boasted a museum, a monument to the poet, Robert Burns, and a celebrated cheese fair. A railway line was in course of construction from Kilmarnock to Darvel, but was not yet completed. This meant that each Friday evening and Monday morning he had to walk the six miles which lay between the farm and Newmiln (the last station on the line). 'That kept me fit', he used to say, 'and did me a lot of good.' The Academy, which was situated in a large building on the top of a hill, was an excellent school where frequent examinations were held which kept the boys on their toes.

'There were fifty or sixty pupils in each class. Not much chance of individual attention. But we worked well. The headmaster was considered to be a pioneer in furthering the study of science in schools. We studied two science subjects each year, mostly theoretical: inorganic chemistry, physiography, magnetism and electricity, heat, light and sound, and physiology.' But this science teaching, according to one of Fleming's contemporaries, was 'primitive', and it would be interesting to know how much benefit Alec derived from, say, the instruction in chemistry which he received at Kilmarnock. The answer to that question is — very little.

This family of farmers attached enormous importance to the education of the young. Alexander Fleming was sent, at different ages, to the best available school in the neighbourhood. The Scots have a sincere respect for learning. Since many of them have to leave their native land and carry on a hard fight for success in London, they know how essential it is to arrive in England with well-furnished minds.

Hugh, the eldest brother, was left to carry on the farm alone. Thomas (always called Tom) had settled in the English capital. It had been his intention to set up in general practice and with this in view he had taken the lease of a house at 144 Marylebone Road, close to Baker Street Station. But patients were slow in coming. He made the acquaintance of a retired ophthalmic surgeon who advised him to specialize in this branch of medicine, and offered to undertake his training. Tom accepted, and somewhat later, when his younger brother, John, joined him in London, the old surgeon suggested that the younger man should learn the craft of optician, and found work for him in a spectacle factory. The choice of firm was unfortunate and it was not long before it got into financial difficulties. The calling, however, was an excellent one.

John Fleming and, later on, his brother Robert, succeeded brilliantly at it.

When it was Alec Fleming's turn, at the age of thirteen and a half, to take the road to London, Tom had just put up a new plate on his front door: 'Oculist.' His strong sense of family solidarity led him to take charge of this second brother, though his own position was far from being assured. It was the family that organized and controlled his destiny. Hugh and his stepmother were running the farm until such time as Hugh should marry. Mrs Fleming's cheeses enjoyed a great local reputation and sold well. For a time, at least, Lochfield was in a position to subsidize Marylebone Road. Six months later, Robert joined Alec, and the four Fleming brothers lived together in London, unostentatiously giving each other mutual support in a strange world. One of their sisters, Mary, kept house for them.

It was a violent change to leave trout-streams, rabbit-warrens and birds' nests for life in a great noisy city where trees and grass could be found only in a few scattered parks and squares. 1895 was the glorious high-spot of old Queen Victoria's reign. The Underground Railway, at that time running on steam, shook the house in Marylebone Road every ten minutes or so. The streets were alive with innumerable vehicles — hansom-cabs, trams and omnibuses — all horse-drawn. Alec and Robert Fleming explored the capital from the tops of buses, where they sat beside the driver and learned much about the language of this foreign country by listening to the abusive exchanges between competing drivers and the remarks made by them to passing pedestrians. The brothers visited the Tower of London, Westminster Abbey, the British Museum and the various picture-galleries. They were happy in one another's company though, faithful to the traditions of their ancestors, they spoke little except when they wished to draw attention to some object worthy of interest.

In the evenings Tom was the life of the party. He had a passion for competitions of every description — geography, history, science. Each of the brothers contributed a penny to the pool and the winner took all. This was an excellent training for examinations. One night Tom brought home a pair of boxing-gloves, and substituted bouts for games. But Mary decided that boxing brought disturbance into brotherly love, and put the gloves in the dustbin. It is scarcely necessary to point out that evening games and daily excursions had to give way to work. First Alec, then Robert, attended lectures at the Polytechnic School in Regent Street. Tom, soured by the difficulties he had experienced in his attempt to set up as a doctor, had turned his back on the liberal professions, and now pinned all his hopes on business. Consequently he entered his brothers' names in the Commercial Section where everything was taught except Greek and Latin.

When Alec entered the school, he was at first placed in a class suited to his age. But so advanced did he show himself to be that within a fortnight he had jumped two classes, with the result that he found himself working with boys considerably older than himself. Scottish methods now showed to advantage. In the beginning, the Fleming brothers' accent caused a good deal of laughter, and this made them very shy. After a while, however, they discovered that, since the English are fundamentally a tolerant race and generous to those who have been unlucky enough to be born on the wrong side of the Border, a slight Scottish accent is an advantage rather than the reverse. It is like some physical infirmity which leads others to show an amused pity for the afflicted. At the same time, there are limits to what can be endured, and the dialect of Ayrshire overstepped all bounds. They did their best, therefore, to correct it, though they never ceased to be markedly Scottish in their talk, outlook and behaviour.

In those last years of the nineteenth century it looked as though the lines along which the family was to move had been laid down for good and all. Tom, whose practice was now growing, had taken a larger house at 29 York Street, where he still found room for his brothers. Mary having married, it was the younger sister, Grace, who now looked after them all. Alec had found employment in a shipping company, the American Line, with offices in Leadenhall Street, and four passenger boats, which, though old, were fairly large. At first he earned the 'princely sum of $2\frac{1}{2}$d. an hour'. He did his job extremely well. He did not like it, but accepted his fate with silent stoicism. John and Robert were both working in a factory producing optical lenses. Hugh was still at Lochfield and preferred his life there to that of his city-bound brothers who, however, were still devoted to the farm and regularly returned to it at holiday-time for the fishing and shooting. But, though they showed little on the surface, they were inwardly seething with plans and could not have endured the thought of spending their lives on a remote hillside.

In 1900 the Boer War broke out. Less than three years after the apotheosis of the Diamond Jubilee, two small agricultural republics at the far southern point of the African continent were putting up a successful resistance against one of the most powerful countries in the world. The London crowds at first treated the unequal conflict as a laughing matter, singing songs about Kruger and promising to eat their Christmas dinner with him in Pretoria. But after several grave reverses, a wave of patriotism swept the country. Volunteers flocked to the colours. John and Alec, to be followed later by Robert, enlisted in the London Scottish, a regiment largely composed of men of Scottish descent. Young doctors and lawyers served in it as simple privates, and the relations between officers and men were considerably more intimate than was usual in the British Army.

The London Scottish was a combination of regiment and club. It ran a swimming club and the Flemings, who were good swimmers, played in the water-polo team. Alec, too, turned out to be a first-rate shot. His gifts of observation stood him in good stead on the range. He remained in the ranks and was indifferent to promotion. He had been drafted to 'H' Company, the last one of all, he said, which marched at the tail-end of the regiment where neither drums nor bagpipes could be heard. This meant that the men could keep in step only by a great effort of attention and determination.

'The men of "H" Company', wrote Fleming, 'were self-opinionated, egocentric, and obeyed no rules but their own.' The surprise of the battalion was great when 'H' Company carried off the 'Celestial', which was a shooting trophy competed for annually. This triumph was partly due to Fleming who, on more than one occasion, attended the National Shooting Week at Bisley. Sporting interests play an important part in all Anglo-Saxon communities. They made of this silent little office-clerk, with the fine eyes and the broken nose, one of the favourites of the regiment.

The number of volunteers was so large that the needs of the Expeditionary Force were greatly exceeded, with the result that most of them never went to the Transvaal at all. Fleming was one of those who stayed at home, and was thus able to enjoy the old family life undisturbed. He went on one occasion with the regiment to Edinburgh. Since there was a shortage of seats in the train, he, being the smallest in his party, was accommodated in the luggage-rack, where he remained for the whole of the journey.

Tom, whose practice was still growing, had moved to a house in Harley Street where all the 'successful' doctors lived. Hugh, at Lochfield, had got himself married, and the 'dowager' Mrs Fleming went south to Ealing, where she kept house for Alec, John and Robert. It was a great joy for the three young men to have their beloved mother with them. Tom, now prosperous, had become reconciled to the liberal professions. He realized that Alec's great gifts had no scope in an employment which did not offer him a future. Why shouldn't he take up medicine? Most opportunely, just as Alec turned twenty, Uncle John died and left him a legacy.

Uncle John had been an old bachelor who had spent all his life farming at 'Low Ploughland'. He left his fortune to his brothers and sisters, or their descendants. It must have been pretty considerable for the place and the period, because an eighth part of an eighth part, which was Alec's share, amounted to two hundred and fifty pounds. Tom advised him to give in his notice to his employers at once, and to use this legacy, with a bursary (should he get one), to the study of medicine. Alec, no doubt, would be starting a bit late, but he never regretted the years which he had spent in a business house. 'I learned nothing academic', he said, 'but I gained much general knowledge, and when I went to the medical school I had a great advantage over my fellow students, who were straight from school and had never got away from their books into the school of life.'

It is true that he had this advantage, but he owed it chiefly to the fourteen years which he had spent close to nature. He had learned, without effort, to use his eyes. The harshness of the climate and the habit of work had turned him into a man who could drive himself hard. As a boy he had, without realizing it, become a naturalist with the habit of noticing everything that went on round him. Fully conscious though he was of his own intellectual gifts, he had remained a cautious, taciturn and modest Scot. Under the surface of his reticence there lay a tenacious love of independence and a simple, sensitive heart. The virtue which he most prized, together with a taste for work, was loyalty. He was determined to be faithful to his family, his regiment and his side: to Scotland and to the British Empire. At twenty there was still something of the child in him, the charm of a child, and also of the boy and the good scholar who wants to do well, and does better than his comrades, to whom his tiny triumphs are the source of a deep and secret happiness.

CHAPTER TWO

THE TWISTS IN THE PATH

'I should see the garden far better,' said Alice to herself, 'if I could get to the
top of that hill; and here's a path ... but how curiously it twists ...'
LEWIS CARROLL, *Alice Through the Looking Glass*

IKE many British institutions, the study of medicine in
England was organized in a haphazard manner without any
central plan. Each of the twelve great London hospitals had
maintained a school long before the creation of the University.
When this was founded, the hospital faculties of medicine formed
part of it, but retained, from the days of their independence, the
right to accept students who did not hold the Secondary Schools
Certificate which was necessary before they could enter a university. These students could obtain a special diploma known as the
'Conjoint', which gave them permission to practise general
medicine, but not to have access to the higher levels of the University hierarchy.

Fleming, who had neither the certificate of matriculation
demanded by the University nor any other form of diploma, had to
pass an examination before he could be allowed to enter a school
of medicine. He took a few lessons and then sat for the examination
of the Senior College of Preceptors. There was good reason to fear
that a young clerk who had had no time for study for the last five
years would be in no fit condition to face so exacting a test. But
Fleming had a solid basis of education (which he owed to the little
moorland school), a prodigious memory, a tempered intelligence
which, like a scalpel, cut straight through to the essentials of any
subject, and a natural gift of expression. When faced by any
definite question, he could write with elegance and clarity. He
passed top of all the United Kingdom candidates (July 1901).

With the certificate firmly in his grasp, he was in a position to
make his choice among the available medical schools. 'In London',
he wrote, 'there are twelve such schools, and I lived about equi-
distant from three of them. I had no knowledge of any of these

three, but I had played water-polo against St Mary's, and so to St Mary's I went.' That he should have chosen a faculty of medicine for purely sporting reasons may seem strange. But the fact that he did so reveals a pleasing and constant aspect of his character — a need to combine the fanciful and the serious. He was the least pompous of men, and his mind could adapt itself to an infinite variety of interests.

St Mary's was not a hospital of ancient lineage. It had been founded in 1854 to serve the Paddington district where, since the building of a large railway terminus, the population had rapidly increased. The foundation-stone had been laid by Prince Albert. Fleming entered in October 1901, and while pursuing his studies in medicine was also reading for the matriculation examination of the University, which he passed with ease in 1902. He next set himself to compete against rivals of many different types and upbringing for the senior scholarship in the natural sciences. His most dangerous adversary was C. A. Pannett, a brilliant student with a far more extensive general culture than Fleming could claim. Nevertheless, the latter again came out top, as he was to do in every competitive test for which he entered, all through his life. The dangerous rival became his best friend and has given a partial explanation of these unvarying successes. 'From the earliest days of his career,' Pannett writes, 'one thing was abundantly clear, that he was a first-rate judge of men, and could foresee what they would do. He never burdened himself with unnecessary work, but would pick out from his text-books just what he needed, and neglect the rest.'

Fleming followed with great attention the lectures of those who were to be his examiners, took detailed notes of what they said and, what was even more important in his eyes, made himself familiar with the character of each. Having done this, he described exactly what questions they would set ... and was rarely wrong. He studied his masters, to some extent, as natural phenomena to be carefully observed, and treated the examination papers themselves as a 'special subject'.

This, however, was no more than one aspect, and a secondary one at that, of his success. He maintained that, given sound common sense and a solid knowledge of the basic principles, a man ought to find it easy to improvise the right answer to any question.

Throughout the whole of his University career he triumphed all along the line by making use of these simple principles, though he made light of his successes. His fellow-students found his memory and his powers of observation astonishing. Very few knew him intimately. Either from temperamental shyness or deliberate reserve, he was slow to make friends. He did, however, belong to the hospital Amateur Dramatic Society, and on one occasion played the part of a woman — Fabriquette, in Pinero's *Rocket* — a sprightly French 'widow', 'whom he made a great deal more attractive than that unprincipled female deserved to be'. The supporting feminine role was filled by C. M. Wilson who, in the far distant future, was to be Lord Moran, and Winston Churchill's doctor.

'I do not remember much', says Pannett, 'about his anatomy and physiology period, except that he seemed to do very little reading. Yet he must have worked extremely hard, since he was one of the outstanding pupils of his year. I, personally, took no part in the activities of the swimming and rifle clubs, and so never saw much of him as a sportsman. I wish I had, because there seems to be general agreement that he revealed his true nature at these times. He seems to have excelled in any game or sport he took up. I don't mean that he reached the front rank, but that he always became proficient in the essentials, and so was more than an averagely good exponent.

'I do know that he delighted in making difficulties for himself, just for the fun of overcoming them. For instance, he once undertook to play a round of golf using only one club. In sports he employed the same methods which he applied to his work. He would set himself to grasp the essentials of a technique, concentrate on them, and so win with ease. Because nothing ever presented any difficulty to him, one might be tempted to call him a dilettante, but that would be quite wrong. He was far too serious, too efficient and too brilliant ever to be described as an amateur. He found a sort of elegance and modesty in concealing all effort.

'I never heard him mention history, music or philosophy, and I was surprised to discover later on that he read the poets of whom, not unnaturally, the Scotsman Robert Burns ranked among his favourites. He never showed that side of himself to me. He did not seem to take even scientific treatises seriously, but appeared

Fleming at the door of the little school house of Loudoun

As a young clerk in the City. About 1900

At work at 29 York Street

Left: Private 606 A cartoon by Donald Gray, 1910

Below: In the hospital laboratory where the discovery of penicillin was made. About 1925

PRIVATE 606

to run through them, and, with an economy of effort, get what he needed out of them, store it up in his memory, and with his fertile brain apply it to his own particular researches — a mark of true greatness.

'During our student years, I competed with him for a number of prizes, but since I always came out second, I soon gave up the unequal struggle.'

All those who were St Mary's students in those years have a clear memory of the two invincible champions, Fleming and Pannett, who between them shared all the prizes. The distinctions won by Fleming covered the whole field of medical studies: biology, anatomy, physiology, histology, pharmacology, pathology and medical practice. But in the evenings at home he was always ready to shut his books and play games with his brothers — draughts, bridge, table-tennis. Anyone would have thought he had nothing better to do. 'When he read a medical book,' says his brother Robert, 'he flipped through the pages very rapidly, and groaned out loud when he caught the author making a mistake. There was a great deal of groaning.'

In those early years of the twentieth century St Mary's Hospital, according to Dr Carmalt Jones, one of Fleming's contemporaries, was a pretty gloomy place. There was nothing 'aesthetically attractive' about the public wards, and the Medical School was even worse: squalid in appearance, ill-lit and poorly furnished. The teaching was a great deal better than the environment. The Professor of Anatomy, Clayton Greene, was dogmatic, lucid and frequently amusing. 'He always appeared in the theatre at nine o'clock to the minute, having changed his overcoat for a long white smock. He illustrated his lectures with beautiful drawings on the blackboard in coloured chalks. When the lecture was over, the students went into the dissecting-room.'

After an initial period of instruction in surgical theory, they were admitted to the hospital proper. In the Casualty Department they learned how to open abscesses, how to probe and dress wounds, and even how to pull out teeth, which they did without a local anaesthetic. They had to manage as best they could with the assistance of the house surgeons who knew very little more than they did. Medical treatment oscillated between science and routine. The professors had individual manias which, for the

C   33

students, had the rigidity of law. The first with whom Fleming worked always treated a pneumonia case by applying an ice-bag to the affected lung. But, when he went on holiday, his substitute was found to prefer poultices. Consequently, when the second lung caught the infection, the patient had a poultice on one side and an ice-bag on the other. He recovered.

In 1905 Fleming spent a month attending outside maternity cases. The husband of the expectant mother would fetch the resident student from the hospital and lead him through a maze of side-streets to his wretched home, which often consisted of only one room. When that was the case, such other children as there might be slept during delivery under the woman's bed. 'Fortunately', says Carmalt Jones, 'in ninety-nine per cent of maternity cases, there is nothing to do but to let nature take her course. Or so we thought.'

During the year which he spent in the study of anatomy and physiology, somebody told young Alec that it would be of great use to him to take the Primary Fellowship in surgery. The registration fee was five pounds. Needless to say, Fleming passed. But he never became a surgeon, partly because he had a dislike of operations on living bodies, but mainly because circumstances were directing his feet into a different path. 'However,' he said, 'being a Scot, I never ceased to regret the five pounds which I had spent to no purpose. I wondered whether I ought not, perhaps, to have a shot at the final. I knew my pathology, but had no experience in practical surgery, nor the chance of getting any. Still, the second fee was, like the first, only five pounds, so I decided to try my luck.'

Much to his surprise he passed this far more difficult test and was entitled, as a result, to put the august letters F.R.C.S. after his name. It began to look as though his career was to be at the mercy of a series of curious accidents. He had adopted the medical profession because his brother was a doctor; he had gone to St Mary's, where he was to spend the whole of his life, because of water-polo; he had become an F.R.C.S. because he wanted to justify the expenditure of five pounds; he was to choose bacteriology, to which he later owed his fame, for a reason no less strange and trivial.

★

THE TWISTS IN THE PATH

The two Fleming brothers, Alec and Robert, were still members of 'H' Company of the London Scottish, and as such took part in the annual camps, the various route-marches and the rifle competitions. Alec loved the life, because it brought him in contact with other Scots. Many years later in 1949, by which time he was a famous man, he took the chair at one of the reunion dinners of the few remaining old-timers of 'H' Company which had been dissolved by merger some thirty-five years before.

'You have had as chairmen at these reunions', he said in his speech, 'colonels, captains, sergeant-majors and such-like. But this is probably the first occasion on which a humble private has presided. As a member of the regiment I was always humble. I never disputed an order given by a sergeant or even a lance-corporal. As to officers, I was so insignificant a figure that I don't think I ever got an order direct from any of them.

'To be humble was a great advantage. There was no need for you to think: you just did as you were told. The officers, on the other hand, had to do a lot of hard thinking, since as often as not they did not know what ought to be done. But they had to do something, or pass the buck to the Colour Sergeant. Probably the Colour Sergeant did not know either, but it was more difficult for him to pass the buck (though he did sometimes manage it), with the result that he had to give some sort of order, whether it was right or wrong. The sergeants were always quite sure of themselves, especially when they knew nothing about what was going on.

'It is a wonderful thing in a Company to remain a private, and to watch others doing the climbing. They do it in such different ways, but all of them are interesting. When I joined "H" Company, it was at a low ebb. The other companies said we couldn't shoot, they said we couldn't drill. After five years, they discovered that we could drill *and* shoot. I remember one Whit Monday when "F" Company thought they had everything in their pocket, but the despised "H" Company suddenly woke up and walked off with all the best prizes. I am not at all sure that the Fleming family was not responsible for this. There were three of us shooting that day ...'

★

Ever since 1902, one of the most brilliant members of the teaching staff at St Mary's had been Almroth Wright. He was already celebrated as a bacteriologist, and had created an inoculation service at the hospital. Wright, who was eloquent, paradoxical and something of a genius, had a number of enthusiastic disciples, among them a young doctor called Freeman, a charming and cultivated man with a fine head of curly hair. He was a good shot and anxious to get new blood into the St Mary's rifle club which, after carrying off the Inter-Hospitals Shooting Cup for several years running, had fallen on evil days. Anxious, as he was, to build up a new team, he asked: 'Are there any territorials among the students?'

Someone answered: 'Yes, that little fellow, Alec Fleming. He's in the London Scottish.'

'What's he like?'

'Quite a decent accent, and wins all the prizes. Apart from that, inscrutable.'

'What's his line?'

'Surgery, but if he sticks to that it'll mean his leaving the hospital. There's only one surgical vacancy, and Zachary Cope's bound to get it.'

'Good shot?'

'First-rate.'

Hearing this, Freeman at once conceived the plan of keeping the first-rate shot at St Mary's by getting him into the Inoculation Service. With this in mind, he approached Fleming and tried to imbue him with his own admiration for Wright. After one of the latter's most brilliant lectures, he turned to Fleming and said: 'Wright's a marvel!'

Fleming, moved by a spirit of contradiction, replied coldly: 'What I want is facts. I've heard nothing from him but airy generalizations.'

All the same, as soon as Fleming had got his diploma, Freeman suggested that he should work in Wright's laboratory.

'Look here, I know you're a good shot ... why not join us in the lab.?'

'How can I do that?'

'I'll manage it.'

Fleming, still tempted by the prospect of a surgical career, hesitated. Nevertheless, like all the students, he was fascinated by Wright, and Freeman was persuasive. 'I plugged the fact that Almroth Wright's laboratory would make a good observation-post from which he could keep an eye open for a chance to get into surgery. I told him, too, that he would find work in the lab. interesting, and that the company there was congenial. The lab., at that time, consisted of only one room where the staff lived a sort of communal life.'

It remained to convince the 'Chief', in other words, Wright. Freeman was perfectly frank with him, and talked about his beloved shooting team. Wright thoroughly enjoyed Freeman's whimsical way of dealing with serious matters. Freeman went on to say that Fleming had a scientific mind, and would make an excellent recruit. To cut a long story short, Wright agreed to the suggestion, and Fleming was taken on to the laboratory staff. He never left it until the day of his death.

Such a method of deciding on a career may seem incredible, casual and irresponsible. 'But I don't think', says Freeman, 'that Fleming ever made plans far in advance. He was content to assemble his facts, and then leave Fate to do the rest.' It is not a bad method, for no one can ever be sure of foreseeing the effects of a decision. A water-polo side had led him to St Mary's, and a shooting team to choose bacteriology. Both choices were good.

Many years after these events, when speaking to an audience of students, he said: 'There are some people who think that medical students should spend all their time learning medicine and should give up games. I don't agree. If a student gave up all games and spent all his time reading text-books, he might know his books better than the next man. I say *might*, for it is by no means certain that he would. He would probably have a better knowledge of what was written in the books, but not of the meaning of what he read.

'You should know even at this stage of your career that there is far more in medicine than mere book-work. You have to know men and you have to know human nature. There is no better way to learn about human nature than by indulging in sports, more especially in team-sports.

'When you are one of a team, you have to play for the side and not simply for yourself, and this is marvellous training for a man who hopes to become a doctor. For even a doctor has to play the game of life, not just for his own material advantage, but for the welfare of his patients, irrespective of financial gain.

'Doctors are, in a sense, a team, and the selfish ones who play only for their own personal ends tend to ruin the team-spirit and lower the standard of their profession.

'Play games, and you will be able to read your books with a greater understanding of your patients, and that will make you better doctors ... True, each one of you will, later, have to specialize in some particular part of the body, but never forget that your patients are live human beings.'

Then, speaking of his own youth, he added: 'Sport has had a considerable influence on my own career. Had I not taken an interest in swimming in my young days, I should probably not have gone to St Mary's Hospital: I should not have had Almroth Wright as a teacher, and it is more than likely that I should never have become a bacteriologist.'

The twists in the path are numerous and surprising. But it is the winding road that gets to the top of the hill.

CHAPTER THREE

THE NATURE OF WRIGHT

It is not often that one has the privilege of working alongside a Master, but
Fate arranged that for me. FLEMING

THE Inoculation Department had started life in 1902 in one small room belonging to the old Medical School at St Mary's. When Fleming joined it in 1906, the one room had expanded to two rooms, both tiny, which had to accommodate the Professor, his assistants and such infectious cases as might be sent for treatment from other parts of the hospital. There was no money to spare and the laboratory owed its continued existence to Wright's generosity. At that time he had a rich practice. Millionaires and members of the British aristocracy would call in Wright for the least ailment — for anything, in fact, from a boil to an attack of typhoid. His large waiting-room at 6 Park Crescent was always crammed with patients, and the greater part of his fees served to maintain the bacteriological laboratory (or, as he called it, 'the lab.').

Almroth Wright thought it useful and, indeed, necessary for a doctor engaged on research to remain in practice — so as to 'keep his feet on the ground'. The observation of living bodies confirms — or rebuts — the findings of the test-tube. The spectacle of human suffering arouses, along with pity, the desire to find a remedy — whence his insistence that a clinic should be attached to his department. 'It wasn't at all a bad thing', says Dr Hughes, who later worked there. 'A man engaged on research who finds nothing has an uneasy conscience. The doctors who worked under Wright, when not busy in the laboratory, carried on with their normal professional duties.'

Wright encouraged his assistants to stay in private practice. Actually it was the only way in which they could make a living, for he paid them little: a hundred pounds a year. He maintained that research should be entirely disinterested. 'We don't pay people to do research: they've got to have work outside.'

Salaries and promotion were decided by Wright, the sole master after God. 'This Service', he said, 'is a republic.' In point of fact, it was an enlightened despotism. The dominant personality of the Chief won not only respect but devotion. The Old Man, as he was called by his collaborators, ruled the family like a stern but fond father. This is how Freeman describes him: 'Wright was, at first glance, an almost clumsy figure with large head, hands and feet. As his great friend, Willie Bulloch, the bacteriologist at the London Hospital, used to say of him, he had escaped being acromegalic only by the narrowest of squeaks. His movements were slow and purposeful. He was a big man with the rounded shoulders of a bench-worker and anti-athlete ... He wore spectacles above which showed strongly marked eyebrows which flickered up and down very rapidly when he was amused or being mischievous. He could almost speak with his eyebrows.' But, though his movements were heavy, he could accomplish the most delicate tasks with his great fingers.

His character was a mass of complexities. All things considered, he was a difficult man. His disciples adored him for his genius, for the way in which he made life amazingly interesting, and because his zest, his love of paradox and his vast culture enabled him to be an enchanting conversationalist. But to different people he showed different facets of his personality. With some he turned into a poet, with others into a naughty child. 'You're so mischievous, Wright,' said his famous friend, Balfour; 'that is why we all like you so much!' Gentle and patient with the sick, he could behave to his colleagues with brutal savagery. In a controversy with a celebrated surgeon, he behaved so ferociously that Bernard Shaw, who knew what he was talking about, said: 'It was Lessing who, according to Heine, not only cut off his adversary's head, but held it up to show that there were no brains in it. Sir Almroth, knowing that this is an anatomical impossibility, puts Sir William Watson Cheyne's brains on his operating table and shows that Sir William has never learned how to use them.'

All his life had been a battle. He was born in 1861 of an Irish Presbyterian father and a Swedish mother, the daughter of Nils Almroth, a professor of organic chemistry in Stockholm. From his earliest youth he had shown a spirit of fierce independence. 'Almroth was one of my failures,' said his mother. 'I could never make him do what I wanted; he always went his own way.'[1]

[1] Leonard Colebrook, *Almroth Wright*, p. 5.

Nevertheless, she was very proud of him, and her other children asserted that, if Almroth had committed a crime, she would have said: 'What a fine, manly thing to do!' Since the Reverend Charles Wright exercised his ministry in Dresden, Boulogne and Belfast, Almroth was brought up by private tutors, and acquired an excellent education. So strong was his passion for languages that at sixty-two he learned Russian, and began at eighty to study the Eskimo tongue.

What he loved best in the world was poetry. He knew by heart great chunks of the Bible, Shakespeare, Milton, Dante, Goethe, Browning, Wordsworth and Kipling. He once reckoned that he could recite two hundred and fifty thousand lines. One might have supposed that, with such tastes, he would have embarked on a literary career. He did, actually, think of doing so, and went for advice to the famous Edward Dowden who occupied the Chair of English Literature at Trinity College, Dublin. When his opinion was asked, Dowden said: 'If I were you, I should stick to medicine. It is the finest possible introduction to life and, if you later show gifts as a writer, your experience will furnish you with a precious fund of knowledge.' This verdict was fully justified, because Wright was to become not only a great doctor but also an excellent writer. Bernard Shaw once said to him: 'You handle a pen as well as I do,' which, coming from Shaw, was a very great compliment; in fact, the only compliment worth anything!

Wright's restless and adventurous mind could not remain permanently satisfied with the ordered existence of a general practitioner. He travelled in Germany and France, visiting a succession of laboratories and striking up friendships with German and French research-workers. For a time he read Law and dreamed of being a barrister. He went to Australia and taught in Sydney. But his ultimate choice was scientific research. He had a passionate desire to see 'what lies on the other side of the mountains', to explore new worlds. He had the good fortune to enter the medical profession at the very time when it was undergoing a profound transformation. The two or three previous decades had seen the beginnings of a movement away from medicine-as-an-art and medicine-as-magic to medicine-as-science.

*

Already, before 1860, certain men of science had been thinking that infectious diseases might be caused by microscopic creatures, though they had not supported this hypothesis with any experimental proof. But between 1863 and 1873 a French doctor, Davaine, had demonstrated that one particular ailment, anthrax, was closely connected with the presence in the blood of certain small objects which he called *bactérides*. A German, Pollender, had reached the same conclusion. Between 1876 and 1880, Pasteur in France and Koch in Germany had thrown open to medical research immense and unexplored territories. Pasteur in the course of a long and prodigiously fertile career proved that numerous infections, till then unexplained, were due to the action of micro-organisms which the microscope made it possible to detect in the blood and tissues of the sick. Round about 1877, the word 'microbe' was invented by Sédillot. Little by little, research-workers had succeeded in establishing a catalogue of the principal microbes: staphylococcus, streptococcus, the typhoid bacillus, the tubercle bacillus, etc. ... The German school had taken the lead in devising bacteriological techniques: culture-medium, staining of microbes, methods of examination.

Thanks to the work of the great English surgeon Lister, Pasteur's discoveries had completely revolutionized the practice of surgery. It is difficult for us today to imagine what surgery was like when Lister was a young man. The cases in which it could be employed were strictly limited. A very high proportion of those operated upon died of general infection, as did, also, a large number of women in childbed. This was known as the 'hospital sickness', and it seemed impossible to find a way of dealing with it successfully. A Viennese doctor, Semmelweiss, had pleaded for the adoption of hygienic methods, but in vain. From the moment that Pasteur showed that no infection could take place without the presence of germs, and that those germs were carried by the air, by the instruments, and by the hands and the clothing of the surgeon, Lister realized that by ensuring the sterility of the wound — that is to say, the absence of all septic germs — the 'hospital sickness' could be done away with, that, in fact, it was no sickness at all, but simply the result of a lack of precaution.

The causes of infection had thus been partially explored. It remained to discover a way of fighting them. Certain facts, known since the days of antiquity, might have been of assistance in providing the research-workers with some sort of guidance. When the plague was raging in Athens, says Thucydides, the sick and dying would have received no attention at all had it not been for the devotion of *those who had already had the plague and had recovered from it,* since '*no one ever caught it a second time.*' It was known, too, that smallpox, one of the worst scourges of the human race up to the beginning of the nineteenth century, which killed or disfigured millions of sufferers, never attacked the same person twice. For more than a thousand years in China, Siam and Persia, various forms of deliberate and protective infection — the pricking of certain areas of the skin with contaminated needles, or introducing portions of smallpox scab into the nose — had been practised. In Baluchistan it was the custom to have cows afflicted with cowpox, which was thought to be a benign variety of smallpox, milked by children with scratches on their hands, the idea being that those children would, thereafter, be immune from infection.

European peasants, too, had had an empirical knowledge of these facts. The attention of the English doctor, Jenner (late eighteenth century), was directed to this phenomenon by a girl keeping cows, to whom, because of certain symptoms, he had said that she might be sickening for smallpox. She replied that she couldn't have the smallpox because she had already had the cowpox. This gave Jenner the idea — remarkable at that period — of determining by methodical experimentation the value of such popular beliefs. He took the very venturesome step of infecting perfectly healthy subjects with the smallpox, after first inoculating (in other words, vaccinating) them with the cowpox, and reached the conclusion that in this way they could be given almost complete immunity.

It certainly was an extraordinary phenomenon. On the practical level it led to the elimination (not without displays of violent and absurd resistance) of a universal scourge — the smallpox: while, on the intellectual, it revealed the fact that men or animals, after the injection of a minute quantity of a dangerous virus, became different creatures, better armed against that same virus, something like a country which, frequently attacked, has learned to keep a suitable defence army ready. 'There is', says Dr Dubos,[1] 'such

---

[1] An eminent research-worker at the Rockefeller Institute.

a thing as biochemical memory, which is no less real than intellectual or emotional memory, and, perhaps, essentially no different
from them.' Just as a shock experienced in infancy is enough
to warp the psyche and to sow the seeds of lasting complexes, so
will the simulacrum of a disease produce deep-seated, and sometimes beneficial, changes in the blood. The organism which has
fought against an evil is no longer a novice: ' ... Thou hast
wrestled with me and art no longer the same man.'

Pasteur had given much thought to the great mystery of infectious diseases, and to Jenner's immunity theory. His powerful
mind refused to admit that the case of smallpox was unique. Immunization *ought* to be possible in other illnesses. But how could
the equivalent of vaccine be found which might be used to combat
other microbes? Chance, which so often comes to the help of those
who help themselves, provided him with a key to this problem in
1880. While studying chicken-cholera he was led to two conclusions: (*a*) that increasing age diminishes the virulence of the pathogenic germ; (*b*) that hens treated with attenuated germs are
rendered immune to virulent ones.

In more general terms, he discovered that a germ becomes
suitable for purposes of 'vaccination' when it has been kept for a
long time in contact with the air. (As an act of homage to Jenner,
Pasteur had extended the meaning of the word 'vaccine'.) How
did all these vaccines work? By provoking a defence-reaction or,
more precisely, by forming in the blood new substances, or 'antibodies', capable of helping the organism to fight, when the time
came, against the *non*-attenuated germs. The threat produced a
mobilization of the defending forces. In 1888, Chantemesse and
Widal proved that even a vaccine composed of *dead* germs could
develop in the blood the strength necessary to overcome the
microbe of typhoid fever. About the same time, Roux and Yersin
found the poison, or toxin, secreted by the microbe of diphtheria.
Then one of Koch's pupils, Behring, revealed the anti-toxic power
of the serum of animals (guinea-pigs and dogs) which had been
treated with repeated small doses of the toxins of diphtheria and
tetanus.

A natural extension of the idea led to this armed and mettle-
some blood, this battling serum, being called to the aid of blood
lying under the threat of any contamination. Behring, pursuing

44

this line of thought, had tried the use of anti-sera for the prevention and treatment of some infections. The principle involved was different from that of vaccination. The serum had to bring to the sick or threatened organism *already formed* antibodies. Behring was only partially successful, but Roux tackled the problem again and, this time, with successful results. At the Budapest Congress of 1894, Roux was able to announce to a gathering of enthusiastic doctors that the serum of an immunized horse, injected into those suffering from diphtheria, could bring about a complete cure. The era of serotherapy had dawned. It was no longer merely a question of preventing the onset of the disease, but of curing those who already had it.

When Wright returned to England from Sydney in 1891, and started to look for a suitable opening, he was delighted, after a year spent in doing odd jobs, to be offered the position of Chief Pathologist in the Army School of Medicine at Netley Hospital. There he found a group of young men whom he inspired with his own passion for research and with his desire to see a new system of medicine developed which should be founded on scientific experimentation.

His pupils admired his devotion to science and his aggressiveness. Never had there been a man less suited to get on with soldier-administrators. Very soon Netley was buzzing delightedly with stories: how one day, having hunted high and low for his laboratory sergeant, he had found him taking part in a parade and had, there and then, hauled him off by the collar of his tunic to get busy with what he described to the horrified military as a 'piece of work worth doing': how he had been told by the 'brass-hats' at the War Office, not to talk so much about blood in his lectures, since after all it accounted for 'only one-thirteenth part of a man's weight', and how, in spite of orders to the contrary, he gave each year, to those passing out from Netley, a revolutionary address on 'Physiology and Belief'.

At the time when he was beginning to teach bacteriology — a science then in its infancy — Wright already foresaw a future in which the diagnosis of infectious diseases would be carried out by precise methods and not merely by listening to the patient's chest and saying, as a certain distinguished doctor was in the habit of doing, 'I think I can detect the influenza bacillus ... by the sound.' Widal and Gruber had demonstrated that the blood of a man suffering from typhoid agglutinates the typhoid microbes and that this process, being specific (that is to say, occurring with the microbial family which is the cause of the disease and with no other), makes diagnosis possible. Wright proved that the same held good of Malta fever, a serious ailment which goats (numerous on the island of Malta) can transmit to humans, a fact which led Metchnikoff, who at that time was teaching at the Pasteur Institute, to tell his pupils, not without humour, showing them a map of the world on which the regions subject to Malta fever were marked: 'You will notice that these are all situated within the British Empire. This is not due to any evil influence of the British, but it merely means that they are the only people who have made a study of Malta fever, and know how to diagnose it.'

From 1895 Wright devoted most of his time to working out how immunity to typhoid could be achieved. In those days it was a dreaded and frequently a fatal disease which was particularly prevalent among soldiers in time of war. A Russian bacteriologist, Haffkine, who was working at the Pasteur Institute and paid a visit to Netley, suggested to him that it might be possible to protect human beings against typhoid by preventive vaccination, as Pasteur had succeeded in protecting sheep against anthrax. It was a question in both cases of stimulating the formation of antibodies in the blood. Typhoid was not, as had long been thought, a disease which affected the intestine only. The microbe, in fact, spread through the whole circulatory system and, by making the patient's blood deadly to the microbe, this invasion would be held in check.

Chantemesse and Widal had shown that animals could be vaccinated against typhoid by means of germs killed by heat. Wright developed a simple technique by which the power of the blood to kill bacteria could be measured. This enabled him to establish as a fact that the blood, after inoculation, can kill from ten to fifty times more bacteria than before and conserves this formidable power for several months. He observed that after inoculation there is frequently a negative phase during which the blood loses this power, accompanied by discomfort and fever, after which a positive period ensues. In short, he brought to a successful conclusion a piece of precise research and, sure of his results, was in a position to advise the War Office to have *all* men going overseas vaccinated. This was in 1898. He was the first doctor to use anti-typhoid vaccines on human beings, though Pfeiffer and Kolle in Germany could boast of a similar success at about the same time.

In spite of favourable results in India and elsewhere, the old medical dug-outs of the R.A.M.C. remained sceptical. When the Transvaal war started, Wright, who wanted to have immunization made compulsory in the Army, was allowed to have the operation performed only on those who might volunteer to undergo it. No more than sixteen thousand out of three hundred and twenty thousand came forward. This was a disappointingly small number. Furthermore, it was not easy to follow up the case histories of those who had been inoculated. In the field-hospitals, when typhoid cases were asked whether they had been vaccinated, they were inclined to answer 'yes' from fear of being 'crimed' if they didn't. A story is told of one sergeant-orderly who in his returns invariably showed as having been vaccinated all men suffering from the disease. 'The fact that they've got it,' he said, 'proves as they've been vaccinated.' Wright was so much enraged by the incompetence of official medical practice that he resigned his post at Netley, greatly though he had liked it. In 1902 he was appointed Professor of Pathology at St Mary's.

There he created the Inoculation Department over which he was to reign supreme for forty-five years. At first, his teaching covered pathological anatomy and histology as well as bacteriology. But by degrees he managed to shuffle off these duties and concentrate his attention on immunology. He was now convinced that all infectious diseases could be cured by the action of antibodies, whether those antibodies existed naturally in the blood, whether their production could be stimulated by a vaccine, or, finally, whether they were introduced by a 'foreign' serum. In that direction, he maintained, lay the future of scientific medicine. 'The doctor of the future,' he said, 'will be an immunizer.' The knowledge that traditional medicine had been able to do so little for the cure of patients afflicted with the most serious diseases plunged him into despair. One evening, when he was speaking to an audience of doctors, he wound up his remarks by saying: 'What it comes to is this, that unless our doctors learn to do something useful, they will find themselves relegated to the position of medical orderlies.' Two doctors rose and left the room.

Meanwhile other scientists had been hard at work trying to find an answer to the question: '*How does the organism, in natural condi-tions, protect itself against pathogenic germs?*' Human beings, after all, had existed long before the advent of preventive vaccines, yet many of them must have found a way of resisting the attacks made on them by germs, as is proved by the fact that the human race has survived. How? A scientist of Russian birth, Metchnikoff, working at the Pasteur Institute, had discovered the essential mechanism of this defensive process in the phagocyte. While observing, in the course of his laboratory work, the transparent larvae of star-fish, he had hit on the idea that certain specialized cells, the police force of the organism, provided a defence for living bodies against harmful intruders. He introduced a number of thorns from a rose tree among the larvae. These thorns were soon surrounded and dissolved. This experiment struck Metchnikoff because its outcome so closely resembled what happens when a human finger is in-fected by a splinter. Pus forms. But what exactly is pus? It is a collection of cells, especially of the white corpuscles of the blood which, in the event of inflammation, work their way through the blood-vessels, surround the microbial germs and 'phagocyte' them, in other words, 'eat' and destroy them.

But how do the phagocytes digest the microbes? Thanks to the action, said Metchnikoff, of certain digestive enzymic ferments which, inside the cells, play a part similar to that of the digestive ferments of the saliva or the stomach. Against this cellular theory of immunity the Germans argued in favour of a 'humoral' theory. They believed in the action of the humours (that is to say, of the fluid substances of the body, and, especially, of blood serums).

Wright, who was a friend of Metchnikoff and also of several German scientists, tried to reconcile the two theories. What he had to say about the matter was roughly as follows. In vaccinated or infected subjects, certain specific chemical principles (antibodies) make their appearance in the blood serum and the humours. The effect of these principles is to reinforce the destructive action of the phagocytes by modifying the superficial structure of the germs, on the surface of which they leave a deposit — one might describe it as 'buttering' them — and so facilitate digestion.

With the help of one of his Netley disciples, Captain Douglas, who had joined him at St Mary's, he undertook a series of remar-kable experiments which made it possible to count with perfect clarity the number of microbes swallowed by each phagocyte. Under the microscope the phagocyte showed as a grey patch, and the microbes it had swallowed as black points inside it. Wright and Douglas noticed that the number of microbes which the defence-cells could absorb depended upon the 'preparation' of the microbes by the substance secreted thanks to immunization. One of Wright's favourite amusements was the invention of words drawn from the Greek. He therefore called this property acquired by the blood, which enabled it to 'butter' the microbes in readiness for the phagocytes' meal, the 'opsonic' power, from the Greek '*opsono*' — 'I prepare food for ...', and the substance itself 'opsonin'. In a serum free from opsonin there is little or no phagocytosis, whereas, when opsonin is present in increased strength as a result of infection or vaccine, phagocytosis is considerable.

Wright attached capital importance to his idea. In the first place, it produced a happy marriage between the cellular and humoral theories. True, it is the phagocytes that destroy the bacteria, but *only* when the latter have been 'buttered' or made appetizing by the humoral opsonin. Further, Wright believed that this theory of his made possible the diagnosis of most cases of infection, since infections increase the opsonic power in the blood over the microbe causing the infection, and over that *only*. (As a matter of fact, the modifications, though real, are so complex that it is difficult to interpret them.) Finally, the measure provided by the 'opsonic index'[1] in any given subject should, he thought, open the way to rational treatment by vaccines or serums, since by establishing the percentage of phagocyted microbes the laboratory worker is in a position to determine the quantity of opsonin in the blood and to say whether it increased, or not, under treatment.

When demonstrated with Wright's brilliant eloquence, the theory of the opsonic index seemed to be a stroke of genius. Medicine was at last becoming an exact science! That was the feeling of a few young and highly intelligent doctors and research-workers who, attracted by the great gifts of the master, were prepared to accept the by no means easy life he offered them. The first team was composed of Stuart Douglas from Netley, Leonard

[1] The relationship existing between the opsonic power of the blood in the subject under examination and that of a subject in a normal state of health, taken as the unit of measurement.

Noon, Bernard Spilsbury and John Freeman. The latter was a man of original intelligence and an excellent scientific writer. He entered the lab. in 1903, became one of Wright's favourite disciples, and was called, by him, his 'son in science'. Freeman, until he married, lived with Wright at 7 Lower Seymour Street. At a later date, Fleming (in 1906), Matthews, Carmalt Jones and Leonard Colebrook joined the team.

A team? It would be more accurate to describe it as a brother-hood, something in the nature of a religious order. It was accepted as an indisputable fact by these men that they had a mission, that they were to devote their lives to the service of science, and that they owed unconditional loyalty to Wright. What was it that gave him this prestige in their eyes? His charm, his intellectual brilliance, his personal passion for research, which kept him working in the laboratory until three or four in the morning, and sometimes until daybreak. What was it that made him spurn all pleasures and even a family life in order to count black points in grey patches? Ambition? Perhaps, in part. He loved authority and longed for fame. But, more than anything else, intellectual curiosity and a profound desire to help human suffering, for he was by nature both sensitive and kindly.

According to Freeman, Wright was led by his passion for work so wholly to neglect his own flesh and blood that his daughter Dolly, having to write a school essay on the pleasures of home-life, concluded it with this sentence: 'It is awfully jolly if Daddy can manage to get down on Sunday to see how his family is getting on ...' One day, when Wright, on arrival at the hospital, was hanging up his hat, Douglas saw a piece of white paper fall out of the ribbon. He picked it up, and read: 'Daddy, three times you have forgotten to put more gas in my balloon, as you promised you would. I have put two empty balloons in the inside pocket of your overcoat. Don't forget this time.' Douglas filled the balloons and tied them to the hat-ribbon. Dolly Wright got what she wanted, at last!

It was not only affection and loyalty, however, that accounted for the admiration felt by these young scientists for their master. His genius justified their enthusiasm. Nor were they alone in their feelings, which were shared by many eminent men who had no connection with the hospital. Often, round about midnight, tea was made in a small room next to the lab., and there many illustrious visitors were entertained: biologists like Ehrlich and Metchnikoff; statesmen like Arthur Balfour and John Burns; dramatists like Bernard Shaw and Granville Barker. People came together from every corner of London and, indeed, of the world, to listen to Wright.

In the house of his great friend, Lady Horner, a celebrated hostess, Wright met most of the members of the Cabinet; among them was Lord Haldane, at that time Secretary of State for War, who was responsible for getting him knighted. Freeman, who read the letter in which the news of this honour was communicated to the Chief, says that it ran more or less as follows: 'Dear Wright, we must have your Typhoid Prophylactic for the Army, but I have failed to convince the head man in the Army Medical Service of this. I have therefore got to build you up as a Public Figure, and the first step is to make you a knight. You won't like it, but it has to be ... Haldane.' Wright, at first, wanted to refuse and said in a disgusted tone: 'They'll even shove it on my gravestone!' but in his heart of hearts he was very pleased.

One evening, when Bernard Shaw was drinking tea in the lab., the question arose of whether a new patient should be admitted. Freeman said: 'We've got too many cases on our hands already,' and Shaw asked: 'What would happen if more people applied to you for help than you could properly look after?' Wright replied: 'We should have to consider which life was best worth saving.' Shaw laid a finger to his nose, and said: 'Ha! I smell drama! ... I get a whiff of a play!'

Not long afterwards, a certain Dr Wheeler, who was a great friend of both Shaw and Wright, warned the latter that Shaw was making him the hero of a play. That was true: it was called *The Doctor's Dilemma*, and it was impossible not to recognize Sir Almroth Wright in its leading character, Sir Colenso Ridgeon. In the first act there is a passage between Colenso Ridgeon (Wright) and an infinitely sceptical doctor of the old school:

SIR PATRICK What did you find out from Jane's case?
RIDGEON I found out that the inoculation that ought to cure
    sometimes kills.

51

SIR PATRICK I could have told you that. I've tried these modern inoculations a bit myself. I've killed people with them; and I've cured people with them; but I gave them up because I never could tell which I was going to do.

RIDGEON (*taking a pamphlet from a drawer in the writing-table and handing it to him*) Read that the next time you have an hour to spare; and you'll find out why.

SIR PATRICK (*grumbling and fumbling for his spectacles*) Oh, bother your pamphlets. What's the practice of it? (*Looking at the pamphlet*) Opsonin? What the devil is opsonin?

RIDGEON Opsonin is what you butter the disease germs with to make your white blood corpuscles eat them.

(*He sits down again on the couch.*)

SIR PATRICK That's not new. I've heard this notion that the white corpuscles — what is it that what's his name — Metchnikoff — calls them?

RIDGEON Phagocytes.

SIR PATRICK Aye, phagocytes: yes, yes, yes. Well, I heard this theory that the phagocytes eat up the disease germs years ago: long before you came into fashion. Besides, they don't always eat them.

RIDGEON They do when you butter them with opsonin.

SIR PATRICK Gammon.

RIDGEON No: it's not gammon. What it comes to in practice is this. The phagocytes won't eat the microbes unless the microbes are nicely buttered for them. Well, the patient manufactures the butter for himself all right; but my discovery is that the manufacture of that butter, which I call opsonin, goes on in the system by ups and downs — Nature being always rhythmical, you know — and that what the inoculation does is to stimulate the ups or downs, as the case may be ... Inoculate when the patient is in the negative phase and you kill: inoculate when the patient is in the positive phase and you cure.

SIR PATRICK And pray how are you to know whether the patient is in the positive or the negative phase?

RIDGEON Send a drop of the patient's blood to the laboratory at St Anne's; and in fifteen minutes I'll give you his opsonin index in figures ...

Fifteen minutes was Bernard Shaw's own rather optimistic reckoning. In point of fact, when patients were numerous, the opsonic index kept these young monks of science awake until dawn.

CHAPTER FOUR

FLEMING AND WRIGHT

It is not the marble halls which make for intellectual grandeur – it is the spirit and brain of the worker. FLEMING

THE introduction of Fleming, a circumspect young Scot, to this talkative and brilliant group conjures up before the mind's eye a curious picture. Far from being inferior to the other members of it, he arrived laden with diplomas and medals, a student already covered with glory, and possessing incontestable references. But his gift of silence appeared to be inexhaustible. 'He could', says Freeman, 'be more eloquently silent than any man I have ever known. He seldom or never gave himself away. In the stress of the moment I sometimes called him a blithering idiot, or used some equally opprobrious epithet. In reply, Fleming would merely look at me with his barely noticeable Gioconda-like smile, and I think he had the best of the exchange.'

The lab. equipment was rudimentary: an incubator, a sterilizer, some Petri dishes, a number of test-tubes and a microscope. Fleming was trained in doing most things with a few rubber teats and capillary tubes, and making most of the gear he needed. At tea-time, whether at night or during the day, he joined the 'family' in the small room which was known as the library, a courtesy title, for it contained no books. Wright, massive and shaggy in his armchair, played the part of a Victorian father from behind his table, while the others crowded together on a settee, or sat on the floor round him. His disciples appeared to look upon him as some immense natural phenomenon. When Dr Robert Debré, a Frenchman, visited St Mary's, he was astonished to see Fleming, solemn-faced and dexterous, go up to Wright while the latter was holding forth and, without a word, prick the august finger so as to get a drop of blood which he needed for control purposes, while Wright went on talking without paying the least attention to this rite.

More often than not these meetings took the form of a long monologue by Wright who sat leaning forward in his chair, slightly terrifying but quite fascinating in his role of feudal lord and unquestioned ruler. No matter what the subject, he was perfectly capable of quoting fluently and at length from Kant, Sophocles, Dante, Rabelais, Goethe and even *Mademoiselle de Maupin*. When important visitors, like Balfour, happened to turn up, it was Wright who answered their questions, or sometimes Freeman. Fleming, as a rule, said nothing. At first he had been amazed at Wright's tremendous vitality and universal knowledge. But he had the precious, if somewhat embarrassing, gift of seeing the weak point in any argument, and driving straight forward. He very soon realized that the Chief's glittering oratorical performances were not always constructed on irrefutable premisses. When the midnight tea became an orgy of metaphysical discussion, he would listen for a long time in silence, and then, with a single word, cause the whole laboriously constructed system to collapse noiselessly. 'Why?' he would say, with assumed innocence, at which there would be a general exchange of glances. For he was perfectly right: why?

Wright valued Fleming for the perfection of his work and his sure judgment. But his silences were in the nature of a challenge, and he enjoyed pulling his leg. Assuming that the young Scot, who never spoke about religion, must be a Covenanter and a Believer, the Old Man would try to provoke some show of emotion on that impassive countenance by indulging in blasphemous outbursts, such, for instance, as putting together two verses from the Gospels in such a way as to produce an absurd or scandalous sentence. Or he would say: 'Fleming, how could the star of Bethlehem be over *one* house? The apparent distance of the stars is such that the same star appears to be over *all* the houses in a village. Isn't that so?' But Fleming never rose to the bait. He knew what his behaviour was supposed to be in the lab.: that of a taciturn Scot, and he conscientiously played up to it.

Wright had a taste for quoting at length from the poets. Often, after a long piece of declamation, he would turn to Fleming, who had his beautiful blue eyes fixed on him, and say: 'What's that?' In the early days, Fleming, as a good Scot, had replied 'Burns' — on principle. Then, having a methodical mind, he established the fact that the Old Man chiefly quoted from three great works, the Bible, Milton's *Paradise Lost* and the plays of Shakespeare. From that moment, whenever Wright jumped on him with the question — 'What's that?', he regularly answered, '*Paradise Lost*,' and one time in three the attribution was correct.

After long days of work, Fleming enjoyed this atmosphere of gay badinage. He did not like people to take serious matters too seriously. He loved having a bit of a game, even where work was concerned. Himself given to teasing, he did not in the least mind being teased in return. But in games, as in everything else, he liked to be top-dog. Calmly, imperturbably, he would study the rules until he had completely mastered them. The really splendid game in the lab. was not conversation but research, and there Fleming triumphed. Though Wright was skilful in technical performance, in spite of his podgy fingers, Fleming, or, as he was affectionately called, 'Little Flem', was even more deft and ingenious. In his hands glass was made to serve the need of the moment. It was pure joy to watch him construct, with incredible rapidity and improvising as he went along, some complicated piece of apparatus. In the truest meaning of the word he was an artist, and his colleagues instinctively spoke of his work in terms of art. 'That experiment of Flem's,' someone would say, 'was a perfect little work of art.' In this way, and without any effort, he retained that contact with nature which is so precious a possession for those who question her, and which the abstract thinker is too apt to lose.

Wright, a scholastic, believed that pure reason or, at least, his own, could discover the laws which govern phenomena. 'Actually, he had a far greater intellectual affinity with St Thomas Aquinas than with Bacon', with Descartes than with Claude Bernard. He believed, of course, in the experimental method: he had carried out innumerable and 'beautiful' experiments, and had owed to them everything he knew, but when Nature gave him a negative answer, it was only after a tough struggle that he could bring himself to accept it. 'The positive spirit', says Alain, 'is a prey to the passions ... The reply given by *things* to our demands and our hopes is not always sufficiently definite to clear our minds of fantasies.' Though Wright, wisely and with perfect sincerity, preached self-criticism, he was not impartial where the choice and

interpretation of his results were concerned. Words held an irresistible attraction for him. There were days when his dialectic,
thickly sown with terms taken from the Greek, and of his own
invention ('cataphylaxis', 'epiphylaxis', 'ecphylaxis'), led his
audience beyond the borders of the real.

Fleming admired his master's genius, was full of praise for his
integrity, and knew that, if Wright sometimes made a mistake, it
was in perfect good faith. But ever since the days of his youth he
had made it a strict rule that he would never cling obstinately to a
preconceived idea if experience proved it to be wrong. His friend,
Professor Pannett, writes: 'He never liked talking, but when he
did make up his mind to express a judgment in words, you could
be perfectly certain that it would be in the highest degree intelligent. Fleming's edged mind and clarity of thought are beyond
dispute.' When Wright, carried away by his own eloquence,
pressed a theoretical conclusion too far, Fleming was always
courageous enough to say, quite calmly: 'That won't work, sir.'
Wright would repeat his argument even more forcibly. Fleming
would listen without interrupting him and then, quite simply, say
again: 'That won't work, sir.' And it didn't.

Though often, with one sharp monosyllable, he would deflate a
too audacious pilot-balloon, he felt, nevertheless, that Wright's
passionate enthusiasm was a useful source of inspiration. The
young Scot might seem cold and collected, but the indomitable,
delightful and sometimes savage Irishman had awakened in him
a spirit of unlimited loyalty. To contradict Wright to his face was
one thing, and Fleming occasionally ventured to do it, but to
argue against the Old Man's ideas outside the lab. was quite
another, and that he never did. He knew perfectly well that some
of Wright's theories were controversial, but he tried his best to
find a solid experimental basis for the Chief's more hazardous
hypotheses. Wright, because of his unbounded self-confidence and
excessive outspokenness, had made a number of enemies in the
world of science. Some there were who attacked his technical
methods: Fleming, on the other hand, attempted with infinite
patience, to perfect them. If Wright believed in a theory which
others held to be debatable, he would return to it again and again,
and prove to those of little faith that the Old Man had been
justified.

He learned much from Wright and it was a stroke of luck for him to have been trained by such a master, but it was also a stroke of luck for Wright to have at his elbow so fiercely impartial and absolutely loyal a worker. This he knew. Though he had a tendency, like many great masters, to think of the mental processes of his disciples as his own personal possession, and to include the results of their work in his 'papers', he often quoted Fleming by name, and realized, many times over, how much he owed to him.

The essential qualities of the young research-worker were a powerful gift of observation, thanks to which no important detail ever escaped him; a piercing insight into the causes implied by this or that established effect; and a high degree of skill in cutting through the tangled minutiae of any problem and revealing the main lines along which inquiry should move. These qualities he used generously in defence of the opsonic index against a deal of sniping. It was said that thousands of 'counts' would be necessary before a reliable estimate could be arrived at, and that, even if the method were correct, it would be utterly impracticable. 'No,' replied Fleming, 'an experienced and intelligent bacteriologist does not need to count as many cells as a beginner.' In his hands everything became easy. Two examples, chosen from the work of the laboratory, seemed to justify the confidence felt by the team in this famous and much-debated method.

One of the workers in the lab., John Wells, who was on holiday in the country, wrote to say that he was suffering from influenza. Wright replied, telling him not to come back until he had completely recovered. Two months later, Wells wrote again: 'I really must get back to work: this influenza seems to be interminable.' He returned and crawled about the laboratory, depressed, feverish and obviously a very sick man. One day, Fleming, who had taken a sample of his blood, showed Freeman two glass slides, and said: 'Would you mind counting these two films?' He had marked them 'A' and 'B', but gave no further explanation. Freeman, after making a careful count, said: 'Blood "B" has twice as much *less* effect upon the microbe as blood "A" ...'

'That tallies with my own finding,' replied Fleming: ' "B" is the control sample; "A" comes from Wells. The microbe is that of "glanders" ... John Wells is suffering from the "glanders" ... Do you remember that young woman whose pony died? ... Wells, on that occasion, handled a culture and probably did not take sufficient precautions ... The pony must have had the "glanders", and John Wells caught the infection ...' Six weeks later the diagnosis was confirmed, and John Wells died from the 'glanders' which, at that time, was incurable.

The other case was that of Dr May, a robust and red-faced Irishman who rejoiced in the nickname of 'Maisie'. Like the others, he had contributed some of his blood to build up a reserve of normal blood for control purposes. Someone put the question: 'Does this total mixture really and truly represent the average blood of the lab. workers?' The opsonic index of the mixture was compared with that of the individual donors. May noticed that his blood differed markedly from that of any of the others. Wright said to him: 'We won't take any more of your blood. You are not normal.' 'Maisie' continued to measure his opsonic index and established the fact that it was diverging more and more from the norm. Wright told him: 'I'm afraid you'll have to leave the lab. You are suffering from a suppressed form of tuberculosis.' 'Maisie' laughed, for he did not feel ill, but, nevertheless, accepted a less exacting post in South Africa. When this became known in the medical world, many pathologists said: 'Wright really is completely mad! He's got in his laboratory a chap who's the very picture of health and, just because this man's opsonic index varies from the norm, he has calmly announced that he is tubercular. Never heard anything so ridiculous!' ... May, however, had not been in Africa two months before the doctors found Koch bacillus in his sputum. The diagnosis by opsonic index had anticipated the clinical diagnosis by several weeks.

It looked, therefore, as though this immense labour had not been in vain. But it condemned Wright's disciples to spend whole nights in the lab. The students of St Mary's knew that if they left a party round about two in the morning, they could always look in for a final mug of beer on Fleming, who at that hour would invariably be found bending over his microscope. They liked nothing better than to find him there — at once unperturbed and welcoming — wearing his neat bow tie and ready to listen to anything they might have to say, while the eternal cigarette dangling from his lips, even when he was speaking, made it more than usually difficult to hear what he was saying.

Another of Fleming's qualities was the masterly manner in which he organized his expositions. From the very first his papers had been noted for the clarity of his scientific style. Wright, whose taste in literature was exacting and reliable, could not help recognizing that Fleming in his precise and sober way wrote well. 'My colleague, Dr Alexander Fleming, has given in the treatise which is prefaced by these remarks of mine an admirable summing-up of the results obtained by the Inoculation Department of St Mary's Hospital ...' Wright had moved on from preventive to therapeutic vaccination, and it is now necessary to give some account of the flow of ideas which had carried him forward in this direction.

To immunize means, when there is any threat of infectious illness, to give to the blood the means of fighting against a possible attack. Jenner's inoculations as well as Pasteur's had been preventive. But Pasteur had also successfully treated those already infected with rabies. How had that been possible? Because rabies in the human being does not develop until some time after the bite has been inflicted by the mad dog. An injection of the virus in an attenuated dose, given during the period of incubation, stimulates the production of antibodies and with them the human system can fight the invasion before it is established; this is still, therefore, a sort of preventive inoculation.

Wright took it as his starting-point. Why, he asked, should one not go farther? Up till then the 'immunizers' had held the view that the invaded body was one and indivisible. But was this view correct? Observation had been recorded of numerous cases of local infections which had not become generalized. A patient might suffer from tuberculosis of the knee without the rest of his body being attacked. To what did this point? To this — that the local natural defences, and they alone, had been carried by the enemy; that the microbial forces had won a bridge-head but nothing more. The general defence mechanism had not been put on the alert.

Could the garrison be mobilized? Yes, said Wright, by means of auto-inoculations. It would be enough, in cases of local infection, carefully to determine the microbes responsible, to prepare from them dead cultures (auto-vaccines), to inject these into the patient, and then study his opsonic index to ascertain the effect of the treatment. Beyond this first area of research Wright could already see vast fields waiting to be explored by vaccine therapy

— e.g. blood poisonings and certain secondary infections which often accompany cancer. An enthusiastic inquirer with a fixed idea can find it everywhere.

There can be no doubt that Fleming, like his colleagues, had a firm belief in vaccine therapy. Indeed, numerous cures brought about by its use were on record at St Mary's. This new conception made a great stir. Bacteriologists from all over the world came to study auto-vaccines and the opsonic index under Wright's direction. It was not easy to find accommodation for them in the two wretched rooms which were all the Department at its disposal; far too little for half a dozen foreign scientists in addition to Wright's six or seven assistants. Patients, attracted by favourable rumour, arrived in a steady flow. It was necessary to take blood-samples, to identify the microbes, to prepare the vaccines, and to keep a watch on the blood of the sufferers by making a count of the number of microbes absorbed by the leucocytes. It was gruelling work, and there was a shortage of everything, of money as well as space.

In 1907 the hospital authorities, who lacked the funds necessary to equip the upper floors of a recently constructed block (the Clarence Wing), offered them to Wright if he would undertake to obtain a subsidy. Wright had rich and powerful admirers. He rallied to his aid Lord Iveagh, Arthur James Balfour, Lord Fletcher Moulton and Sir Max Bonn. Between them they rapidly collected the sum needed. In addition, as soon as the laboratories were equipped, arrangements were made with a large firm of pharmaceutical chemists, Parke Davis & Co., to supply them with vaccines, serums and antitoxins for distribution. From that moment, the Department had permanent resources, but these were used to expand the laboratories, and the research-workers continued to be paid about what sweepers would earn today. In 1909, the constitution of the Inoculation Department was definitely established at a meeting held at the House of Commons under the chairmanship of Balfour. The Department now became entirely independent. Its administration was vested in a committee which met only when Wright thought it necessary to call it together. Wright and two other members constituted a quorum. In this way was the benevolent tyranny of the Old Man legitimized.

Few women ever came to the laboratory except when Wright

had prepared what his friend Ehrlich called a *Damenprogramme*. On these occasions, Lady Horner, Mrs Bernard Shaw and other privileged females were put *au fait* with the latest discoveries by means of a number of spectacular demonstrations. Wright affected a profound contempt for the intelligence of women, and many of the 'midnight teas' were devoted to his diatribes against the sex. 'The continual over-estimation of the feminine intelligence', said Wright, 'is very largely due to conjugal infatuation. Everyone must have noticed that wives who love their husbands adopt their ideas ... I once heard a mother say of her daughter, "she is so devoted to her husband that if he turned Mohammedan tomorrow, she would follow suit"...'[1]

He maintained that the passions are almost always engendered by bacterial toxins. His taste for Greek words led him to explain the need felt by so many men and women to press against one another, to clasp their arms round the beloved object, and to lean his (or her) head on her (or his) shoulder, as a *stereotropic* instinct, in other words, the desire to find something solid to lean on. He had written a whole book against Votes for Women which, at that time, were being violently demanded by the Suffragettes, and had collected all the most wounding things that the most famous authors had said about the 'second sex', from Michelet's 'A man loves God: a woman loves a man', to Meredith's 'I expect that Woman will be the last thing civilized by Man' and Dr Johnson's remark that 'there is always something a woman will prefer to the truth.'

The man who would pursue a great design and work without intermission should, according to Wright, live completely separated from women, a rule which he applied rigorously in his own case, for he kept his family in the country while he himself lived in London. The laboratory was his home. 'Before making a decision on any subject, a man should always have numerous conversations with those who are expert in it' was another of his sayings. And so it was that he surrounded himself with disciples. Some of them, like Freeman, stimulated him and led him on to make his most brilliant repartees: others, like Fleming, gave him their sureness of judgment, technical skill and sturdy good sense, though at times they might be silently rebellious.

[1] Sir Almroth Wright, *Alethetropic Logic* (Heinemann, 1953), p. 40.

Fleming had quickly fitted into this new world which he had entered quite by chance. The work demanded more of human nature than human nature could give. Every morning the young men had to make the rounds of the wards, for Wright still clung to the view that research-workers should also be practising doctors. The afternoon began with a 'consultation' at which those cases regarded by the old-fashioned doctors as hopeless were examined. Samples of blood were taken and labelled. Fleming was always anxious to get these preliminaries over quickly, for he was in a hurry to get back to the laboratory and prepare his slides. After dinner these innumerable specimens were studied. The workers used their own blood for control purposes. 'We were', says Colebrook, 'so many human pincushions.' All this was not without danger.

Meanwhile, though never abandoning these exacting labours, Fleming continued to read for his final medical examinations which he passed in 1908, coming out, as usual, top, and being awarded the Gold Medal of the University of London. Nor should it be forgotten that at this time, too, and without any preparation, he sat for and got his F.R.C.S. As though this were not enough, he wrote a thesis on 'Acute Bacterial Infections' for one of the prizes regularly offered by his own Faculty (St Mary's), and again headed the list, winning the Cheadle Medal. His success was announced in the *St Mary's Hospital Gazette* as follows: 'Mr Fleming, who recently was bracketed for the Gold Medal and who seems to have taken the Fellowship in his stride, is one of Sir Almroth Wright's most enthusiastic followers, and we see great distinction in store for him in the future.' The far-sighted author of this article was Zachary Cope, who later became Sir Zachary Cope and a great surgeon.

Fleming's thesis on bacterial infections and the means of fighting them constitutes, as it were, a prefiguration of the line of research which the author was to follow all through his life. In it he presents an inventory of the contents of the arsenal at that time available to the medical profession in its war against bacteria: surgery, where the centre of infection is accessible; antiseptics; general methods of increasing the patient's resistance; the use of products which have an effect upon certain specific bacteria (quinine for malaria; mercury for syphilis, etc.); ways of increasing the exudation of the blood-lymph into the infected tissues; and, naturally, serums and vaccines.

He gave the place of honour in his essay to Wright's vaccine therapy. The latter's enemies asked ironically: 'What is the point in adding dead microbes to a body which is already carrying on a battle against living ones?' — and, with an air of triumph, brought up against him the phenomenon known as infectious endocarditis, where, the valves of the heart being contaminated, the microbes are continually shed into the general circulatory system. According to Wright's theory, this process should be a natural form of vaccination, and there should follow an increase in the resistance of the organism. In fact, nothing of the sort occurred. The blood did not produce antibodies.

Fleming, having come up against this obstacle, ventured to put forward an hypothesis. The intravenous route, he suggested, was not suited to the injection of a vaccine. But this theory still needed to be confirmed by experiment. Being unable and unwilling to use a patient for this purpose, he became his own guinea-pig and submitted to an intravenous injection of a staphylococcic vaccine. This was a rather courageous thing to do. Intravenous injections were held at that time to be dangerous, and no one could say with any certainty what the consequences might be. One Saturday he had a hundred and fifty million dead staphylococci injected into a vein. On the Sunday he had a feeling of nausea, a headache and a high temperature. Given such symptoms, it was reasonable to expect an increase of resistance in the blood. There was, however, none, whereas the same quantity of staphylococci administered hypodermically caused it to rise sharply. This seemed to justify the hypothesis that inoculation into the blood-stream, which occurs naturally in endocarditis, is a bad method, which produces the maximum toxic effect with the minimum of immunization. The results of the experiment had been what the young doctor had expected.[1]

This thesis on the infections is important, providing us, as it does, at the very dawn of a life devoted to medicine, with a picture of the direction that life was to take. All through his working career, Fleming was to seek one thing, and one thing only: a means of fighting infections which at that time were looked upon as the

[1] *St Mary's Hospital Gazette*, 1908.

most dangerous of all the scourges of the human race. For this line of research he felt himself to be well equipped. He was a born naturalist, and was fully conscious of his abilities. It would, therefore, be a great mistake to think of him as an embarrassed and discontented man living in a refined, literary circle much superior to anything to which he had been accustomed. For soured and querulous persons he felt nothing but contempt. 'Alec was always happy, and always on top of his work', writes one of his colleagues, Dr Hollis; 'there was never any sign in him of bitterness or fatigue ... His attitude to his research-work seemed to be a combination of humour and seriousness.' Here, too, is what Professor Cruickshank thinks: 'He tolerated, and was probably amused by, sophistication in life, and by the kind of intellectual philosophy in which Almroth Wright indulged. Although he took little part in argument, one gets the impression that, even in his early days, his opinion was greatly respected.' His own infrequency of speech did not at all depress him. He liked listening. It was one of his strong points. Wright's tremendous personality dominated the scene, but the tranquil Fleming, for ever at his side, was loved and esteemed.

CHAPTER FIVE

THE PRENTICE YEARS

Science is the tool and the reinforcement of the spirit, and the spirit will find its salvation, not in turning back upon itself, which is the pursuit of a shadow, but in seeking out the object and grappling with it. ALAIN

WRIGHT and his disciples believed in vaccines and the opsonic index. They proved their faith by devoting their days and their nights to the practice of their religion. Other scientists in other parts of the world were hoping to conquer the dangerous microbes by other means. One of Wright's German friends, a scientist in horn-rimmed spectacles, with bright eyes and a loud, cheerful voice, was looking, in a mood of passionate confidence, for the 'magic bullet' which should kill the invaders without harming the invaded.

Born in 1854, Ehrlich had been a student at the time when the great German dye-enterprises were coming into their own. Being a chemist as well as a doctor, he had been deeply interested, while still a young man, in the colouring of animal and human tissues. This staining turned out to be selective; that is to say that a particular dye became fixed to one particular part of the body. For example, methylene-blue coloured predominantly the nerve tissue, and this made it possible to follow the course of the nerves. Ehrlich had also established the fact that the noxious microbes 'took' certain colorants better than the cells of the organism which harboured them.

Why? For the same reason, said Ehrlich, who was accustomed to thinking as a chemist, that the toxins of diphtheria attack the cardiac muscles, or those of tetanus the nerve-cells, in a selective manner, which is as much as to say that there is a chemical affinity between the molecules. It follows, therefore, that the beneficent antitoxins must consist of molecules which, by affinity, are led to combine with the toxins and neutralize them.

In 1904, Ehrlich, who at that time was Director of the Institute of Serotherapy in Frankfurt, embarked with his assistant, a Japanese doctor called Shiga, on an immense programme of experiments. He tried out all his coloured projectiles against the trypanosomes — a more than usually formidable species of parasite. Following the practice of Maurice Nicolle and Mesnil, he employed particularly active products — the trypan-red and the trypan-blue — with reasonably encouraging results. Shortly afterwards he was to win his greatest victory, not against the trypanosomes, but against the pale treponema, or spirochaete, which causes syphilis, and this by employing not dyes but arsenical compounds. One may not always find what one is looking for but, if one looks hard enough, one often finds something. Ehrlich scored a bull on a target at which he was not aiming.

In the sixteenth century, Paracelsus had tried using arsenic against syphilis, but without much success, and consequently doctors turned to mercury, and were to remain loyal to it for a long time. Between 1905 and 1907, the chemists had produced an arsenical compound — atoxyl — which had the desired effect both on the trypanosomes and the spirochaetes. Unfortunately, this product, in spite of its name, was toxic. Ehrlich set himself, therefore, to transform atoxyl and to make a new magic bullet of it. The necessary research demanded infinite patience. For each new derivative of atoxyl which the chemists created under Ehrlich's direction, it was essential to determine, first of all, the curative dose, the one that would destroy the microbes (C), and then the maximum dose which the body could tolerate (T). The relationship $\frac{C}{T}$ indicated the efficacy or the danger of the drug. If C was greater than T, then obviously the new product was worthless. Thousands of mice and guinea-pigs were sacrificed in this battle. In 1909 the compound No. 418 seemed to offer hope, but no more than hope. Ehrlich, exhausted but enthusiastic, continued with his massacre of mice. At last, in May 1909, the compound 606 destroyed all the trypanosomes without killing either mice or guinea-pigs. Some time later, when the substance was used for treating syphilitic lesions in rabbits, complete cures were achieved in three weeks. From now on, so it seemed, a magic bullet really did exist with which to attack and overcome one of humanity's worst enemies. It flew straight to the target, namely, the parasite, without doing any harm to the sufferer's tissues. Ehrlich gave it the name 'salvarsan' (that which saves by arsenic).

Ehrlich was a pleasant companion and a passionate talker. The freakishness of his mind delighted Wright, and he was soon a great favourite at the lab. When he came to London to lecture on chemotherapy (which Wright, punctilious in all linguistic matters, tried, in vain, to rename 'pharmacotherapy') he entrusted some doses of salvarsan to the scientists of St Mary's and, at once, Fleming became a past master in the art of applying the new treatment. This was no easy task. The substance rapidly became oxidized when in contact with the air, and the intramuscular injection was extremely painful. Ehrlich's new Japanese assistant, Hata, a technician of quite extraordinary skill, had administered salvarsan to rabbits by the intravenous route, but in 1909 few doctors knew how to make an injection into the blood-vessels.

Dr G. W. B. James remembers how in 1909 he and a friend watched Flem give 606 to a patient. These young men of St Mary's knew and admired Fleming as the winner of the Gold Medal. 'I have a vivid recollection of him standing beside the bed in a long white coat,' says Dr James, 'setting up a glass reservoir containing a yellow fluid, inserting a needle into a vein on the patient's arm, and running the fluid directly into the blood stream. It must be remembered that intravenous therapy was new and strange to the students of 1909 or 1910. This vivid picture of Flem has always had a dramatic value for me, for, in addition to the exciting intravenous method, there was the rapidity with which the 606 took effect, so different from the slow working of the mercurial treatment with which I was familiar from my having attended in the Out-Patients Department of the hospital.

'I remember speaking to Flem (greatly daring) while he was at the bedside, and asking him what the yellow fluid was. His manner was slightly alarming in those days. He fixed me with a blue eye, and gave me the chemical formula of 606: "Dioxy-diamide-arsenobenzol-dehydro-chlorine."

'I was none the wiser.

' "What is it you want to know?" he asked.

' "Well, sir, just look ..."

' "What d'you think this is?" — and he pointed to the man in the bed, who only too visibly was suffering from the most horrible syphilitic lesions.

'We both of us replied: "Syphilis."

' "And how would you treat it?" said he. "Mercury, I suppose, eh? Well, just you watch. This stuff acts much more rapidly."

'When I came to know him better, I realized that his icy and laconic manner had no hostile intention but was "just Fleming". After we had left the patient's bedside on this now far-distant occasion, Flem took my friend and me into the laboratory where he worked, and told us the whole story of salvarsan, impressing both of us with his encyclopedic knowledge. At that phase of a student's life, a difference of four years in age means a great deal. I know that my friend and I felt that we had "discovered" Flem. Certainly we found him a most stimulating and interesting teacher and, looking back, I realize how good he was to two eager and callow youths. When leaving us, he said: "Come back and take a look at this chap tomorrow." We did so. Everything was clean and cleared up. We were staggered, and he thoroughly enjoyed our stupefaction.

'After that he was always willing to see us. The amount of work he put in at the lab. was tremendous. One of the most interesting occupations was to sit and watch him making things out of glass and tubing. He seemed able to do anything with molten glass, constructing not only the pipettes he needed for his work, but small models of every sort of animal. One, I remember, was a cat which he moulded from red-hot glass. When it had cooled it looked positively alive, and he added a whole series of tiny creatures running away from pussy.

'We remained good friends until his death. I was constantly impressed by his fidelity in friendship. It seemed to be impossible ever to offend Fleming. One could say exactly what one thought to him — things, very often, which another person would have taken in bad part, but not so Fleming.

'He had a somewhat materialistic outlook in medical matters — as was probably inevitable, given the nature of his work — and found it very hard to accept what he called the "rot" talked by psychologists. We had many tussles in later years, after I had specialized in psychiatry. He stuck doggedly to his scientific facts. Either bacteria existed or they didn't. He was determined, I felt, never to go beyond facts which could be seen and measured. I remember trying to explain to him the theory of the unconscious mind. "What's the use of talking about the unconscious mind?" he protested. "There's no such thing. If you are unconscious, you don't *have a mind* for the time being."

'The only time he listened, with a somewhat humorous and inquiring look on his face, was when I asked him to tell me how much of an iceberg is visible above water. He said he had no idea. "One-eighth," I told him. "The other seven-eighths are beneath the surface, and the invisible part is like the unconscious mind." A mischievous twinkle came into his eyes. One never knew what he was really thinking, or whether one had convinced him. He loved argument, and contradicted for the sake of contradicting. He could infuriate you as an adversary even though he was on the best of terms with you as a friend. In his own field, he was invincible. His knowledge of bacteriology was monumental.'

He could never resist the pleasure of bringing 'down to earth' any interlocutor who had taken flight into those 'upper regions' which he considered to be inaccessible. Once, when arguing with a friend of his about the Universe, Time and Space, he said, showing his watch: '*This* time is quite enough for me.' So impenetrable was the mask he habitually wore that one could never be sure whether he was just enjoying an argument as an argument, or was serious. Only the twinkle in his eyes gave him away to those who knew him.

In collaboration with Colebrook, he published in the *Lancet*, a note on 'The Use of Salvarsan in the Treatment of Syphilis'. The results had been astonishing and, from now on, he had great hopes of chemotherapy. Wright, on the other hand, was sceptical. At the beginning of his career, he had said: 'The doctor of the future will be an immunizer,' and he stuck to that opinion. 'My anticipations have already been justified. I do not know anybody who, having tried vaccine therapy in the treatment of local bacterial affections, has not been convinced of its efficacy. The time when the doctor will be, for the most part, an immunizer is visibly drawing nearer.' In spite of his honesty of mind and his long intimacy with Ehrlich, he watched with a suspicious eye the entry of chemical remedies on the scene. To the Medical Research Club he declared: 'The use of chemotherapy for the treatment of bacterial infections in human beings will never be possible.'

His disciples were less dogmatic. They were beginning to realize that the opsonic index, interesting though it might be, was unlikely to become a factor in ordinary practice, because of the superhuman work it entailed. Only Wright's prestige and authority could keep his team of brilliant young men in the laboratory, night after night, counting microbes. Some of them found it very difficult to stay awake when they resumed their duties next morning, though Flem, after a sleepless night spent with his eye to the microscope, was able to retain his capacity for work. He would be the first to turn up, looking as fresh and alert as though he had just got back from a country holiday. Several of the research staff — Fleming, Noon, Brinton — had to run a practice outside laboratory hours in order to make a living. Freeman, who had taken a house at 30 Devonshire Place, provided consulting-rooms for his colleagues. Fleming and Colebrook were for some time, thanks to Ehrlich, almost the only doctors in England to make use of salvarsan, and this very soon resulted in a flow of patients. At that time it was necessary, when employing the treatment, to inject great quantities of the liquid. Fleming had invented a very simple apparatus (two glass jars, a syringe, two rubber tubes, and two taps with double nozzles) which made possible the treatment of four patients in the same time as would previously have been occupied in making a single injection. In the London Scottish, from which more than one unhappy victim of the pale tryponema had recourse to him, he was known as 'Private 606', and a caricature showed him armed with a syringe in place of a rifle. He loved the spectacular character of salvarsan cures.

His diagnoses were absolutely reliable. Professor Newcomb gives a characteristic example of this. A patient suffering from an ulcer on the lip had been for six months in University College Hospital for tubercular ulceration. Every known treatment had been tried, but without success. Then the patient was sent to St Mary's for vaccination. The ulcer continued to get worse. One day, the doctor in charge of the case being absent, Fleming took his place for twenty-four hours. Now medical etiquette lays it down that a deputy must never modify a treatment. But Fleming, who cared little about orthodoxy, at once did three highly irregular things. He took a sample of the man's blood, gave him an injection of salvarsan, and sent Newcomb a section from the tissues, labelled: 'Ulcer of the lip: tubercle?'

'Well,' says Newcomb, 'I thought — according to Flem it's tubercle, so tubercle it is … but there was one odd thing about it, it was full of plasma cells. So I wrote it up as "Tubercular lesion of the lip. Great number of plasma cells present, probably the result of secondary infection". Next day, at lunch, Flem gave me a solemn look and said: "Funny sort of tubercular lesion I sent you the other day, wasn't it?" I said: "Yes, it was, rather." "Very funny indeed," said Flem. "I treated the patient with salvarsan and the thing healed up completely. Extremely odd tubercular lesion to yield to salvarsan like that!" He never let me forget it and, whenever I got a bit uppish, would say "What about that tubercular lesion of the lip?" '

'I think it says a lot for Flem's character', writes Dr Fry, 'that everyone liked him, though he was always right, and always had the last word. People don't usually like those who are always right. But he was so nice about it, that you couldn't not like him. Of course he couldn't resist saying "I told you so," but he said it as a child might have done. He loved pulling your leg if he had done something better than you, and enjoyed it all thoroughly. By great good luck, there were very few in the lab. who hadn't got a sense of humour. No one without it would have lasted long with Wright and Fleming always ready to poke fun at them, each in his own way.'

There were times at the laboratory teas when Fleming seemed to take an impish pleasure in saying something about somebody which would compel the blushing victim to stammer out a denial. 'Did you know, sir,' he would say, for instance, 'that Giles is in love?' The question, put to the Chief, before an audience consisting of the whole of the lab. staff, had the effect of a stone dropped into a pond. Flem took a particular pleasure in studying the reactions produced by such utterances. He never said anything malicious, but found much amusement in the horrified explanations of the particular colleague to whom he might have drawn attention with his chaff.

His sometimes caustic humour was not resented. 'We were all very fond of Flem,' says Freeman, 'he was a lovable character, but not expansive. He would answer a question in one word, and then go mum when the others joined in. We used to say that he was a typical Scot, and that his conversation consisted mostly of grunts. It wasn't, of course, strictly true, but just a little joke between us and him.'

He was always ready to help a friend. Hayden, one of the doctors at St Mary's, had fallen a victim to poliomyelitis and was partially paralysed. This disaster was made the worse for him by reason of the fact that he had a family to keep. 'The legs have nothing to do with science,' Fleming told him. 'If you want some real work to do, come along to the lab.' He found no difficulty in persuading Wright to take on this excellent research-worker and Hayden used to move about the laboratory in a wheel-chair. The team was a happy and united family with a strong feeling of solidarity. When Hayden died, his colleagues, though they had little money to spare, took it upon themselves to educate his two sons.

This comradeship in work and play had a sort of cosy charm unlike anything to be found elsewhere. Dr Porteous, who joined the Department in 1911 as a junior, found the climate of the lab. delightful. 'A lot of people had told me that Fleming was reticent and forbidding, but I never found him so. The impression he made on me was that of a kindly colleague who was always ready to help a newcomer. His enjoyment of fun some-times led him to indulge in practical jokes, as when, for instance, he put a smear of Plasticine on the lens of a microscope, to see how the victim would react. It was true, of course, that he was always a bit shy, but his shyness never came from lack of self-confidence. *He knew that he knew*, and that gave him a great feeling of security. Certain inhibitions, dating from far back, made it difficult for him to express himself freely about anything invol-ving the emotions. But where a practical problem was concerned, he would deal with it easily, directly and unaffectedly. If one of his colleagues, even Wright, put forward some technical absurdity, he would cut it to pieces in fine style. But he found it impossible to talk about his feelings, and those of others, when they were publicly displayed, made him uncomfortable. He was inclined to think exaggerated and highfalutin what anybody less severe would have thought only human.'

With a friend of whom he was genuinely fond, and who obviously took pleasure in being with him, he would drop his rather dour mask for a second or so, and his whole face would light up. His look of rather tense concentration would break into a charming smile, and an almost touching expression of sweetness would show in his blue eyes. But such occasions were exceptional, and never lasted for long. In spite of his small stature, which his great breadth of shoulder seemed to make more obvious, one always got the impression that he was 'a presence'. Of this he was not aware and suffered much from being a small man. Speaking of the son of a friend who was sitting for an examination, he said: '*He* doesn't need to bother about exams: he is tall, and tall people can do anything and go anywhere!' There was about his walk a sort of easy swing, accompanied by an almost aggressive hunching of the shoulders. This curious gait may have had something to do with his having worn a kilt when in the London Scottish, but it was also a form of challenge, an exhibition of self-confidence. The way in which he could control his body was exceptional and accounted for his skill in shooting and at croquet, in which game his proficiency was almost uncanny and quite fascinating.

In London he had got to know several people who had no connection with either the hospital or his own family. An Australian doctor named Page, who was on a course at St Mary's, introduced him to friends of his, the Pegrams, who lived in Warwick Gardens. He was a great success with them, more especially with the small, twelve-year-old Marjory Pegram. 'Alec', she writes, 'was then in his late twenties, a serious and silent young man, with a massive head, beautiful eyes and broad, strong hands. He had a simplicity of mind which made him really enjoy playing with a child, and he would invent games with a zest which was completely free from any hint of condescension. To me he was the ideal companion. We used to play eccentric games of golf together which were terribly exciting.

' "I'll tell you what," he would say, "you do the whole round with a putter and I'll beat you with nothing but a niblick." I knew that he would, and he always did. On wet days he devised elaborate games of golf on the carpet, where it needed extreme delicacy of touch to make the ball stop dead on one small spot. But Alec could always do it.

'My parents were devoted to him and my mother talked to him as though he were the same age as me. "Now, Alec, don't be silly!" she would say when he made one of those outrageous assertions which he loved to toss into a conversation to liven it up. One of his favourite gambits, which unfailingly got a rise out of her, was to say, apropos of one of his miraculous cures: "Oh, it was nothing to do with me; he'd have got well anyway," or to reply, if somebody asked him what some patient he had cured had been suffering from: "Damned if *I* know!" '

Marjory Pegram had an uncle, a painter named Ronald Gray, who was afflicted with tuberculosis of the knee. Fleming suggested vaccine therapy, looked after Gray with the utmost devotion, and cured him.

He was less successful with Marjory herself, who was prone to attacks of asthma. He tried so many treatments on her that she was nicknamed in the family 'Alec's guinea-pig'. She loved her visits to the laboratory, which she found mysterious and fascinating. She admired especially the glass slides on which the stains had made little patches. 'One day Alec told me that there was a new method of finding out to what asthmatics were sensitive, and in some trepidation I bared my thigh on which Alec made a series of scratches and then dropped different liquids into them, saying, as he did so, "eggs, feathers, horsehair, seaweed, fish" — and so on. We then sat in breathless silence to see if any of them became inflamed. The result was bitterly disappointing, since only seaweed showed anything at all. Alec said, the next time we met: "Did you have a very sore leg?" "Yes," I said, "I did." "I thought as much," he remarked gaily, "you see, I did it all wrong!"'

'He had some curious mannerisms which enthralled me. When asked a question, there was always a time-lag before he answered and, when the answer came, he shut his eyes. The far-back-in-the-throat Scottish "l" was exaggerated with him into something more like a guttural French "r", and this made it difficult for foreigners to understand him when he said "I must take a specimen of your blood" …'

Ronald Gray, at the time when Fleming was looking after him, lodged with a Mrs Hammersley, the wife of Hugh Hammersley, who was one of the directors of Cox & Co., the Army agents. She had a lovely eighteenth-century house and a wide circle of friends among painters and writers. George Moore, Wilson Steer and Ronald Gray were 'regulars' of long standing, and their conversation was animated and witty.

At Gray's bedside Fleming met Mrs Richard Davis, a good-looking and elegant woman, the daughter-in-law of an anti-quarian dealer in Bond Street who was a specialist in old French furniture. She was brilliantly intelligent and entertained many artists and men of letters in the lovely house which she and her husband had in Ladbroke Terrace. The whole of this group immediately attached itself to Fleming. His medical skill amazed them and they were impressed by his modest silences. Ronald Gray had to go twice a week to St Mary's for treatment. Mrs Davis used to go with him, and Sir Almroth, who loved the company of artists, invited them to have tea with him. Fleming, now more sociable and tame, called Mrs Davis 'Davey' and used to greet her, when she visited the laboratory, with 'Oh! I *am* glad to see you! I badly need some of your delicious blood!'

His new friends decided that Flem must go out more, relax a bit, and learn to dance. Mrs Davis was on intimate terms with the Wertheimers, rich collectors known all over the world and great patrons of the arts, whose portraits were painted by Sargent (the whole family is now in the Tate Gallery). Fleming was delighted at discovering under their roof a world which was entirely new to him, the existence of which he had never so much as suspected. Their house was more like a palace, full of beautiful furniture and rare porcelain, with a perfectly trained staff, and a table which abounded in delicious food and wines. Fleming loved going there and meeting the artists who frequented it. He had a natural good taste and all his life long, so far as his means permitted, was an assiduous attendant at auction-sales, and built up a collection of *objets d'art*.

Once a week the Wertheimers, who had installed a ball-room, invited their daughter's friends to what, in those days, were called 'hops'. Fleming often took part in them, though he never became a good dancer. It was then that he ordered his first dress-suit and solemnly said to the tailor: 'Don't make me look like Carl Brisson, but a sober scientist.' (Carl Brisson was a very charming musical-comedy star!)

It was Ronald Gray who introduced him to another pleasant

circle, which was to play a great part in his life, The Chelsea Arts Club. It had as its premises an old house in a quarter traditionally associated with painters and writers. Strictly speaking, only artists were eligible for membership, but there were a few honorary members, of whom Fleming was one. He made a point of treating his fellow-members free, and got them into St Mary's whenever he thought that any of them needed a period in hospital. He got into the habit of going to the club for a game of snooker whenever he had a free hour or so.

The other players soon noticed his schoolboyish zest for the game, his dislike of playing 'for safety', his obvious delight when he brought off a good stroke and balls went bang into the pockets. If ever anyone offered him gratuitous advice on how to play a shot, he would immediately relapse into silence, stare at the speaker for a few moments, and then play the shot in his own way — often a very unorthodox one. Frequently those who were looking on were staggered by the success of these unusual methods.

If, after the spin of a coin had decided the opposing sides, the odds, on form, seemed to be against him and his partner, he played with an even greater zest than usual. 'I often played with him against reputedly better men', says A. Murray, 'and we quite frequently won. We were both stubborn Scots, determined not to be outdone by mere Englishmen.'

Gray told him that he would have to paint a picture to justify his admission to the club. Fleming said he was sorry, but he wasn't an artist. Gray forced a brush into his hand, and *ordered* him to paint a farm scene. Much against his will, Fleming produced a cow, though it was difficult to recognize it as such.

'Thank you,' said Gray, 'it is a masterpiece, and exactly what I wanted.'

Some time later, he took Fleming to an exhibition where the famous picture was prominently displayed. The painter of the 'Portrait of a Cow' was much amused, the more so since several critics were loud in their praise of his 'sophisticated naivety'. He heard two elderly ladies of distinguished appearance discussing his 'work'. 'Perhaps you are right,' said one of them, 'this modern art must mean something, though I confess that I cannot make out what it is.'

To make quite certain that his election to the club would

stand, he asked one of his friends, Dr E. J. Storer, to buy the picture — he himself providing the money. It then occurred to him that he would also have to pay the gallery's commission. An agreement was therefore come to that Storer should do no more than ask the price and then declare that it was too high. The committee fell in with this little plot and Fleming was made a life-member. He constantly, until the day of his death, met most of the great artists of the day there. He had a great fondness for the place and soon became very popular among his fellow members.

The Chelsea Arts Club gave an annual fancy-dress ball. Mrs Davis and Ronald Gray dragged him to it. But he had to take a partner, and Steer suggested a pretty girl, Lily Montgomery, who had often sat for him. Flem went as a negro and thoroughly enjoyed the evening. In the following year he again went to the ball, this time with his friend Dr Porteous, both of them dressed as little girls in short red frocks and black stockings. Even bacteriologists can unbend on occasion.

At the laboratory, he went on with his own work in addition to his routine duties. In 1909 he published in the *Lancet* an excellent article on acne. He next devised a simple modification of the Wasserman Reaction in the diagnosis of syphilis, a small-scale reaction requiring only a tiny blood-sample drawn from the tip of the finger in a capsule. He enjoyed nothing better than tinkering and mending defects in pieces of laboratory equipment with any odd thing that came to hand, a bicycle-clip, for instance. Little by little, he elaborated, for his own use, a philosophy of research. This consisted in making no rigid plans, but in going on with his regular work with one eye always cocked so as not to miss the unexpected and gauge its importance.

The Chief still played the part of an inspired Olympian. One of Wright's virtues was that he allowed his disciples complete freedom in research. He himself continued to devise new and difficult techniques. One of these he called 'wash and afterwash'. It enabled them to make, in the specially long capillary stem of a pipette, serial dilutions of infected material.

When Freeman and Noon went, at the invitation of Professor

Jules Bordet, to demonstrate these techniques at the Pasteur Institute, Maurice Nicolle said: 'These methods are more suitable for conjurers, or as a means of amusing children.' That was true. They demanded great dexterity. They delighted Fleming. He knew that they were complicated, but also that he was more able than anybody else, thanks to his own skill, to operate them. Besides, the Chief championed them, and Fleming was nothing if not a loyal disciple.

There was merit in his loyalty, for in the world outside St Mary's the waves of hostility now breaking over Wright were becoming more and more violent. Some of his fellow scientists had invented a nickname for him, 'Sir Almost Right', and even inside the hospital many of the doctors and surgeons were growing sceptical about therapeutic vaccines. Vaccinate in order to prevent — YES: vaccinate in order to cure — NO. 'Wright', says Professor Newcomb, 'produced storms wherever he went.' Some scientists used to say that his work was all nonsense. Fleming continued to support his master strongly and, if there was a storm round him, he was sure to be in it.

Some of the big-wigs of Harley Street, annoyed by Wright's contempt for what he called 'non-scientific medicine', took their revenge by denying the results obtained at St Mary's. The statisticians, who had already been up in arms against Wright in the days of anti-typhoid vaccination, now returned to the charge. Wright replied by saying that for facts as different among themselves as are medical cases mathematical statistics should give way to what — again inventing a name — he called the 'diacritical judgment', that supreme quality of the human mind which makes it possible to pronounce on individual, and not concordant, phenomena. He added: 'Diacritical judgment is notably lacking in women and in Bernard Shaw.'

There were times when even the disciples had doubts. 'In our enthusiasm', said Colebrook, 'we had attached too little importance to the *vis medicatrix naturae*.' Was it by vaccine therapy or by nature that local infections were cured? In fact, ulcers did close, tubercular glands did disappear, boils were reabsorbed. Obviously there were cases of failure, but when these occurred the reason given was that the infection had become generalized before treatment. Another charge brought against the St Mary's team had to do with the sale of vaccines by the Inoculation Department to a large firm of pharmaceutical chemists. But what was wrong with that? The sums produced by these sales were used exclusively in developing the laboratories. The research-workers, including Wright, were still in receipt of ludicrously inadequate salaries.

Wright had made still other loud-voiced enemies by reason of his attacks on the Suffragettes. He obstinately maintained that there is an unbridgeable gulf between the functioning of the male and female minds. In this connection Colebrook quotes something Wright once said about women: 'The reason we feed them and keep them is that they shall have no freedom of expression.' He had written a whole book, *The Unexpurgated Case against Woman Suffrage*, for the purpose of showing that the Suffragettes were unsatisfied women who dreamed of an epicene world ('epicene' from the Greek '*epikoinos*', common to, or identical with, both sexes) in which men and women should work as equals, shoulder to shoulder at the same tasks. In fact, said Wright, women were receiving preferential treatment and preventing men from doing the best work of which they were capable. This was a doctrine which he could impose within the four walls of his own laboratory, but in the world at large the powerful forces of femininity held it to be an abomination.

Finally, Wright delighted in adopting for his own purposes the policy of 'divide and rule'. He told Freeman that he looked upon him as his 'son in science', and that, as such, he would one day take his place as the Head of the Department. But he had made almost identical promises to Fleming. Was he deliberately trying to foster an antagonism between two men who, though very different from one another, had so far been friends? By reason of his title as Director, of the prestige which his work legitimately gave to him, and of the financial support which he could secure for the Department, he continued to wield the supreme power of an absolute monarch. Leonard Noon and John Freeman had carved out for themselves a small, self-governing principality within which they concentrated on hay-fever and allergies in general, with considerable success. Fleming, for his part, worked directly with the Chief.

This he did not in the least mind, for he felt a deep veneration for that illustrious and picturesque figure. He admired the Old

Man who for so many years, seated at his work-table, 'using ridiculously simple equipment, a few test-tubes, glass slides and pipettes, a few rubber teats, some scraps of cardboard, a little paraffin and sealing-wax, and with no other resource than the inexhaustible ingenuity of his mind and the dexterity of his hands', had devised a whole arsenal of microtechniques for following and measuring the processes of infection and immunity. This hard and monotonous existence, devoted to the cause of science, gave Fleming a deep and secret happiness.

Would he some day have the good fortune to make the brilliant discovery which so much enthusiastic work and so hard a discipline deserved? Breathing the air of the laboratory in which 'the delicate scent of cedar-oil mingled with that of melting paraffin', he felt a profound satisfaction in the knowledge that he had been born into an extraordinary epoch which was witnessing a continuous revolution in the theories and practice of medicine. Within fifty years, Pasteur — whom Fleming regarded as the ideal of what a scientist should be — Behring, Roux and Wright had transformed the control and treatment of infectious diseases. With the coming of Ehrlich and salvarsan hope had dawned that chemotherapy might become a practical reality. What of the future? Only a small number of micro-organisms were killed by 606. All the others were still invincible. The solution of the problem of how they could best be attacked must, thought Fleming, be linked with the natural defences of the human body. The more one studied these tiny mechanisms, the more marvellous did they seem.

But he was careful not to let himself be lured away into expressing general ideas. His job was to demonstrate facts without any additional padding. Being his own technician, he worked every hour of the day and had no time for talking. At the lab. his colleagues set their watches by the moment of his daily arrival. He valued a skilfully constructed piece of apparatus, a 'neat' elaboration of a method, more highly than any theory. Wright's intelligence did not impress him: it was the man he loved. Deep down, Fleming was sensitive and affectionate, but his shyness made him brusque. Often of an evening in the laboratory a heated discussion would start, then lose direction and seep away into the sand. Flem would be there, listening attentively, but taking no part in the debate until, just as the arguments were becoming quite crazy, he would jerk all the great minds back to earth with a brief, quiet remark in which there was no hint of 'showing off'.

Others overestimated the results of their experimental work. He, on the other hand, was inclined to underestimate his. Wright said to him one day: 'You treat research like a game: you find it all great fun.' It was perfectly true. He liked having fun. In Freeman's house, where he had a consulting-room, he liked, whenever possible, to slip away and, with Mrs Freeman, play at pitching coins on to a small square of the drawing-room carpet. At the laboratory, his 'amusements' were ingenious, practical and precise. In his childhood he had learned to use his eyes, and he never forgot anything he had seen.

CHAPTER SIX

THE WAR OF 1914-18

The greatest derangement of the mind is to believe things because one wants
to believe them and not because one has seen that they are. BOSSUET

'A barrowful will do, to begin with.'
'A barrowful of *what?*' thought Alice. LEWIS CARROLL, *Alice in Wonderland*

ONE day in 1912, young Dr James, paying a visit to St Mary's after the completion of his studies, saw a sturdy, bronzed soldier, in the field uniform of the London Scottish standing at the top of the steps. It was Fleming. He was just back from the annual camp and James was staggered to learn that a doctor of his quality, a learned bacteriologist, should be willing to go into training as a simple private. 'At that time', says James, 'I had no military experience. The idea of sharing a tent with six or seven other men filled me with horror ... I ventured to ask him how he managed to keep his equipment so spotless, his rifle and boots so clean in spite of the rain and mud. He gave me an icy-blue and rather terrifying look, and replied with his habitual brevity: "By bloody hard work!"

'My former meetings with Fleming had left me with a lively sense of admiration. Finding my hero transformed into a soldier gave me something to think about. I had been taught by my Nonconformist upbringing to think of war as a crime. I believed that no one went into the Army unless he had something to reproach himself with, and that all officers were more or less like the immoral Cavaliers who had taken up arms in the Civil War against the Puritans. The realization that one of my most highly esteemed seniors, with a remarkable record of work, was prepared to risk his life as a soldier of the King, made me revise my views about the possibility of a war.'

Actually, war did not break out until two years later. Fleming had left the London Scottish in April 1914, because the training periods did not fit in with his work at the hospital.

★

A month or two after the beginning of the war Wright was given the rank of colonel and sent to France to establish a laboratory and research centre at Boulogne-sur-Mer. He took with him Douglas as a captain, Parry Morgan, and Fleming who sported the two stars of a lieutenant in the R.A.M.C. Colebrook joined them later. Freeman went first to Russia to prepare vaccines against the cholera and then proceeded to the laboratory at Boulogne. This was officially attached to the hospital established by the English Army in the Casino. To begin with, the bacteriologists were accommodated in an appalling basement through which a drain-pipe ran, so that the whole place stank. Every morning at six o'clock a sapper sergeant poured some cresol into the pipes, but the sickening stench persisted.

Sir Almroth reacted in no uncertain manner (he could be most effectively brutal on occasion), and got the fencing-school on the top floor allotted to the research staff. Naturally it contained none of the equipment needed by a laboratory — no benches, no running-water and no gas. The ingenious Fleming did yeoman service. Bunsen-burners were kept going on methylated spirit, and the incubators were heated with paraffin stoves. For such work as demanded the use of glass, he contrived a very effective blow-pipe out of rubber tubes and a pair of bellows mounted on a petrol-tin. He said, later, that he had never had a better laboratory.

In war as in peace, nothing could disturb his habitual composure. 'My first impression of Lieutenant Fleming', says his former orderly sergeant, 'was of a short, pale officer who never said more than he had to, but carried on calmly and efficiently with his work. When Captain Douglas went sick, Captain Fleming (he was promoted by that time) took over the command. Captain Douglas had always been chaffing and swearing when he talked to me about service matters. The first time I gave Captain Fleming some papers requiring his signature, he was busy with his microscope. I waited respectfully until he could give me his attention. At last, he raised his head, took a pencil and, without asking me for a word of explanation, signed the vouchers. On such occasions as I had to make a report to him, I got the feeling that he wasn't interested, though he was — much more than I thought. He took the whole thing in, solved the problem on the spot, and ended up with: "Right, Sergeant, carry on." '

Throughout the war the amount of work done by the Department was tremendous and enormously beneficial. The question was no longer one merely of vaccines, though Wright (like Vincent in France) had fought tooth and nail to get anti-typhoid vaccination made compulsory in the Army. It saved thousands of lives, but the wounded brought other problems, most of them urgent and distressing. Wright and his assistants on their way to the laboratory had, every morning, to go through the wards, where they could see for themselves the terrible effects of explosives more powerful than those used in any previous war, and the infections set up in open wounds by earth and scraps of clothing. The surgeons despairingly drew the attention of the bacteriologists to innumerable cases of septicaemia, tetanus and, especially, gangrene. Every day convoys of wounded men arrived with splintered bones, torn muscles and severed blood-vessels. Within a very short space of time the patient's face would become ashen in colour, his pulse would weaken and his breathing diminish almost to nothing. This was the effect of gas-gangrene and meant certain death.

How was it to be dealt with? 'In this war,' said Sir Alfred Keogh, Head of the Army Medical Services, 'we have found ourselves back among the infections of the Middle Ages.' Since the time of Lister, surgeons had got into the habit of relying on antiseptic and, especially, aseptic treatment. Except in certain cases of road-accidents, the wounds with which they had had to deal were reasonably clean, and they had learned how not to infect them. Lister had introduced the system of passing smocks, gloves and instruments through an antiseptic preparation. Later, everything which had to come in contact with the patient was first sterilized by heat. It looked as though 'hospital sickness' had been conquered once and for all. But in the terrible butchery of 1914, by the time the injured reached hospital, their wounds were already crawling with microbes. Any poor wretch who happened to have fallen in a field or on a road was bound to have picked up any number of deadly germs. Fleming, examining odds and ends of uniform, found in them microbes of every description. As to manure heaps, they were infested with germs.

What was to be done? Fleming made a careful study of recently infected wounds, and noticed a remarkable fact. Phagocytosis was more active in them than in wound infections observed in ordinary civil practice. The leucocytes had devoured, and killed, an enormous quantity of microbes. Why? 'In normal times,' he said, 'infections occur more or less spontaneously in individuals, who for some reason or other have become less resistant to the infecting agent. In civil practice also the bacteria have frequently an enhanced virulence, due to their passage from one individual to another. In war, on the contrary, a strong and healthy man when wounded finds himself suddenly and violently infected by microbes the virulence of which has been weakened as the result of living in unfavourable conditions. It is, therefore, only natural that phagocytosis should in these cases be greater. But why, then, in these conditions, should the infection in war-wounds be worse? Because the projectile has produced a very extensive destruction of tissues. Not only do dead tissues provide a good culture medium for microbes, they actually prevent the healthy phagocytes from reaching them.' His first piece of advice, therefore, to the surgeons was: remove all necrotic tissues as soon as possible.[1]

He had learned from his experience as a research-worker to have a solid respect for the natural defence-mechanisms of the human body. What happened in the case of a wound relieved of dead tissues and left to the processes of nature? The healthy leucocytes, penetrating the walls of the blood-vessels, attacked in strength, and cleansed the wound by absorbing the microbes. What was the cause of this 'diapedesis', or migration, of the white corpuscles? To say that a 'positive chemotaxis' attracted the phagocytes to the toxins, was merely to stress, once again, the soporific effect of opium. But, whatever the cause might be, the effect was certain. What mattered, therefore, was to let the natural defences of the body have free access to the microbes.

The army doctors were lacking in neither courage nor devotion, but they were now finding themselves face to face with a new problem. In the absence of adequate direction, they stuffed wounds with antiseptics, often chosen in a rather haphazard manner. That was strictly in accordance with the instruction which they — and Fleming, too — had received as students. 'I remember', he said, 'that I used to be told to be most careful to use antiseptics in the dressing of wounds — carbolic acid, boric acid, peroxide of hydrogen. I could see for myself that these antiseptics did not kill

[1] Alexander Fleming, *Lancet*, September 18th, 1915.

all the microbes, but was told that they killed some, and that the results were better than if no antiseptics had been used at all. At that time I was in no position to argue.'

At Boulogne he could see that antiseptics were powerless, that microbes abounded, that the wounded were dying. Being nothing if not thorough, and suspicious of all *a priori* ideas, he devised a series of brilliant experiments for the purpose of bringing various antiseptic dilutions into contact with different forms of microbial infection. These showed that not only did the antiseptics do nothing to prevent gangrene, they seemed actually to promote its development.

Of course, in certain cases of superficial infection there was an advantage to be gained in using solutions sufficiently concentrated to destroy the bacilli. True, they also destroyed some of the cells of the body but, since this process took place on the surface, the surgeon could then remove the dead tissues. But cases of superficial infection were rare. Modern explosives produce deep wounds which are more than just simple cavities. Scraps of underclothing and other dirty objects, driven inwards by the explosion, penetrate deeply into the tissues. The injuries with which Fleming had to deal presented multiple anfractuosities, corners and crannies which might be compared to the configuration of the Norwegian fjords, and infection broke through the walls of these. Such antiseptics as were then in use were powerless to get at the tissues. Was it possible to sterilize these ragged recesses? In order to find the answer to that question, he hit on the idea of modelling an artificial wound in glass. After first making the closed end of a test-tube red-hot, he drew out, on the inside, several hollow excrescences to represent the anfractuosities of the wound. Next, he filled the tube with a serum previously infected with faecal matter. The general result gave a diagrammatic, but sufficiently exact, picture of a war-wound.

He then put the tube into an incubator and left it there for the night. Next morning the serum, invaded by microbes, had a muddy appearance and stank. The tube was then emptied of the serum and refilled with an antiseptic solution strong enough to kill the microbes. After certain intervals, not always the same, he emptied the tube and filled it again with *non-infected* serum. After incubation, this serum, which had begun by being sterile, was as muddy and stinking as the first. No matter how many times the operation was repeated, the result was the same. What did that prove? Obviously that, since the new serum had been originally free of contamination, microbes must still be lurking in the anfractuosities of the tube. From this he concluded that it was not possible to sterilize a war-wound with the then-known antiseptics.

Once more the question arose, what was to be done? Wright's answer was — leave the natural defences of the body to do their work, and *help them*. The leucocytes which flocked through the walls of the blood-vessels formed a pus the action of which was powerfully beneficial. Wright and Fleming had demonstrated by experiment that fresh pus destroys the colonies of microbes. To this bactericidal power of healthy leucocytes there is no limit, provided they are present in sufficient numbers. The best form of treatment, therefore, would be the one which would mobilize armies of leucocytes and cause the greatest possible quantity of fresh lymph to exude from the walls of the wound. Wright showed by laboratory tests that this action could be produced by using a high concentration of saline solution. Fleming confirmed these findings by experiments made on actual wounds.

The same cause explains the successes obtained in the field by the French physiologist, Carrel, who introduced the system of washing out wounds with Dakin's solution (hypochlorite of soda) which, like the high concentration of saline solution, stimulated an intense exudation of fresh lymph. Fleming, knowing that antiseptics rapidly lose their bactericidal properties when in contact with pus and tissues, wanted to see how long Dakin's solution remained active in a wound. He found that ten minutes after instillation, this antiseptic ceased to be dangerous to microbes. 'Yes,' was his conclusion, 'Dakin's solution gives good results, but, like the highly concentrated saline, *only because it helps the natural defences*. It's lucky', he added, with a touch of humour, 'that it loses its antiseptic action so quickly. In ten minutes it can't do much damage, and, after that, nature has two hours' rest in which to recuperate without being interrupted.'

Fleming's later discoveries have thrown his work during the war into the shade. But those qualified to judge (Dr Freeman, for instance) are of the opinion that he never conceived anything more perfect or more ingenious than those brilliant experiments by which he demonstrated the danger to human tissues of antiseptics when wrongly used.

Bernard Shaw, a frequent visitor to Boulogne, was cock-a-hoop. 'We are left in the hands of doctors who, having heard of microbes much as St Thomas Aquinas heard of angels, suddenly concluded that the whole art of healing could be summed up in the formula: Find the microbe and kill it ... The simplest way to kill most microbes is to throw them into an open street or river and let the sun shine on them ... But doctors instinctively avoid all facts that are reassuring, and eagerly swallow those that make it a marvel that anyone could possibly survive three days in an atmosphere consisting mainly of countless pathogenic germs. They conceive microbes as immortal until slain by a germicide administered by a duly qualified medical man ... In the first frenzy of microbe-killing, surgical instruments were dipped in carbolic oil, which was a great improvement on not dipping them in anything at all and simply using them dirty; but as microbes are so fond of carbolic oil that they swarm in it, it was not a success from the anti-microbe point of view ...'[1] Here Shaw did not understand, or pretended not to understand. The instruments were genuinely sterilized because in their case the strong concentrations were inoffensive. Lancets do not have vulnerable cells.

But though Shaw may have been amused, the pundits were shocked. Wright who, with his customary quickness of mind and his passionate enthusiasm, had concentrated all his attention on this problem, the solution of which might save thousands of lives, increased the number of his lectures to English and French doctors. In 1915, he addressed the Royal Society of Medicine in London on two separate occasions. He did his best — and this, for him, meant a great effort — to keep his talks at a purely practical level, with his literary genius in abeyance. He did all he could not to be aggressive or ironical, his object being to convince without giving offence. In this he did not succeed. Self-satisfaction is so strong an emotion that it will deny the most obvious facts in the interest of a pride which is quick to take offence. The President of the Royal College of Surgeons, Sir William Watson Cheyne, who, having been a friend of Lister and spent his life in carbolic acid, was pleased to regard these new ideas on the surgical treatment of

[1] Bernard Shaw, Preface to *The Doctor's Dilemma*. Standard edition, 1932, pp. 21-2.

war-wounds as amounting to an attack upon his own honour and that of his master — quite wrongly, for Wright and Fleming had the greatest respect for Lister, but conditions were different. Consequently, Sir William thundered from the mountain-top of his authority.

This was, to say the least, unwise, for Wright, when touched on the raw, could be a ferocious controversialist. On September 16th, 1916, he published in the *Lancet* an admirably written reply which, in fact, amounted to a pamphlet. He lacked neither authority nor competence, since he and his assistants had had recent and extensive experience of war-wounds. Sir William Watson Cheyne had admitted that, when infection had been active for ten or twelve hours, the chance of doing much good with antiseptics was very small.

'But', replied Wright, 'in war, a wounded man who has been left for a long time on the battlefield, then slowly transported in an ambulance, can rarely receive attention within those limits of time which you appear to think necessary for successful treatment. And once the proper moment for the use of antiseptics has gone by, what is your programme? So far as I can make out, you haven't any. You say, in effect: "I have opened the wound, I have inserted a drain, I have washed the affected parts of the body with a weak antiseptic solution, and I am not prepared to give further thought to the problem."

'For my own part,' continued Wright (and here we are summarizing his argument), 'I take a diametrically opposite view. So far as the sterilization of war-wounds is concerned, I share with all those who have had the same experience in France as myself, the feeling that serious wounds inflicted in battle are never sterilized, and *never can be*, by the application of antiseptics. I have, therefore, strongly put forward the view that we must help the body, by *physiological* means, to combat bacterial infection. By stimulating a plentiful flow of lymph, we can aid the fluids in the blood to act upon the infected tissues. The more fresh serum we can produce, the more we can accelerate the migration of the leucocytes, the more we can assist in the destruction of the infecting microbes ... It seems to me that Sir William Watson Cheyne is blind to all these problems. He has not even caught a distant glimpse of the towers of that city in which we are seeking to arrive ...'

He then produced overwhelming arguments to show that his illustrious opponent seemed to have not the remotest idea what an experiment was. 'Let us consider what the necessary qualifications for a practical scientist are ...' Sir William had referred to a case of a gaping fracture sterilized by Lister. 'All that this passage in Sir William's text shows is that a muddled mind and deficient logic can draw false conclusions from a genuine clinical observation ...' One of the objections put forward to Sir William's contention had been that Sir Almroth Wright's physiological treatment must be effective since so many doctors had been using it at the front for some considerable time. 'I have nothing to do with the actions of men at the front,' Sir William foolishly replied, 'to say nothing of the fact that a well-known piece of mechanism, known as discipline, operates in the field ...' In other words, since Wright was a colonel, his word must always be law in military circles. But so far was this from being true that Wright had asked the army surgeons, no matter what their rank, to think for themselves, and verify from their own experience the experiments carried out in the little laboratory at Boulogne, all of which were objective, simple and irrefutable.

No doubt, though Wright was an individualist and boasted that he had never taken orders from anyone, he considered that in so grave, so tragic, a situation, it was impossible to let every regimental medical officer go his own sweet way. In peace the practitioner works in a familiar and well-explored field. In wartime, on the other hand, he finds himself having to deal with unfamiliar problems, and forced to take decisions on the spot. It is essential, therefore, that his seniors and advisers shall make available to him the results of experiments carried out by others. Thus, for instance, Wright was totally opposed to the immediate evacuation of the wounded to England ... After an exhausting iourney, he argued, they would be in no fit state to undergo operations which, carried out on the spot, would have a far better chance of being successful. 'We accumulate surgeons in France and wounded men in England ... It looks as though the problem, as set by the Army, is never to have the wolf, the lamb and the cabbage all together on the same side of the river ...' It was a matter of regret to him that the medical administration of the armies in the field, excellent though it was in dealing with the feeding and transportation of the wounded, seemed unable to shoulder the responsibility of solving such far more important problems as those affecting the improved treatment of the wounds themselves.

He, for his part, went to infinite trouble to make generally known what he thought to be the truth. At Boulogne he delivered a lecture: 'On the Proper Methods of Judging Different Types of Treatment'. 'Our task,' he said, 'is to find the truth and to convince others that it is the truth. The medical organization of our armies is such that it becomes necessary to persuade all the doctors who are working in the field. It is not enough to win over their superior officers because there can be no certainty that they will issue orders ...' He was urgent in putting forward a suggestion that a 'Medical Intelligence and Investigation Department' should be set up at the War Office. Its duty would be to study all the problems arising out of war conditions, not only as they concerned wounds, but other matters as well, such as epidemic jaundice, trench-fever and the causes of nervous break-down among air-pilots. Its decisions would be accepted by all. Since he had many friends in the world of politics, he went in person to London to put his point of view to the Secretary of State for War, Lord Derby, and to Arthur Balfour. But the opposition of the 'high-ups' in the Army Medical Service was violent. Sir Arthur Sloggett, the D.G.M.S., loudly denounced the scheme, said that Wright should stick to his laboratory work, and went so far as to demand his recall. He failed to get it, but Wright, too, failed to get what *he* wanted.

Dr James, at that time a battalion M.O., visited the Boulogne Casino on his way back from leave. There he saw Fleming and Colebrook. His first reaction, when he compared the almost academic calm of the laboratory with the din of battle, the dirt, the stench and the nervous tension in the forward aid-posts, was one of faint irritation. These back-area doctors, he thought, have too easy a life! Wright lived in a charming house on the Boulevard Daunou, where Lucienne, an excellent French cook, looked after his comfort. But it was not long before he noticed how much thinner Fleming had grown and how worn-out he looked. In conversation with him, he soon realized that these same 'back-area' doctors were working night and day, and that their only wish was to do everything they could to help the fighting men. Fleming, more eloquent than usual, explained to him the experiments he was conducting and the very precise ideas he had formed about what was necessary if that great enemy of the wounded, infection, was to be overcome. 'What we are looking for,' he said, 'is some chemical substance which can be injected without danger into the blood stream for the purpose of destroying the bacilli of infection, as salvarsan destroys the spirochaetes.' They had not yet found such a substance, but the team had already collected a number of very important facts. These enabled them to avoid the more fatal mistakes and to help the organism of the wounded man in its curative work. James took back with him to his battalion several new, precise and sound ideas on the treatment of wounds.

There was no lack of visitors to the Casino. Bernard Shaw turned up on several occasions. Wright and he spent long nights in front of the fire discussing the relative importance of philosophy and medicine. One evening, when they were deep in argument, the chimney caught fire and the room was soon full of smoke. Lucienne and Freeman took turns in going into the street to see whether the roof was alight. Shaw and Wright, completely undisturbed, went on with their discussion.

The famous American brain-specialist, Harvey Cushing, stayed for a while with Wright. Though the two men were very different in temperament, they liked each other enormously. Though Cushing, like Fleming, had a matter-of-fact mind, he was greatly entertained by Wright's passionate tirades on women, the Catholic Church and intellectual integrity. While the talk was going on, on one occasion, the fire died down. Wright got it going again with the help of a newspaper and, since he had theories about everything under the sun, explained that, to keep the paper from catching fire, one must always on the first sign of combustion make a hole with a poker in such parts of the paper as had turned black. Cushing, much amused by this fire-surgery, called the method 'Wright's Punctures'.

Cushing was Surgeon-in-Chief of the American Hospital provided by the University of Harvard, which had recently been transferred to Boulogne. Another Harvard professor, Roger Lee, was the Head Physician. He knew Wright by reputation because of anti-typhoid vaccination. (During the Spanish-American war, for every one man who died of wounds, a thousand succumbed to typhoid.) He had done some laboratory work on the opsonins and was delighted to learn that the famous Wright was under the same roof with him. He lost no time in paying him a visit and found him surrounded by Fleming, Freeman, Keith and Colebrook. 'I was at once attracted by Fleming,' he says, 'though he hardly spoke.' The attraction was mutual and the two men remained lifelong friends.

Among other visitors were Robert W. Bliss, the United States Ambassador in Paris, and several Frenchmen: Professor Pierre Duval, Jacques Calvé and Dr Tuffier. Wright got along very well with the French, who shared his taste for general ideas. Freeman soon grew tired of Boulogne and went to work in Paris. On leaving, he said to Fleming: 'You know, Flem, we two ought to be playing a more active part.' A grunt was the only answer he got. Fleming was thinking that the research-work at Boulogne might well save the lives of innumerable wounded men.

At the time of the First World War, the British had not, as had the French, the feeling that war is a quasi-religious ceremony, an act of sacrifice to be made with a becoming sense of gravity. They regarded it as a point of honour to relax occasionally, to seem to have time on their hands. A few miles behind the front the officers fished for trout and went sea-bathing. An eye-witness relates how one day Captain Fleming and another scientist — 'I rather think it was Wright himself—feeling the need for exercise, had a wrestling-match. Just as both of them were rolling on the floor, the door opened to admit a delegation of high-ranking French army doctors. The wrestlers jumped to their feet and at once embarked upon a learned scientific discussion. But I shall never forget the expression on the faces of those French medical generals.'

Nothing could well have been less in accordance with army conventions than the life led by this little group of scientists in uniform. So careless was Wright of his appearance that his orderly sergeant, Clayden, insisted on putting him through a dress-parade every morning, so as to make sure that he had got his belt on properly, etc. 'One day', says Clayden, 'I noticed that the seat of his trousers was torn and that a piece of his shirt was showing. I didn't quite like to mention it, so I told Captain Fleming and said that he really ought to draw the Colonel's attention to it. His reply was: "Do it yourself." So I went straight up to Sir Almroth, stood to attention, clicked my heels (which always earned me a mocking smile from the Colonel), and said, "*There's a hole in the seat of your pants, sir.*" He looked at me. "That's a nice way to talk, Sergeant, I must say! I suppose you think the nurses will be shocked. Well, what do you suggest I should do about it?" "I think, sir, the best thing would be for you to send your driver back to your billet for another pair." "What a brain!" he said. Captain Fleming and I had a good chuckle, and then everyone settled down to work.'

On Sundays Fleming and two of his colleagues (Thomson, an Irishman from Belfast, and Dr Keith, a Canadian) used to play golf at Wimereux. The links were situated on the sand-dunes which lie along the Channel coast. It meant a walk of a couple of miles or so northwards from Boulogne, but that didn't frighten the old foot-slogger of the London Scottish. Nevertheless, if an empty staff car happened to pass, the three musketeers would stop it. A somewhat self-important colonel regularly put in an appearance on the links. Fleming, a silent humorist, thought it great fun, when he was out of sight behind a dune, to drop the colonel's ball into the hole, and the colonel, thinking he had achieved the miraculous feat of holing out in one, was duly elated.

Fleming was far from being a brilliant player. As always, he wanted to improvise a secondary game within the game proper. To vary the proceedings, he adopted a number of non-regulation methods. He would, for instance, lie on the ground and use a reversed putter as a billiard-cue, or turn his back to the hole, and putt between his legs. Sometimes the results were successful. The others accused him of cheating, but that didn't worry him.

Keith, the Canadian, had become one of Fleming's great friends. He had done his medical studies at various American universities and, in the eyes of the English, he was a *Yank*. Fleming's practical mind was much to his taste, because it was so effective. 'We found this research group more than usually interesting,' says Keith, 'because it kept in constant touch with the doctors and surgeons who looked after the wounded. The exchange of views which went on between them turned out to be useful and exciting. At tea-time, Boulogne being the great supply port for the B.E.F., there was always a crowd of guests, and the talk grew animated. Though Fleming said little, he did a great deal to keep the conversation at a practical level with his felicitous and opportune remarks. His views on the work done by the others, though penetrating, were always mixed with the milk of human kindness. His breadth of outlook reminded me of the best of our American research-workers, and it played a great part in the birth of our friendship.'

In 1918, a special hospital (No. 8 Stationary) was established at Wimereux to deal with fractures of the femur involving deep laceration. It was decided that a special study should be made there of septicaemia and gas-gangrene. 'It was a proud moment for me', says Dr Porteous, 'when I was sent to this hospital as a bacteriologist working under Fleming's orders. He was in charge of the laboratory, and we shared a hut. Our lab. was a wooden shed. The walls were covered with "pin-ups", pictures of phago-cytes with, here and there, an illustration from *La Vie Parisienne*.' Fleming was still busy with his study of antiseptics and the saline treatment of wounds. He did a great deal of work on the septi-caemias caused by streptococci and, with Porteous, tried to establish the conditions which would make this form of infection less frequent. He also practised transfusion, brought the method to a fine point, and published his results in the *Lancet*. Transfusion was not yet a familiar routine. The blood donors were volunteers, who were encouraged by the promise of extra leave. To keep himself physically fit, Fleming had laid out two golf-holes on a piece of grass behind the hut and the two friends played there at night, with candles in the holes, whenever wind and air-raids permitted.

The great 1918 epidemic of Spanish flu kept the doctors hard at it night and day. The unexpected rate at which the sufferers were dying was heartbreaking. The orderlies themselves went sick with it. Quite often Fleming and Porteous themselves had to carry corpses to the improvised cemetery. Gas-gangrene was still raging and the stench was appalling, flies became a positive scourge, until Fleming devised a method of 'bringing them down' by spraying them with xylene out of a syringe. He studied the Pfeiffer bacillus which was said to be causing this notorious form of flu. To be sure, it was found in ninety per cent of those suffering from it, though in general this particular bacillus is not regarded as being very dangerous. Fleming wondered why it should suddenly have produced this deadly epidemic. He attempted to grapple with the problem and discovered that there were several variants of the Pfeiffer bacillus and that it was not always the same but one or other of those variants which was found in people suffering from Spanish flu. He concluded, therefore, that the illness was caused by some agent other than the Pfeiffer bacillus which, in itself, was only the germ of a secondary infection. He was right, but that did not do much to help the sufferers.

'The picture I have of him', says his sergeant, 'is that of a short R.A.M.C. officer carrying a tray loaded with pipettes, Plasticine, platinum wire and a spirit lamp, standing on a cold winter's morning, with ice and snow everywhere, in a tent heated by a brazier, with me carrying out an autopsy on a table, while on another table another corpse lay awaiting its turn! We had six autopsies to do that morning! It was Christmas Day and from each of the bodies Captain Fleming took specimens.'

In spite of all their efforts, the hospital doctors never succeeded in protecting the wounded from gas-gangrene. Fleming was in despair. 'Surrounded by all those infected wounds,' he wrote, 'by men who were suffering and dying without our being able to do anything to help them, I was consumed by a desire to discover, after all this struggling and waiting, something which would kill those microbes, something like salvarsan ...' In this way he was driven back again on to the problem with which he had been obsessed when he wrote his thesis on 'How to Overcome Infectious Diseases'. But by this time Foch, in a sequence of unexpected blows, had shattered the enemy front. The war ended in November 1918. In January 1919 Fleming was demobilized.

CHAPTER SEVEN

CHILDREN AND MEN

Children attracted him by their natural enjoyment of simple pleasures. In the same way he had a great love of nature, birds, flowers and, of course, trees, and knew a great deal about them. PROFESSOR CRUICKSHANK

O N December 23rd, 1915, while on leave, Fleming had got married. When he returned to Boulogne and, after a while, started talking of 'my wife', his friends at first refused to take him seriously. They could not imagine him as a married man. They insisted on seeing a photograph of Mrs Flem. He had one sent. But by scientific minds this proof was not accepted as sufficient, and they had to wait until the war was over before coming to terms with so surprising an idea. But he really and truly had married Sarah Marion McElroy, a trained nurse who ran a private nursing home in York Place, Baker Street. She was its proprietor, and numbered among her clientele several aristocratic patients who, having once had experience of her establishment, would go nowhere else when they were ill.

Sarah, generally known as 'Sareen', was born at Killala, Ballin, County Mayo, Ireland. Her father, Bernard McElroy, owned one of the largest farms in the neighbourhood. He was an admirable man, mad about sports, and very much under the influence of his wife who ruled both farm and family. There were many children of the marriage, including twins — Elizabeth and Sarah. Four of the daughters had been trained as nurses. Sarah started her hospital career in Dublin. In the house of the celebrated surgeon Sir Thornby Stoker, for whom she worked, she met many famous writers — George Moore, W. B. Yeats, Arthur Symons and others. But she took very little interest in literature and none at all in men of letters. What she loved was her profession and an active life.

At the time when Fleming first met her, Sareen was a white-skinned blonde, with pink cheeks, grey-blue eyes — Irish eyes — and an expressive face. Her charm lay in her extraordinary vitality, her manifest kindness, her gaiety and the self-confidence which accounted for her success. She was drawn to the young Scottish doctor who was so serious, silent and temperate — in fact, the very opposite of herself in all respects. It was to her credit that she had divined beneath the outward show of modesty and reserve a hidden genius which at once won her respect. 'Alec is a great man,' she said, 'but nobody knows it.'

It seems probable that she had had to give him a good deal of encouragement before he could bring himself to propose. She long remembered his shyness. He was incapable of expressing his feelings, and never ceased to be surprised that people found it so difficult to understand what he meant. Much later, when she was seriously ill and felt that she was dying, one of her women friends said to her: 'You *mustn't* die. What would your husband do without you?' 'Oh!' she replied, 'he'll marry again,' and then added with a smile, 'but whoever it is, she'll have to do the proposing!' The fact remains that she always knew how to pierce the armour of silence which protected the sensibility of the strange young man, and loved the beautiful blue eyes which held, deep down, a flicker of impish kindliness.

She was Irish and, therefore, a Catholic. But he never showed the faintest sign of aggressiveness in the matter of her religion. He was more than tolerant, and went so far as to say to a woman friend: 'Why don't you take Sareen to Mass?' He thought that Catholic education was excellent, especially for young girls. 'It is an admirable thing for them to have a convent training,' he said, 'it's good for their morals.'

Sareen's twin sister, Elizabeth, the widow of an Australian, not long afterwards married Alec's brother, John, who was as brilliant, gay and loquacious as Alec and Bob were silent. There were not many points of resemblance between the two women. Sareen was strikingly exuberant, Elizabeth calm and rather sad. Sarah, impetuous and a born fighter, argued in the Irish manner — the manner of Shaw and Wright — with a hearty contempt for her adversary. Fleming, for his part, showed neither displeasure nor anger. Like so many Scots, he had to be known through and through before one could be certain whether he was annoyed or pleased. His motto seemed to be: 'Anything for a Quiet Life', and he really was prepared to sacrifice a great deal so long as he was left in peace to get on with his work.

For this work Sareen had a deep respect, and helped it by bringing to her husband a degree of freedom from money worries. She sold her nursing home, and made Alec promise to give up 'practising' so that he could give all his time to research. This showed great unselfishness on her part, for, since their means were slender, it meant that she would have to do without servants and undertake all the household chores. She also condemned herself to seeing very little of her husband, who spent all his evenings at the laboratory. She had to be resigned to leading a fairly solitary existence, and going to the theatre either alone or with friends.

Those of her husband had at once adopted her. In the course of the several visits he had paid to the Pegrams' cottage in Suffolk, Fleming had become greatly attached to that lovely county. His wife and he used part of the money which came to them from the sale of the nursing home in buying a country house, 'The Dhoon', at Barton Mills, a charming village adjoining the one in which the Pegrams lived. The house was old, with a gravel drive lined by shrubs leading to an attractive glazed front door, flanked by stone seats. It carried with it a fair amount of land and a stretch of river which was reached by a rustic bridge leading to an island. There was good rough fishing — pike, perch and gudgeon — and Alec, being a keen observer, soon got to know the habits and hiding-places of the pike.

He and Sareen between them transformed the meadow and orchard round the house into a well-designed garden which eventually showed a fine profusion of flowers. Clearing the ground took several years, but they both had 'green fingers'. They established a large kitchen-garden, two greenhouses, a vine, and peaches which they trained against a wall. On the river-bank they built a boat-house in which they kept a punt.

Dr and Mrs Fleming spent their week-ends and holidays at The Dhoon. On March 17th, 1924, Sareen gave birth to a son, Robert. It was then that she adopted the habit of settling into The Dhoon during the summer months with her small boy and several nephews. Fleming was left on his own in London, but went into Suffolk every week-end and for the whole of August. He adored his child and would often get up in the middle of the night and tip-toe across to make sure that he was well covered up and was sleeping quietly, just as, so many years before, his mother had done with him in the moorland farm. Later on, he gave up golf entirely in order to play with Robert. Children attracted him because they had his own precious gift of finding happiness in simple things. He had a tremendous love of nature – of birds, flowers and trees – and tasted once again in his country home some of the pleasures of his childhood.

He took a never-failing delight in fishing, swimming and, more than anything else, in gardening. He had an original taste in flowers, his favourites being the giant dahlias and 'love-lies-bleeding'. He liked sowing or planting out in those months of the year which were not advised by the experts, just in order to prove that the experts were wrong. 'A gardener must never be impatient,' he said. 'Flowers grow in their own time and one does more harm than good if one tries to hasten the process. One can protect them against the weather: one can see that they get food and drink, but it is only too easy to kill them when either is too strong or too plentiful. They are responsive to kindness, but they can also withstand any amount of hard treatment. In other words, they are like human beings.' This heretical gardener had some astonishing successes. 'He just went up to some improbable tree when it was in full leaf, wrenched off a branch, stuck it in the ground, and lo and behold, it produced roots!' says Marjory Pegram.

His wife turned out to be no less ingenious and freakish than he was. He spoke with admiration of everything she did: her cooking; the things she bought; the things she planted. They loved and respected one another, and both had a taste for old and beautiful objects. They hunted the local antique shops for furniture. The most affable of hosts, they had friends to stay each week-end. Sareen coped with everything. Her energy was well-nigh miraculous. She mowed the lawn, did the weeding, planted the flowers, polished the furniture, cooked the meals. 'She does all the work,' said Alec with a laugh, 'and provides all the conversation.'

Sareen maintained that that was why they got on so well together. He never answered questions and nothing could make him lose his temper. Their visitors found this traditional confrontation of Scotch and Irish endlessly amusing. The river, and a golf-links not far away, provided additional entertainment. In the evenings they played croquet and putted on the lawn, and when it grew dark, continued the game by candle-light, as Fleming had

learned to do in the old Wimereux days. But he was never satisfied with ordinary croquet. Keen, as he always was, to contrive a
game within a game, he was for ever making new rules which he
observed with an almost religious scrupulousness. Staying at
The Dhoon was always great fun.

As husband and as father he was still his old imperturbable self.
'I never knew him to be put out', says Dr Gerald Willcox. 'One
day, at The Dhoon, he took me out fishing in a boat with his
small son. All of a sudden he hooked a pike. The boy, mad with
excitement, jumped up, and fell into the river. Fleming remained
seated, his attention divided between the pike, which was fighting
like a mad thing, and me, for I was trying to fish the child out of
the water; but not for a moment did he let go of his rod ...'
Another evening, when there was a fireworks display in the garden,
one of his friends, wishing to test his host's legendary impassivity,
let off a rocket between his legs. Fleming never turned a hair,
but simply said, quite calmly: 'Squib gone off.'

Sareen organized children's parties. Her husband took charge of
the games and thoroughly enjoyed himself. He frequently arranged
competitions, for which he offered prizes, and always knew what
the young people would most like, because he had remained one
of them. He certainly felt as happy with them as with grown-ups.
Short though his holidays were, he devoted several days every year
to running a garden fête for the village. The marvellous times
that were had in his garden are still talked about at Barton Mills.

In London he had taken a lease of another charming house in
Danvers Street, in the very heart of Chelsea, with which part of
the Town and himself the Arts Club already formed a bond.
There he entertained several artists who lived in the neighbourhood. Sareen was completely at her ease with them. She had a
passion for youth and liked to be surrounded by pretty young
women. Not only was she completely without jealousy: she enjoyed
looking at them as she enjoyed looking at the beautiful objects for
which she had developed a taste. Fleming did more listening than
talking, but never gave the impression that he was bored. On the
contrary, he greedily absorbed everything that was said, took an
amused enjoyment in it, and hoarded it in his memory. But he had
a horror of dirty stories and never laughed at them. If somebody
embarked on one, he would sit with his eyes shut until it was over.

On all other occasions, he overflowed with innocent gaiety. Even in London he found pleasure in games. He had a special liking for spillikins at which his perfect control of his hands, which never trembled, usually gave him the victory.

The Belgian professor, Gratia, tells how he once spent an evening in Chelsea and was present when Fleming interrupted the conversation of several extremely eminent bacteriologists in order to organize, with absolute seriousness, a game of shove-ha'penny. 'I have known people who used to get annoyed at this pleasing display of childishness,' he writes, 'but should one not rather regard it as an expression of the strength of character of a people who can shoulder the most formidable responsibilities with a smile, and relapse wholeheartedly into foolery with an appearance of imperturbable gravity?'

Sareen was far from having luxurious tastes, but she loved embroideries, china and old glass, which she collected with the complete approval of her husband. She was not particularly interested in clothes, except when it came to 'dressing up', and was only too delighted when she could make a wrap out of an old evening dress. She trimmed her own hats and exhibited them proudly to her women friends, pointing out how silly it was to spend money on such things. Those who did not know her well, occasionally, in the early days of their acquaintance, showed some surprise at her abrupt manners, which were those of a woman accustomed to command. But they very soon came to realize that behind the outward appearances lay a fund of warm feeling and affection. Though she was a careful housewife, she was very generous not only to her friends, nephews and nieces, but also to those whom she employed. In short, the couple was no less liked in Chelsea than at Barton Mills, and Fleming's private life was happy and uneventful.

The same could not be said of his professional career. In 1921, Wright had made him Assistant Director of the Department. Freeman, who was his senior in age, was deeply affronted. Had not Wright always called him his 'son in science' and said that the succession should fall on him? He later realized that Wright 'moved in a mysterious way'. You never knew when the Old Man would be up to his tricks. But, at the time, Freeman believed in perfect good faith that the appointment had been engineered by

Fleming, who, in fact, had been very much distressed by the whole business. The peace of the lab. was put in jeopardy. Freeman, in order to get away from the team, devoted all his time to the Allergy Service, of which he was now undisputed head since the death of Leonard Noon. He did some remarkable work there, especially on the pollens.

Cliques began to form. Personal passions had torn a breach in what once had been a united scientific family. Fleming's position as Wright's deputy became difficult. He could not endure quarrels, nor could he understand them. The Old Man, who had handed over to him the whole administrative side of the Department, would occasionally, as a result of prodding from one or other of his favourites, interfere and flagrantly reverse instructions issued by Fleming. In silence, the latter did everything he could to conciliate opposing groups, so as to avoid irritating his master, and to do and say nothing that might brush his colleagues up the wrong way. He tried to let his promotion sink into oblivion. Modest, efficient, but fully conscious of his duties, he saw to it that the Department should function properly, and also because of a deeply felt and compelling need that justice should be done. In the interests of a cause which he believed to be good, he was prepared, when necessary, to face the Old Man's anger. Those whom he protected never knew that he had done so, unless accidentally.

Dr Dyson gives a good example of this. He had had reason to think that Wright had treated him in an arbitrary and unfair manner. He complained to Fleming. 'I had hoped that he would say: "You are perfectly right, Dyson, and I will support you tooth and nail" ' ... But not a bit of it. He listened without saying a word and Dyson went away feeling intensely annoyed. It was only many years later that he learned that Fleming had on that occasion conducted his defence with the utmost vigour, though without saying a word to anyone about what he had done.

Fleming was now installed in a tiny laboratory near the staircase. From the window he could see a pub, the Fountains Abbey, and a street, Praed Street, with its clutter of junk-shops. Dr Todd, a brilliant hand at research and a tremendous worker, shared it with him. It was not long before a newcomer, Allison, joined them. In their company Fleming could forget all about quarrels and devote himself to his favourite game — research. From time to time the cliques would provoke storms, some of them big, others trivial. To all of them Fleming presented a front of passive resistance. The loyal secretary of the Service, Craxton, still remembers the anguished astonishment with which he once said to him: 'Craxton, why must people be so difficult?' But the mood would pass and he would turn again to his work. Allison often used to hear him humming a song. It was always the same song. 'I don't remember the exact words, but it was about a "dicky-bird" who was quietly sitting on its nest when a hawk swooped down and tore it to pieces.' No doubt his liking for this melancholy ditty arose from the fact that he saw himself as a quiet little bird continually menaced by more than one hawk. But there was no bitterness in him. The song was his way of laughing at himself, and quickly made him forget his troubles.

During the war, St Mary's had for the first time admitted women students. They had helped to keep the Medical School going in the absence of the men, but when the war was over, their continued presence led to storms. One group of male students demanded their removal. Some of the doctors thought that this would be unfair, and put their names to a counter-petition. One of them, a man named Fry, had been taken on at the lab. on Fleming's recommendation, and he felt responsible for him.

'You are making a great mistake, Fry. The Old Man will never forgive you. He hates women students.'

'I don't think he'll take it too hard. But whether he does or he doesn't, my signature stands.'

Fleming's prudence appeared to be excessive. Wright bore no grudge against the heretic. He was delighted to have such a chance of letting himself go and getting a lot of fun at Fry's expense.

The Medical School could no longer carry on without a considerable subsidy from London University. The buildings were in a bad state of repair and the professors were so badly paid that they could not afford to give much of their time to teaching. By great good fortune, a new and energetic dean, Dr Wilson (later, Lord Moran) was elected. But he had a difficult battle to fight. When the members of the Universities' Commission turned up at St Mary's, all went well until they reached the Pathology and

Research Department.[1] There the ironical Wright told them a few home truths and they took to their heels in terror.

Meanwhile, the brilliant and persuasive dean had managed to convince a few powerful individuals that the training of doctors was becoming a problem of national urgency. One of his friends, Lord Revelstoke, the chairman of Baring Brothers, gave him twenty-five thousand pounds to be spent on St Mary's Medical School. Another of his friends, and a patient of his, Lord Beaverbrook, visited the hospital incognito to draw his own conclusions. He visited the Out-Patients' Department and then went into the small canteen reserved for those awaiting attention.

'How much does a bun cost?' he asked. The answer was: 'Three ha'pence, but if that is more than you can afford, you can have it for nothing.'

This must have pleased Lord Beaverbrook, for some days later he asked Dr Wilson to come and see him.

'I know,' he said, 'that you are thinking of rebuilding your School. How much do you need?'

'Sixty-three thousand pounds.'

Lord Beaverbrook immediately opened a credit for that amount in Wilson's name.

While waiting for the reconstruction to be completed, the dean proceeded to reform the method of recruiting students. Among Fleming's papers there is the following note: 'St Mary's. Went through a bad time in the 'twenties. Students then recruited by examination. Only thing required, being clever with exam. papers. The School did not shine either from the quality of its students or from that of its work. Then new dean established system of scholarships on principle of Rhodes Foundation. We got number of good athletes, and School improved.' Dr Wilson thought that the choosing of students recommended by their headmasters and then interviewed by himself was a better system than examination for collecting a body of men of high quality. 'In this way', writes Zachary Cope, 'the School got a regular flow of students of good intelligence, exceptional character and proficiency at games.' This was fully in accordance with Fleming's doctrine.

[1] The new name of the Inoculation Department.

At the laboratory life gradually recovered its pre-war rhythm. There was not very much measuring of the opsonic index now. Wright was out of patience with that method and condemned it with a vigour as excessive as his former enthusiasm had been. Such prejudiced judgments were the price that had to be paid for his genius. He was still interested in metaphysical problems. 'In all my life,' he said, 'I have suffered from only two ailments, nettle-rash and philosophic doubt. The second is the worse of the two.' He believed more strongly than do most men with a scientific outlook in the possibility of reaching the truth by the use of logic and pure reason. His intellectual approach was not that of an Englishman. He inspired personal affection in all who knew him, but unquestioning confidence only in a few. Not many young foreign doctors now visited his Department.

With Fleming and Colebrook he continued, long after the war was over, his private campaign against antiseptics. In 1919 Fleming was chosen to give the 'Hunterian Lecture', a solemn oration delivered every year in memory of the great surgeon, Hunter. He chose as his subject: 'The Action of Physical and Physiological Antiseptics upon a Septic Wound', and treated it in a masterly fashion. 'There were,' he said, 'during the war, two schools of thought about the treatment of wounds: the one, *physiological*, which concentrated on the body's natural agents of protection; the other, *antiseptic*, the object of which was to kill the microbes in the wound by means of a chemical agent ...' He explained once again why Sir Almroth Wright and his disciples belonged to the first of these schools.

Why? Because experience had shown that antiseptics, excellent though they might be for *preventing* infection, were powerless to suppress it once it was established. This he had often demonstrated, but he now added that, even if antiseptics had been inoffensive (which was not the case) they would still have constituted a psychological danger. 'It is very difficult for the surgeon not to be deluded into the belief that he has, in the antiseptic, a second string to his bow, and, consequently, it will tend to make him less careful in his surgical treatment of the wound. If he knows that he has nothing to fall back on, then, even with the most conscientious individuals, the surgery will improve. Because of this alone, it would be well if the treatment of the wound with antiseptics in the early stage were abandoned and the surgeon left to rely on his skill alone. All the great successes of primary wound treatment have been due to efficient surgery, and it seems a pity that the surgeon should wish to share his glory with a chemical antiseptic of more than doubtful utility.'[1]

But, even though he did belong, with his master, to the physiological school, no one knew better that infection often overcomes the natural defences, that the surgeon is sometimes powerless. Like Ehrlich and many others, he would dearly have liked to find the 'magic bullet' — something which should be as fatal in its effects upon the invaders as it was inoffensive to the cells of the human body.

[1] *The British Journal of Surgery*, 1919.

CHAPTER EIGHT

FIRST HOPE: THE LYSOZYME

... sometimes a man whose intelligence is arrested by things which do not strike others, who, knowing how to use his eyes, looks hard at what the others do not see. LERICHE

Never neglect any appearance or any happening which seems to be out of the ordinary: more often than not it is a false alarm, but it *may* be an important truth. FLEMING

'IN 1922', writes Dr Allison, 'I went to St Mary's to work in the Inoculation Department with Fleming. From the very first he started to pull my leg about my excessive tidiness. Each evening I put my "bench" in order and threw away anything I had no further use for. Fleming told me that I was a great deal too careful. He, for his part, kept his cultures sometimes for two or three weeks and, before finally getting rid of them, looked very carefully to see whether by chance any unexpected or interesting phenomenon had appeared. The sequel was to prove how right he was and that, if he had been as neat as I am, he would probably have found out nothing new.

'About a month or two after I had started working with him, he was busy one evening cleaning up several Petri dishes which had been lying on the bench for perhaps ten days or a fortnight. As he took up one of the dishes in his hand, he looked at it for a long time, showed it to me, and said: "This is interesting." I had a good look at it. It was covered with large yellow colonies which appeared to me to be obvious contaminants. But the remarkable fact was that there was a wide area in which there were no organisms; and another, farther on, in which the organisms had become translucent and glassy. Beyond that, again, were organisms which were in a transitional stage of degradation, between the very glassy ones and those which were fully developed with their normal pigment.

'Fleming explained that this particular dish was one to which he had added a little of his own nasal mucus, when he had happened to have a cold. This mucus was in the middle of the zone containing no colony. The idea at once occurred to him that there must be something in the mucus which dissolved or killed the microbes in its immediate neighbourhood, and then became diffused in such a way that it progressively contaminated the already developed colonies. "Now, that really is interesting," he said again. "We must go into it more thoroughly." His first care was to pick off the organism and to stain it by gram. He found it was a large gram-positive coccus, not a pathogen, and not one of the known saprophytic organisms commonly met with, but obviously a contaminating organism which was more likely to have been in the atmosphere of the laboratory and may, of course, have blown in through the window, from the dust and air of Praed Street.

'The next step in the investigation was to try again the use of nasal mucus, and he tested some for its effect on this large gram-positive coccus, not on a plate but in a tube. He made a culture of the organism in broth and added nasal mucus to it. To his great surprise and mine, the opaque suspension of organisms became, in the space of a few minutes, completely clear — "clear as gin," he said at the time. Immediately afterwards, and in the same conditions, he tried the effect of tears. A single drop of tear-fluid dissolved the organisms in probably less than five seconds. It was astonishing and thrilling.

'For the next five weeks, my tears and his were our main supply of material for experiment. Many were the lemons we had to buy to produce all those tears! We used to cut a small piece of lemon-peel and squeeze it into our eyes, looking into the mirror of the microscope. Then, with a Pasteur pipette, the point of which had been rounded in a flame, we collected the tears which we proceeded to put into a test-tube. In this way I often collected as much as $\frac{1}{4}$-$\frac{1}{2}$ c.c. of tears for our experiments.'

Visitors, men and women alike, were put under contribution in this matter of tears. The *St Mary's Hospital Gazette* published a drawing which depicted children coming, for a few pennies, to the laboratory, where one attendant was administering a beating, while another collected their tears in a receptacle on which was written the word 'Antiseptics'. Even the laboratory attendants were condemned to undergo the 'ordeal by lemon', but they got threepence each time. They kept regular accounts and were paid for all their tears at the end of the month. Once, when Fleming noticed that the eyes of one of these men were very red, he remarked: 'If you cry often enough, you'll soon be able to retire!'

These experiments had proved that tears contain some substance which can dissolve certain microbes with surprising speed. 'It was possessed', said Fleming, 'of extraordinary power. Up till then I used to wonder at the much slower action of the antiserum which, when added to an infected broth warmed in an incubator or in the water bath, takes some considerable time to dissolve the microbes, and then only incompletely. But when I studied this new substance, I put into a test-tube a thick, milky suspension of bacteria, added a drop of tear, and held the tube for a few seconds in the palm of my hand. The contents became perfectly clear. 1 had never seen anything like it.'

The phenomenon was indeed very impressive, and Fleming was the first person to observe it. The double piece of luck had been miraculous, for the mysterious substance had been brought in contact with the one microbe which was most sensitive to its action. All the same, though its power of dissolving (and so, killing) had been demonstrated in a more spectacular fashion in the case of the yellow 'coccus', which was inoffensive, the substance also dissolved, though more feebly, other microbes, some of which were pathogenic. In a series of experiments, Fleming showed that it had the properties of an enzyme (natural ferment).

What should this substance be called? As usual, the question was debated in the library, round the tea-table. Wright, as we have seen, delighted in constructing words from Greek roots. Since the new substance was a species of enzyme, its name must end with the syllable 'zyme'; and since it dissolved, or 'lysed', certain microbes, it was agreed to given it the name of 'lysozyme'. As to the microbe so easily 'lysed', Wright named it *'micrococcus lyso-deikticus'* — from *'lysis'* (dissolution) and *'deixein'* (to show): in other words — the organism which makes it possible to show, or note, a power to dissolve.

Fleming continued tenaciously with his investigation of the lysozyme. Since he had made the initial discovery, an idea had been taking form in his mind and becoming more and more insistent. How did it happen that a natural secretion of the body should possess such great strength as a bactericide? Obviously because it had a protective effect on exposed surfaces. This was a necessary provision of nature since, did it not exist, the human species would have died out long ago, or would never have developed at all, seeing that, from the moment of birth, human bodies are in contact with the innumerable germs which air, earth and water contain. At every moment of our lives microbes are being deposited on the surface of the skin, and are penetrating into the nose, the mouth and the alimentary canal. Many of these microbes are harmless, some are even useful and, for example, facilitate digestion. The organism tolerates them, but resists any attempt they may make to get beyond the mucous membrane or to multiply too rapidly.

The blood and its army of phagocytes provide one part of this system of natural defences. But there are certain sensitive and fragile areas, such as the conjunctiva of the eye, the membrane of the nose, and the mucous membrane of the respiratory channels, which are exposed to airborne microbes, and do not have the advantage of an abundant blood-flow. These parts of the body cannot be left without protection. It looked as though lysozyme might be one of the body's natural defences and, if the hypothesis could be verified, it seemed probable that this substance, or other substances of the same type, would be found distributed all over any animal body — whether of a man, a bird or a fish — and that this peculiarity would be present, too, in the vegetable world.

Fleming, therefore, organized a series of experiments with the object of showing that lysozyme would be found in other secretions and even in tissues. He discovered that a nail-paring, a scrap of skin, a drop of saliva or a few hairs, when introduced into a test-tube, exercised the same miraculous solvent action. He got into the habit, when speaking to his students about natural defences, of asking them to take a cutting from the edge of one of their finger-nails and place it in a microbial suspension. The instantaneous effect amazed them — 'especially as they had recently come from the hands of a physiologist who had taught them that finger-nails consist of inert tissue.' Meanwhile, as he went on with the researches, he was finding more and more lysozyme everywhere: in the secretions of the buccal mucus; in the sperm of all animals;

Captain Fleming in the laboratory at Boulogne

Tears embedded in the form of a T in agar which was then flooded with a coccus. There is no growth of the coccus for some distance from the tears

sheet of growth of coccus away from Tears.

Zone of inhibition

Tears imbedded in agar

Lady (Sareen) Fleming,
(d. 1949) and Robert

One of Sir Alexander's own
paintings, done at Barton
Mills

in the spawn of the pike; in a woman's milk; in the tip of a stalk; in leaves.

All the growing things in the garden were tested. Tulips and buttercups, nettles and peonies, were found to contain lysozyme. The turnip had an unusually large amount. But the richest store was egg-white. Fleming demonstrated that egg-white, when diluted in sixty million times as much water, was still capable of dissolving some microbes. The egg, therefore, possesses considerable power as a bactericide, and it needs to, for the white, and even the yolk, of an egg provide a marvellous culture medium for microbes. The shell of an egg is not impervious to them: consequently, if eggs can remain sterile for several days in a dairyman's shop-window, where they are exposed to the attack of every kind of germ, the reason must be that they have some form of natural protection. 'It looks,' said Fleming to his colleague, Ridley, 'as though the surfaces most exposed to infection are also the best protected. For instance, the slime secreted by an earth-worm is a highly potent bactericide.' He found lysozyme in the blood, especially inside the leucocytes and in the fibrin of clots. 'Would not this be,' he asked, 'a protective mechanism for open wounds, which rapidly become covered with a layer of fibrin and leucocytes, both of which are rich in lysozyme?'

Yes, lysozyme really did seem to be the body's natural antiseptic, the cells' first line of defence against microbic invasion. Fleming had every right to be proud of his work. He had discovered a new and very important aspect of those natural defences of the human body to which he had devoted so much study, in the worship of which he had been brought up by Wright. Not so very long ago, Metchnikoff had demonstrated the fact that certain special cells, the phagocytes, opposed the invasion of microbes. Fleming had found that these cells contained lysozyme. Was it not possible, therefore, to conclude that lysozyme was one of the weapons employed by the leucocytes in their battle against the microbes?

As to the skin and the mucous membranes, Metchnikoff had thought that they were protected only by mechanical means. 'Nature', he had said, 'does not use antiseptics to protect them. The fluids which bathe the surface of the mouth and other mucous membranes are not bactericidal, or only very imperfectly so.

Nature removes from the mucous membranes and the skin quantities of microbes by epithelial desquamation,[1] and these are then expelled by the liquid secretions. Nature has chosen this mechanical procedure, just as the surgeon replaces the antisepsis of the mouth with a lavage of salt water.' In 1921 most bacteriologists held this opinion.

Fleming had just proved that Metchnikoff's argument must, on this point, be modified. 'From the aforementioned experiments', he said, 'it is clear that these secretions, and the greater part of the tissues, have, in a very high degree, the power to destroy microbes.' This discovery was one of capital importance. But Fleming never used the word 'discovery'. It was one of those 'big words' which he disliked. He always said 'my observation'. But, whether discovery or observation, this one gave him more satisfaction than any other. So great was his secret elation that in the first paper which he wrote on lysozyme he, as a rule so prudent, so reserved — he, who either from temperamental shyness, or in reaction from Wright's passion for vast abstractions, would never permit himself to talk of anything but facts — opened the flood-gates of his caution to a tide of wonderful hypotheses.

Not only was this discovery of his tremendous in its own right; it also brought to a head ideas which he had been pondering for a very long time. Somewhat later, in one of his rare moods of expansiveness, he said to Ridley: 'When I was a young doctor in the '14-'18 war, the Old Man was very much concerned with the power of the blood to kill bacteria by means of its own leucocytes and serums. But I realized that every living thing must, *in all its parts*, have an effective defence-mechanism; otherwise, no living organism could continue to exist. The bacteria would invade and destroy it.' Ridley adds: 'He left me in no doubt that he had disclosed to me in that simple sentence "every living thing must in all its parts be protected" something fundamental in his thinking. This, I believe, was the star that guided him all through his professional life.'

Against what microbes was lysozyme effective? Fleming devised an ingenious method by which to arrive at an answer to this question. He hollowed out in a gelatinous substance contained in a Petri dish either a hole or a gutter, in which he placed some agar

[1] Elimination of the superficial layers of the epidermis in the form of small scales.

impregnated with lysozyme. Next, he 'planted' certain microbes, some in streaks perpendicular to the gutter, others in lines forming the radii of a circumference of which the hole was the centre. Some of the microbes developed right up to the gutter or the hole. They were obviously insensitive to lysozyme. Others stopped short at a greater or less distance, and this distance marked the measure of their sensitiveness.

Unfortunately, lysozyme, which was so powerful against the inoffensive microbes, turned out to have a much weaker effect upon the dangerous germs, the pathogenic ones. Nothing, thought Fleming, could be more understandable. For what were the pathogenic germs if not those which could penetrate the defences of the organism, establish themselves and cause infection? Now, had they been as sensitive to the action of lysozyme as, for instance, the yellow 'coccus' (*lysodeikticus*), they would have been destroyed by the defenders, they would have been unable to establish themselves and do harm, and this in itself would be contrary to their own definition.

Does not all the difference between 'pathogenic' and 'non-pathogenic' lie precisely there? he reflected. Certain microbes can infect certain varieties of animal and not others; certain tissues, and not others. Is the solution to the problem of predilection to be found in a difference of the quantity or the quality of lysozyme in these animals or tissues? Starting from this hypothesis, Fleming conceived one of those experiments which were always so simple, but never failed to go straight to the heart of the problem.

He tried the effect of human tears on three groups of germs. The first was composed of one hundred and four inoffensive species, found in the air of the laboratory. The second contained eight germs, pathogenic to some animals, but not to human beings. The third was made up of germs which were pathogenic to human beings. The results were exactly what he expected them to be. The lysozyme exercised a very powerful action on seventy-five per cent of the first group, and on seven species (out of eight) of the second. Its action was weak in the third group, though not completely absent. Consequently, if the amount of lysozyme in the organism were increased, it might be possible in that way to stop the development of certain dangerous microbes. There was material here for investigation.

Fleming asked Dr Allison to join him in a programme of research along these lines. But before making further experiments, he read a paper on his discovery and on the conclusions he had drawn from it, in December 1921 to the Medical Research Club, a scientific body of respectable age (it had been founded in 1891) which was both exclusive and influential. The reception accorded to the paper was cold beyond belief. Not a single question was asked and no discussion followed the reading. Only utterly worthless papers were treated in this manner. Sir Henry Dale, who was among those present, has written: 'I very well remember his interesting paper, and the way in which we all of us said: "Charming, wasn't it? Just the sort of naturalist's observation Fleming *would* make" ' — and that was all.

This icy reception of so original a study hurt Fleming's feelings, for beneath his impenetrable mask he was extremely sensitive. But it did not stop him. He prepared another paper on the same subject which Wright presented to the Royal Society in February 1922.[1] But, once again, it did not receive the attention it deserved. Fleming without being unduly upset continued with Allison's help to work on the substance, in the importance of which, despite the indifference of his peers, he persisted in believing. Between 1922 and 1927, they published a further five brilliant papers on lysozyme. They made an attempt to extract it in its pure state, but neither of the two men was a chemist (Fleming used to say that he would fail in an examination in elementary chemistry), and in the laboratories of the St Mary's Research Service there was no chemist or biochemist to be found. They could not isolate lysozyme, though they noted that alcohol could precipitate it, without destroying it.

Having observed that lysozyme found in egg-white was a hundred times more concentrated than that found in tears, they used it for their experiments and established conclusively that the substance, at a concentration double that to be found in tears, had a bactericidal action on almost all the pathogenic germs and, in particular, on the streptococci, the staphylococci, the meningococci, and the bacillus of diphtheria. They even tried the effect of egg-white, administered by mouth, on the streptococci of the

---

[1] 'On a Remarkable Bacteriolytic Element Found in Tissues and Secretions', *Proceedings of the Royal Society*.

intestine. Having made certain that lysozyme was not destroyed by the gastric juices, they chose a patient who had an abnormal quantity of streptococci in his intestine and made him swallow the white of four eggs every day. The streptococci returned to normal. Encouraged by this temporary success, they prescribed egg-white for several patients presenting the same anomaly, who complained of fatigue and 'migraine'. They obtained a change for the better in the symptoms. With prudence and honesty they concluded that: 'This may, of course, have been merely a psychological effect, or it may have been due to a temporary action of the lysozyme on the streptococci.'

Fleming, all this while, was going on with his general study of antiseptics. The purpose of it was the same: to conquer the infections. In 1923, the combined efforts of several research-workers in the lab. produced a new and effective technique for this type of investigation. Elliott Storer, who had thought it out, called it the slide-cell (a slide divided into cells) method, but the slides prepared by him gave disappointing results. Wright, who realized the value of this technique, perfected it, and Dyson added a further improvement. It had everything in it to please Fleming: it required skill in its manipulation; it cost nothing; and it could be worked with small quantities — a great advantage where human blood was concerned.

The slide-cell consisted of two slides of glass separated by five strips of Vaselined paper, placed at regular intervals at right-angles to the longest axis of the slides. The space between the slides was thus divided into four equal compartments, each one of which could contain a small quantity of blood. (Fleming had noticed that the paper on which a certain medical journal was printed had the ideal thickness required for the strips. When he was describing the method in his lectures, he would say, with perfect gravity, and much to the surprise of his students: 'For the Vaselined strips you should use the *Journal of Experimental Pathology*.')

The small compartments were then filled with defibrinated blood infected with the microbes to be studied, sealed at the two open ends with paraffin, after which the whole slide-cell was placed in the incubator. The microbes multiplied in colonies which, in this thin layer of blood, were easy to count. For instance, it was possible to observe that, if about one hundred staphylococci were put into a compartment containing normal blood, the leucocytes killed, on an average, ninety-eight per cent of them, so that only two of the colonies developed.

Fleming thought that this was an ideal technique for making a definitive study of the action of the antiseptics on the leucocytes. In the compartments of the slide-cell he mixed blood with more and more concentrated solutions of the antiseptic which he wanted to study. He noticed that the antiseptic killed the leucocytes at concentrations far below those required to kill the bacteria and so there were concentrations in which all the leucocytes, in other words all the defenders, were killed, while *all* the staphylococci flourished: a hundred microbial colonies were counted in each compartment instead of only two *without* antiseptics. His conclusion was as follows: 'These experiments show that there is little hope that any of the antiseptics in common use could be successfully introduced into the blood stream to destroy the circulating bacteria in cases of septicaemia.'[1] By this beautiful and simple experiment, he had proved irrefutably that the antiseptics then in use destroyed the leucocytes in much weaker solutions than those which would have enabled them to act upon the microbes.

On the contrary, when the slide-cell was used to study the action of egg-white on the phagocytes, Fleming and Allison observed that 'whereas egg-white, in marked contrast to the chemical antiseptics, has no destructive effects on the leucocytes, it has considerable inhibitory or lethal effect on some of the bacteria'. They made the experiment of giving intravenous injections of an egg-white solution to a rabbit, and then measuring the bactericidal power of its blood. There were no unfortunate consequences. The anti-bacterial power was markedly enhanced. 'And it is possible', wrote Fleming, 'that in cases of generalized infection with a microbe susceptible to the bacteriolytic action of egg-white ... the intravenous injection of a solution of egg-white might be beneficial ...'[2] This was an important conclusion, for, with it, Fleming, the victorious adversary of antiseptics, was affirming

---

[1] 'A Comparison of the Activities of Antiseptics on Bacteria and on Leucocytes' *Proceedings of the Royal Society*, B, vol. XCVI, 1924.
[2] 'On the Antibacterial Power of Egg-White', *Lancet*, June 28th, 1924.

that he had no prejudice against chemotherapy, provided the product employed did not destroy the natural defences of the blood.

But in order to make a series of intravenous injections without danger, it would have been necessary to rid the lysozyme of egg-white. Fleming and Allison, as we have seen, had attempted, without success, to extract lysozyme in its pure state. In 1926, a young doctor named Ridley came to do research work in Wright's laboratory. He was not a professional chemist, but he knew a great deal more about chemistry than did his colleagues. Fleming asked him to extract lysozyme in its pure state. Ridley tried, but unsuccessfully. Fleming was greatly disappointed. 'It is a pity,' he told Ridley, 'because if we had this substance pure, it ought to be possible to maintain in the body a concentration which would kill certain bacteria.'

Later, as we shall see, a biochemist did manage to purify and crystallize lysozyme.

Fleming was an obstinate man. He continued to make a study *in vitro* of the action of other products upon the bactericidal power of the blood. He wanted, for instance, to measure the action of salt. He found that every saline concentration which departed from that normally found in the human body weakened the phagocytes.

What would be the effect *in vivo*? In order to find out, he gave an intravenous injection of hypertonic salt (that is, a solution of greater concentration than the normal concentration in the organism) to a rabbit. The first injection was too strong. The rabbit had convulsions and for a few seconds seemed to be on the point of dying. Two minutes later, however, it had got over the shock. Fleming examined its blood. At first, and for as long as the concentration of salt in the animal's blood remained above the normal, the result was identical with that obtained *in vitro*. The bactericidal action of the blood was diminished. But, to his great astonishment, Fleming discovered that, after two hours, the concentration of salt in the blood having returned to normal, the bactericidal power of the blood was greatly enhanced, and this lasted for several hours.

Having perfected the experiment in such a way as to give a quantity of salt so little above the normal that it caused the animal no distress, Fleming tried his hypertonic salt on a patient. An intravenous injection produced an increase of the bactericidal power without causing the slightest discomfort.[1]

He made further experiments on patients whenever his medical colleagues allowed him to do so. But, generally speaking, he was given only desperate cases, and even those very rarely. One or two other doctors made similar experiments and observed that the results were good. But they did not continue. Fleming was very fond of this little discovery and always regretted that it had been more or less ignored. He could not understand why greater advantage was not taken of a treatment which was wholly inoffensive and was probably more effective than the therapeutic vaccines. His sixth paper on lysozyme was written in 1927. It deals with an important phenomenon. By exposing microbes to increasing concentrations of lysozyme and picking up the few survivors, he had managed to create 'strains' of the famous yellow coccus, or of the faecal coccus, eighty times more resistant than had been originally the case. Had these microbes, in developing greater resistance to lysozyme, also become more resistant to the action of the blood? Experiment showed that they had. Why? As we have seen, Fleming had found lysozyme in the phagocytes. Since the increase in resistance to lysozyme kept *pari passu* with resistance to phagocytosis, did it not look as though the action of the phagocytes was, in part, due — as he had already thought it was — to the lysozyme which they contained?

As in his first paper, he here found himself faced by problems of the greatest importance. The pathogenic germs are enemies dangerous to man, because they force the natural defences. Could it be that lysozyme had in primeval times been an all-powerful weapon supplied to primitive man by nature to protect him against *all* germs? Might not the pathogenic germs be, in fact, descendants of the few germs which, having resisted lysozyme, had acquired an ever-increasing power of resistance, until they had become capable of overcoming nature's other defences? If that were so, could one not, by selection, transform an inoffensive into a virulent germ? This was the subject of his sixth paper.[2]

[1] 'On the Effect of Variations of the Salt Content of Blood on its Bactericidal Power *in vitro* and *in vivo*', British Journal of Experimental Pathology, vol. VII, 1926.
[2] *British Journal of Experimental Pathology*, vol. VIII, 1927.

Why was it that this series of superb studies, which had opened up new and vast horizons, attracted so little attention from British scientists? Was it due to the fact that Wright at that time was 'slowing down', and that the enemies of his school were now inclined to accept with a considerable degree of suspicion the work carried out in his laboratory? Fleming, loyal as ever, said that the fault was his, and that he should have presented his findings in the matter of lysozyme to an audience, not of doctors, but of physiologists, who would, most certainly, have been interested. However that may be, the indifference of his colleagues to work which, in spite of his modesty, he knew to be remarkable, made him more silent and reserved than ever, but also stronger. His judgment was not influenced by that of others. His momentum had by no means come to a halt. All through his life he never abandoned the search for a substance which would kill the microbes without weakening the phagocytes. He had looked for it, with his master, in the vaccines. He had hoped that he had found it in lysozyme, a substance which could have reconciled the physiological and the antiseptic schools, because it was an antiseptic enlisted in the service of the body's natural defenders. Being a tenacious scientist who was sure of his facts, he still looked forward to a future in which *his* lysozyme would play an important part.

Nor was he wrong. Even today much work is being done on lysozyme. It interests bacteriologists because it dissolves the mucins with which the microbes are covered; industrialists because it protects foodstuffs from infection (the Russians use it for preserving caviare); doctors, because, when added to cow's milk, it reproduces the component structure of human milk, and also because they use it in the treatment of eye and intestinal affections. All this has come about because an attentive observer, when about to throw away a contaminated culture, looked at it carefully, and said: 'This is interesting.' The discovery which was received with icy silence in London in 1921, has in the space of thirty years become the subject of two thousand papers. Alexander Fleming always said: 'We shall hear more about lysozyme one day.' Who knows?

In the laboratory, those who held aloof from cliques realized its value. Martley, a charming bearded Irishman and one of nature's gentlemen, said to Pryce in 1927: 'Fleming's the really intelligent chap ... If the Old Man had been the author of those experiments with lysozyme and other things, what a sensation there'd have been!' At the first International Congress of Microbiology, held in 1930, Jules Bordet, a Belgian scientist, a former pupil of Pasteur and President of the Congress, spoke in his opening address of Fleming's work on lysozyme in the highest terms. Fleming, completely taken by surprise, was tremendously pleased.

CHAPTER NINE

THE MOULD JUICE

God took care to hide that country till He judged His people ready
Then He chose me for His whisper and I've found it, and it's yours.
                                                        RUDYARD KIPLING

IN most of the great scientific discoveries there has been one part deliberate research and one part luck. Pasteur, a man of unusual firmness of purpose who sought the truth with a combination of pure reason and experiment, was sometimes helped by Chance. He was called upon to deal with *ad hoc* problems which later were to lead him to general conclusions. If he had not been appointed to a professorship at Lille, if the distillers and brewers of the neighbourhood had not gone to him for advice, he might perhaps not have come to take an interest in fermentations, though, his genius being what it was, he would have discovered something else. Fleming had for a long time been hunting for a substance which should be able to kill the pathogenic microbes without damage to the patient's cells. Pure chance deposited this substance on his bench. But, had he not been waiting for fifteen years, he would not have recognized the unknown visitor for what it was.

Once again, as at the very beginning of his career, he had just been taking stock of the weapons which medicine could employ against the infections. The means of defence were woefully inadequate, but he refused to give up hope. 'At present', he wrote, 'there seems little chance of finding any general antiseptic capable of killing bacteria in the blood stream, though there is some hope that chemicals may be produced with special affinities for special bacteria which may be able to destroy these in the blood, although they may be quite without action on other and, it may be, closely allied bacteria.'

He was studying a new antiseptic, mercuric chloride, which killed streptococci, though, as always, at a degree of concentration

123

which the human body could not tolerate. He put the question to himself whether, by injecting it into the blood stream in weaker doses, it might not be possible to achieve a degree of concentration which would not destroy either the human cells or the streptococci, but *might* have the effect of making the latter more fragile and, consequently, more vulnerable to the action of the phagocytes.

His laboratory was still small and encumbered. An accumulation of culture dishes was piled in apparent disorder, though he could always find the one he wanted without a moment's hesitation. His door was almost always left open and any young research-worker in need of some variety of microbe or of some particular implement was given a warm welcome. Fleming would stretch out an arm, lay his hand at once on the required culture, give it to the intruder, and then, usually without uttering a word, go back to his work. When the air in the tiny room became stifling he would open the window which looked on to Praed Street.

In 1928 he agreed to contribute an article on the staphylococci to a vast undertaking — *A System of Bacteriology* — to be published by the Medical Research Council. Some time before this, his colleague, Merlin Pryce (now Professor Pryce) had, while working with him, devoted a certain amount of study to some abnormal forms, mutants, of these microbes.

Fleming, who liked nothing better than to give a helping hand to the young, wanted to quote Pryce in his article. But the latter had left Wright's department before he could complete his researches. Being a conscientious scientist he did not want to publish his results without verifying them, and his new job gave him insufficient leisure in which to do this quickly. Fleming, therefore, had to work again over the ground already covered by Pryce, and set himself to study numerous colonies of staphylococci. In order to examine these colonies, cultivated on agar in Petri dishes, he had to lift the lids of the dishes and leave the contents for some considerable time exposed under the microscope, which meant running a risk of contamination.

Pryce went to see Fleming in his little laboratory, where he found him, as usual, surrounded by innumerable dishes. The cautious Scot disliked being separated from his cultures before he was quite certain that there was no longer anything to be learned from them. He was often teased about his disorderly habits.

He was now to prove that disorder may have its uses. With his rough humour he reproached Pryce for obliging him to re-do a long job of work, and, while speaking, took up several old cultures and removed the lids. Several of the cultures had been contaminated with mould — a not unusual occurrence. 'As soon as you uncover a culture dish something tiresome is sure to happen. Things fall out of the air.' Suddenly, he stopped talking, then, after a moment's observation, said, in his usual unconcerned tones: 'That's funny ...' On the culture at which he was looking there was a growth of mould, as on several of the others, but on this particular one, all round the mould, the colonies of staphylococci had been dissolved and, instead of forming opaque yellow masses, looked like drops of dew.

Pryce had often seen old microbial colonies which for various reasons had dissolved. He thought that probably the mould was producing acids which were harmful to the staphylococci — no unusual occurrence. But, noticing the keen interest with which Fleming was examining the phenomenon, he said: 'That's how you discovered lysozyme.' Fleming made no answer. He was busy taking a little piece of the mould with his scalpel, and putting it in a tube of broth. Then he picked off a scrap measuring about one square millimetre, which floated on the surface of the broth. He obviously wanted to make quite sure that this mysterious mould would be preserved.

'What struck me', Pryce says, 'was that he didn't confine himself to observing, but took action at once. Lots of people observe a phenomenon, feeling that it may be important, but they don't get beyond being surprised — after which, they forget. That was never the case with Fleming. I remember another incident, also from the time when I was working with him. One of my cultures had not been successful, and he told me to be sure of getting everything possible out of my mistakes. That was characteristic of his whole attitude to life.'

Fleming put the Petri dish aside. He was to keep it as a precious treasure for the rest of his life. He showed it to one of his colleagues: 'Take a look at that,' he said, 'it's interesting — the kind of thing I like; it may well turn out to be important.' The colleague in question looked at the dish, then handed it back with a polite: 'Yes, very interesting.' But Fleming, in no way discouraged by this manifestation of indifference, temporarily abandoned his investigation of the staphylococci, and gave himself entirely to studying the surprising mould.

What exactly is a mould? It is one of those tiny fungi, green, brown, yellow or black, which proliferate in damp cupboards or on old boots. This type of vegetation results from 'spores' — smaller than a red blood corpuscle — reproductive organs which float in the air. When one of them settles upon a suitable medium, it germinates, buds and puts out shoots in every direction until a soft mass forms.

Fleming transferred several spores to a dish containing agar and left them for four or five days to germinate at room temperature. He soon obtained a colony of the mould similar to the first one. Then he planted in the same agar different bacteria in isolated streaks, forming, as it were, the radii of a circle with the mould as centre. After incubation, he noticed that certain microbes survived in close proximity to the fungus — the streptococci, the staphylococci and the diphtheria bacillus, for instance, whereas the typhoid and influenza bacilli were not affected in the same way.

The discovery was becoming tremendously interesting. Unlike lysozyme, which acted more especially upon the inoffensive microbes, this mould seemed to produce a substance which could inhibit the growth of microbes which caused some of the most serious diseases. It might, therefore, have an immense therapeutic value. 'Here,' said Fleming, 'it looks as though we have got a mould that can do something useful.' He cultivated his *penicillium* in a larger receptacle containing a nutritive broth. A thick, soft, pock-marked mass, at first white, then green, then black, covered the surface. At first the broth remained clear. After several days, the liquid assumed a vivid yellow colour. What mattered now was to find out whether this liquid also possessed the bactericidal properties of the mould.

The methods perfected in 1922 for lysozyme suited Fleming's purpose admirably. He hollowed out a gutter in a dish of agar, and filled it with a mixture of agar and the yellow liquid. Then microbes were planted in streaks, perpendicularly to the gutter, up to the very edge of the dish. The liquid appeared to be just as active as the original mould. The same microbes were affected. There was therefore in the broth a bactericidal (or bacteriostatic) substance produced by the mould. How great a strength did it have? Fleming experimented with weaker and weaker solutions — a 20th, a 40th, a 200th, a 500th. Even this last still arrested the development of the staphylococci. The mysterious substance contained in the golden liquid appeared to be endowed with quite extraordinary power. Fleming at that time had no means of knowing that the proportion of the active substance in the 'juice' was scarcely more than one in a million. The proportion of gold in the sea is greater than that.

It was important now to identify the mould. There are thousands of moulds. Fleming's knowledge of mycology (the science of fungi) was no more than elementary. He turned to his books, rummaged about in them, and decided that the substance in question was a penicillium of the genus *chrysogenum*. There happened just then to be at St Mary's a young Irish mycologist, C. J. La Touche, who was assisting Freeman in his researches into asthma. Freeman had got hold of him because a Dutch research-worker had put forward the theory that many cases of asthma among those living in damp rooms were due to moulds. La Touche was a sensitive individual who found the restless atmosphere of the Inoculation Department little to his liking. But he had made his colleagues aware of the importance of moulds, and they had affectionately nicknamed him 'Old Mouldy'.

Fleming showed his fungus to La Touche who, after studying it, decided that it was the *penicillium rubrum*. The bacteriologist deferred to the expert and in his first paper on the subject gave to his mould the name prescribed by La Touche. Two years later, the famous American mycologist, Thom, identified the fungus as a *penicillium notatum* (close to the *chrysogenum* which had been Fleming's first diagnosis). La Touche very graciously wrote to Fleming, apologizing for having misled him. Fleming learned from Thom's book that the *penicillium notatum* had been originally recognized by a Swedish chemist, Westling, on a specimen of decayed hyssop. This reminded Fleming the Covenanter, of Psalm 51: 'Purge me with hyssop and I shall be clean' — the first known reference to penicillin.

Meanwhile, his experiments on the bactericidal action of the

liquid had convinced him that he was in the presence of a phenomenon of antibiosis. The mould, a rudimentary living creature,
produced a substance which killed other living creatures,
microbes. The peaceful co-existence of the two species was not
possible.

That living creatures could be caught up in a vital and murder-
ous struggle, the spectacle presented by the world had always
proved. They squabble over food, air and living-space. Sometimes they complement each other, the one providing what the
other lacks, and, when that happens, a shared life, a 'symbiosis'
is possible. More often, however, proximity is fatal to one of them.
In 1889 the Frenchman, Vuillemin, had for the first time employed the word 'antibiosis', defining it thus: 'When two living
bodies are closely united, and one of the two exercises a destructive
action on a more or less extensive portion of the other, then we can
say that "antibiosis" exists.'

A striking example is that of all the infectious microbes which
are ceaselessly being emptied into water and soil. Most of them do
not survive, and this must needs be so, since, otherwise, neither
men nor animals could live at all. What is it that destroys these
microbes? To a very great extent, the sun, but also the action of
other microbes which are inoffensive, or even beneficial, to human
beings. There are ancient Greek texts which point out that certain
epidemics cause the disappearance of other ailments.

In Lister's Commonplace-Books (now in the library of the
Royal College of Surgeons), we find under the date November
25th, 1871, the following observation: in a glass tube containing
urine, Lister noticed the presence of numerous bacteria, but also of
some granular filaments which he recognized as mould. Seeing
that the bacteria seemed to be in poor condition, he made several
experiments for the purpose of determining whether the growth
of mould had the effect of making the liquid an unfavourable
medium for bacteria. These experiments were inconclusive and
he abandoned them. But he had noted that the presence of a soft
mass (which he thought was *penicillium glaucum*) on the surface of the
tube 'was making the bacteria completely immobile and languid'.[1]

[1] *Annals of the Royal College of Surgeons*, vol. VI, February 1950. When, some years
later, Lister's notes were communicated to Fleming by Lord Webb-Johnson, President
of the College, who had just presented the Gold Medal to him, he said, in his reply:
'What a pity that his experiment of November 1871 did not come off. He had

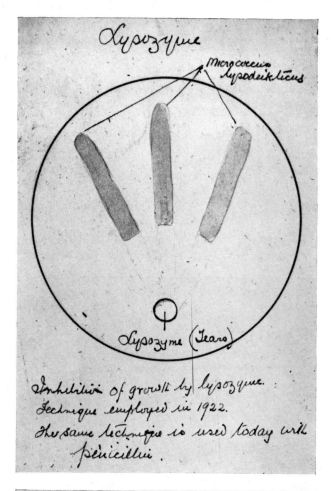

Lysozyme

Micrococcus lysodeikticus

Lysozyme (Tears)

Inhibition of growth by lysozyme.
Technique employed in 1922.
The same technique is used today with penicillin.

Fleming's drawings of the inhibitory effects of lysozyme and egg white on the growth of bacteria

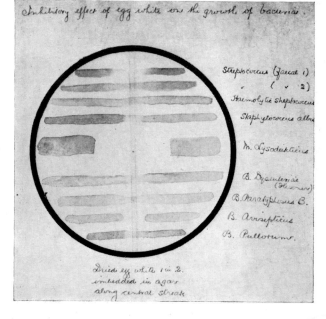

Inhibitory effect of egg white on the growth of bacteria.

Streptococcus (faecal 1)
(" 2)
Haemolytic Streptococcus
Staphylococcus albus

M. Lysodeikticus

B. Dysenteriae
(Flexner)
B. Paratyphosus B.
B. Anisepticus
B. Pullorum.

Dried egg white 1 in 2.
imbedded in agar
along central streak

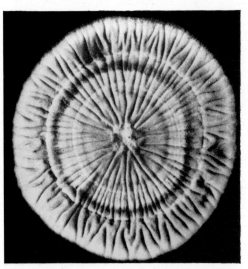

Above: Fleming's original laboratory notes the first use of penicillin to cure bact infection in man

Left: Colony of the mould *penicillium notatum* solid medium

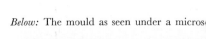

Below: The mould as seen under a micros

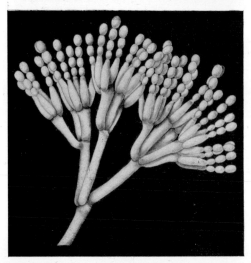

He supposed that what was happening was a competitive struggle for oxygen, the penicillium absorbing that contained in the broth and blocking the surface.

In 1877, Pasteur and Joubert had noticed that the anthrax bacillus, when injected at the same time as inoffensive bacteria, produces no infection of the animal. There, again, an antagonism is set up, and the anthrax bacillus is vanquished. 'In the inferior organisms,' Pasteur wrote, 'still more than in the great animal and vegetable species, life hinders life. A liquid invaded by an organized ferment, or by an aerobe, makes it difficult for an inferior organism to multiply ...' Farther on, having pointed out that a common bacterium introduced into urine at the same time as the bacterium of anthrax prevents the development of the latter, he adds: 'It is a remarkable thing that this same phenomenon occurs in the bodies of those animals which are most prone to contract anthrax, and we are led to the surprising conclusion that one can introduce a profusion of the anthrax bacterium into an animal without the latter contracting the disease; all that is needed is to add common bacteria to the liquid which holds the bacterium of anthrax in suspension. These facts may, perhaps, justify the greatest hopes from the therapeutic point of view.'[1]

In 1897, Dr Duchesne, of Lyon, gave to his thesis (inspired by Professor Gabriel Roux) the title: *Contribution à l'étude de la concurrence vitale chez les micro-organismes. Antagonisme entre les moisissures et les microbes.* 'It is to be hoped', he concluded, 'that if we pursue the study of biological rivalry between moulds and microbes, we may, perhaps, succeed in discovering still other facts which may be directly applicable to therapeutic science.' In this case, too, the search was not continued.

We see, therefore, that antibiosis was already a known phenomenon. But in 1928 the 'climate' of the scientific world was not

[1] Pasteur, *Works*, vol. VI, p. 178.

the idea of penicillin, but he had the wrong mould, or the wrong bacteria, or both. If Fate had been kind to him, medical history might have been changed, and Lister might have lived to see what he had always been looking for – a non-poisonous antiseptic. From the time of Pasteur and Lister workers have been trying to kill one microbe with another. The idea was there but the performance had to wait until Fortune decreed that a mould spore should contaminate one of my cultures, and then for a few years more, until chemists busied themselves with the products of this same mould to give us pure penicillin. Lister would indeed have rejoiced to have had such a thing.'

favourable to research along those lines. In fact, the reverse is true. All former experiments had demonstrated that every substance fatal to microbes *also* destroyed the tissues of the human body. This seemed almost self-evident. Why should a substance which was poisonous for certain living cells *not* be so, as well, for others, no less delicate?

'The fact', said Fleming, 'that bacterial antagonisms were so common and well known hindered rather than helped the initiation of the study of antibiotics as we know it today.' Such facts no longer produced the least excitement, and gave birth to no hope of a new therapeutic development. More especially was the atmosphere hostile in Wright's department. The Chief was convinced that the only means of helping the natural defences of the body was still immunization. Fleming himself had shown by a brilliant series of experiments that all the antiseptics had proved abortive. He had discovered a natural defence, till then unknown — lysozyme. He had tried to increase its concentration in the blood, but without success. Outside the world of the greater parasites (trypanosomes, spirochaetes), Ehrlich's 'magic bullet' remained a dream. Wright could say again, as he had said in 1912, that 'the chemotherapy of human bacterial infections will never be possible ...'

Fleming, an observer without preconceived ideas, did, however, see a flicker of hope in his 'mould juice'. Might not the substance for which he had been looking all through his working life be found there? Though that distant flicker was, as yet, feeble, he decided to neglect nothing which might enable him to achieve success. He gave up all other work to concentrate on this research.

What he did has now to be described.

CHAPTER TEN

PENICILLIN

Fortune favours the prepared mind. PASTEUR

All the same, the spores didn't just stand up on the agar and say 'I produce
an antibiotic, you know.' FLEMING

THE mysterious mould from Praed Street produced a substance which stopped the growth of certain pathogenic
microbes. The first point to get clear was: 'Have other
moulds the same power?' Fleming's friends remember the time
when he would stare at every mouldy surface, his eyes glinting
with curiosity, and be for ever asking whether they hadn't got any
rotting old shoes to give him. The sculptor Jennings, a member of
the Chelsea Arts Club, recollects how on one occasion Fleming
suddenly addressed a general question to the artists clustered
round him: 'If any of you chaps has got a pair of mouldy old shoes,
I'd very much like to have 'em.' When somebody asked what for,
he said: 'Oh, for something I'm doing at the lab.'

Experiment showed that the other moulds which he tested did
not produce an antibacterial substance. His penicillium, therefore, was more than ever worth looking into. What he needed
now, in order to get on with his research-work, was a great
quantity of 'mould juice'.

For some time a young assistant, Stuart Craddock, had been
working with him. Fleming had asked him to help with his study
of mercuric chloride and to see whether, by injecting it in very
small doses, it might be possible, not to kill, but to inhibit, the
microbe, and so facilitate the work of the phagocytes. 'If he told
me once, he told me a hundred times', says Craddock, 'that
the only usable antiseptic would be one which would arrest the
growth of the microbes without destroying the tissues. On the
day when such a substance should be discovered, he said,
the whole treatment of the infections would be transformed.'
That was the *leit-motif* of his scientific life.

Very soon Fleming told Craddock to abandon mercuric chloride

131

at once and devote his attention to the production of mould juice. They began by cultivating the penicillium in a meat-broth at a temperature of just under 100° Fahrenheit. Then, the mycologist La Touche said that the penicillium would be happier at about 69°. A large black incubator was installed in the room where Craddock worked. The latter planted the penicillium in a number of flat bottles of the kind used for preparing vaccines, and left them in the incubator for a week. In this way he obtained from two to three hundred cubic centimetres a day of the mysterious substance, and this he put through a 'Seitz' filter with the aid of a bicycle pump — a somewhat primitive method.

Fleming studied the cultures in order to determine on what day of growth, at what temperature, in what nutritive medium, he would get the greatest yield of the active principle. The methods he had perfected in the old lysozyme days enabled him to measure the antibacterial strength and to standardize the concentration of the cultures. He observed that if the broth was left at laboratory temperature, its antibacterial strength rapidly diminished. This meant that the marvellous substance showed a disquieting degree of instability. He discovered that it became more stable if the alkaline reaction of the broth (pH9) were changed to a neutral reaction (pH6.8).

At last he was able to submit his 'juice' to the test which no antiseptic had so far passed successfully — that of toxicity. To his great — and silent — joy, he observed that 'the toxicity to animals of powerfully antibacterial mould broth filtrates appeared to be very low. Twenty c.c. injected intravenously into a rabbit were not more toxic than the same quantity of broth. Half a c.c. injected intraperitonically into a mouse weighing about 20 g. induced no toxic symptoms. Constant irrigation of large infected surfaces in a man was not accompanied by any toxic symptoms, while irrigation of the human conjunctiva every hour for a day had no irritant effect. *In vitro*, penicillin which completely inhibited the growth of staphylococci in a dilution of 1 in 600, did not interfere with the leucocytic function to a greater extent than did ordinary broth.'[1]

It was all becoming tremendously interesting. 'There', says Craddock, 'was the antiseptic of his dreams, a substance which,

[1] *The British Journal of Experimental Pathology*, 1929.

even in diluted form, remained bactericidal, bacteriostatic and bacteriolytic, without producing any harmful action on the blood.' Craddock just then was suffering from an infected antrum. Fleming washed out the sinus with penicillin-broth. In his laboratory notes we read: 'January 9th, 1929: mould filtrate antiseptic power on Craddock's antrum. Swab from antrum on blood-agar: 100 staphylococci with myriads of Pfeiffer around. Then 1 c.c. mould filtrate put into right antrum. Swab three hours after on blood-agar. One colony of staphylococci and a few colonies of Pfeiffer. In films as many bacteria seen after as before but mostly phagocytosed.'[1]

Thus, even when immensely diluted, the substance killed nearly all the staphylococci. That it would have no action on the Pfeiffer bacillus, Fleming had expected, since it was one of the microbes which had shown resistance in the early experiments. The result of this first and modest therapeutic attempt with raw penicillin on a human being was not too bad.

Craddock also tried to cultivate penicillin in milk. After a week the milk had curdled and the 'juice' had turned into something resembling Stilton cheese, which Craddock and another patient ate, with results that were neither harmful nor beneficial. Fleming had asked his colleagues at St Mary's to let him try his filtrate on infected wounds. One of the cases on which the 'juice' was tried was that of a woman. Coming out of Paddington Station she had slipped and fallen under a motor-bus. She had been taken to St Mary's with a terrible open wound in her leg. An amputation was performed, but she developed septicaemia and it was quite certain that she would die. Fleming, when his opinion was asked, judged the case to be desperate. Then he added: 'Something very odd has happened in my lab. At this very moment I have got a culture of a mould which destroys staphylococci.' He tried soaking a dressing in the 'juice' and applying it to the surface of the amputation. He had not much hope that this application would do any good. The concentration was too weak, and the damage too generalized. The effect was nil.

But he remained just as much convinced as ever of the importance of his discovery. Sir Alexander McCall tells how, one day in 1928, 'Alec and Mrs Fleming spent a Sunday with us. Alec

[1] ibid.

brought a glass slab from his pocket, showed it to my wife, and expressed the opinion that from this slab things would come which would create world-wide interest. My wife, just to pull Alec's leg, said that it was "only a dirty slab".'

About this time it occurred to Fleming that the substance discharged by the mould into the culture broth deserved a name. The one he gave it, 'penicillin', is, as he said later, a word of 'perfectly orthodox formation'. 'Penicillin' comes from 'penicillium', as 'digitalin' from 'digitalis'. Since he had not isolated the active antibacterial principle, he continued to apply the name to the raw filtrate, but his conversation, as well as his papers, leaves no doubt that what interested him was the antibacterial substance contained in the filtrate.

What he wanted now was to extract this active principle. As has been already pointed out, he was not himself a chemist, and there was neither a chemist nor a biochemist on Wright's staff. In one of his moments of paradox, Wright had said: 'There is not enough of the humanist in chemists to make them suitable colleagues.' There is no reason whatever why a biochemist should not be an excellent humanist, but the fact remains that chemistry was not represented in the laboratory, unless we accept as a chemist the young doctor, Frederick Ridley, who, though an amateur, had proved to be skilful up to a point. In 1926, Fleming, having noticed his competence, had asked him to purify lysozyme. Now he begged him once again to make, in association with Craddock, an attempt to extract the antibacterial principle of penicillin.

'So long', says Craddock, 'as penicillin was mixed with the broth, it was obvious to all of us that it could not be used for injections until it had been freed from foreign proteins' (a series of protein injections would have caused anaphylactic accidents). It was essential that extraction and concentration should be attempted before any serious therapeutic use of the substance could be made. 'I have always thought', Craddock continues, 'that the end aimed at in extracting and purifying penicillin was to make it suitable for purposes of injection. When Fleming had started me working on mercuric chloride, he said that it might be possible to use it intravenously in doses sufficiently massive to inhibit bacterial growth without killing the patient, and I am sure he had the same thing in mind with regard to penicillin, provided we could extract it from the broth as a stable and pure substance.'

In this way it came about that two young men who had only just finished their medical studies, set out to find the solution of a chemical problem which proved to be an extraordinarily difficult one. The astonishing thing is that, though they did not know it, they came within measurable distance of success. 'Ridley', says Craddock, 'had sound and pretty advanced ideas about chemistry, but when it came to methods of extraction, we were driven back on to books. We read up a description of the classic method: using acetone, ether or alcohol as solvent, and evaporating the broth at a fairly low temperature, because we knew that great heat would destroy the substance; working in a vacuum. We knew very little when we began. We knew just a little bit more when we had finished: we learned as we went along.'

They worked in a narrow sort of passage, which contained a sink, where in the old days the nurses had washed out bed-pans, filled hot-water bottles and kept specimens of urine. It dated from the time before the laboratory had been installed in this wing of the building. They chose it because there were running water available and a water pump. They had to construct their own apparatus from what odds and ends they could find. They evaporated the broth by vacuum, because they could not use heat for fear of the penicillin vanishing. After evaporation there remained at the bottom of the bottle a brown, syrupy mass in which the strength of the penicillin was about ten to perhaps fifty times greater than that measured in the broth. But this 'melted toffee' could not be used. Their aim was to obtain pure penicillin in the form of crystals.

'We were full of hope when we started', says Craddock, 'but, as we went on, week after week after week, we could get nothing but this glutinous mass which, quite apart from anything else, would not keep. The concentrated product retained its power for about a week, but after a fortnight it became inert.' Later on (when the brilliant work of Chain had made possible the extraction of pure penicillin) they realized how close they had been to success. 'We could not know at the time that we had only one more hurdle to cross. We had been so often discouraged. We thought we had got the Thing. We put it in the refrigerator, only to find, after a week, that it had begun to vanish. Had an experienced chemist come on the scene, I think we could have got across that last hurdle. Then we could have published our results. But the expert did not materialize.' And so it was that the attempts at extraction were abandoned.

There were also personal reasons why the two young doctors should give up. Craddock had just got married and was about to go to a better paid post at the Wellcome Research Laboratories. Ridley, who was suffering from boils, had tried various vaccines in vain and had become discouraged. He abandoned the problem of penicillin in favour of a cruise which he hoped might cure him. An ironical feature of his case is that if he had succeeded in the business of extraction, penicillin would have put an end to his boils! When he returned, he gave the whole of his time to ophthalmology, in which he later specialized. It was, after all, but natural that both men should be out of love with the research-work they had been doing. Chemistry was not their speciality. They had made an immense effort and worked for several weeks, only in the end to find themselves with a 'batch' which had vanished almost at once.

Fleming had not taken an active part in their labours. 'I am a bacteriologist,' he had said, 'not a chemist.' He had asked his two 'amateur experts' to take over that side of the work and had waited, full of hope, for their results. Meanwhile he had prepared a paper on penicillin which he read on February 13th, 1929, to the Medical Research Club. Sir Henry Dale, who was then its chairman, remembers the reactions of the audience. They were more or less the same as they had been in the case of lysozyme. 'Oh, yes, we said, Fleming does observe that sort of nice thing.' It is certainly true that he never knew how to present his findings in the best light. 'He was very shy, and excessively modest, in his presentation, he gave it in a half-hearted sort of way, shrugging his shoulders as though he were deprecating the importance of what he said ... All the same the elegance and beauty of his observations made a great impression.' That impression may have been real enough, but nothing in the strangely superior and sullen attitude of his listeners gave any indication of it.

When a paper has been found interesting, it is always followed by questions, and the greater the interest aroused, the more numerous are the questions. The reader stands at his desk, waiting for them. If none comes that period of waiting in the silent room is a terrible ordeal. Fleming experienced it when he spoke of penicillin, as he had done, formerly, when he spoke of lysozyme. Not a single question was asked, whereas, the next paper: 'On the Nature of the Lesion in Generalized Vaccinia' provoked a lengthy discussion. The icy reaction to something which he knew to be of capital importance appalled him. In 1952, when he was at the summit of his fame, he was still talking about 'that frightful moment'. But in 1929 he gave no sign of disappointment. He knew the value of what he had done and that knowledge gave him strength and made it possible for him to remain unshaken in his belief.

He had now to prepare for publication in the *British Journal of Experimental Pathology* a report on penicillin. This first paper is a triumph of clarity, sobriety and precision. In a few pages it covers all the facts. It does justice to the efforts made by Ridley to purify the substance. It shows that penicillin, since it can be dissolved in pure alcohol, is neither an enzyme nor a protein. It speaks of the innocuousness of the substance when injected into the blood stream and says that it is more effective than any other antiseptic and can be used in the treatment of infected surfaces. It states that he is engaged in studying its value in the treatment of pyogenic infections. In the final summing-up, it recapitulates all these points and, in particular, the following: '(1) A certain type of penicillium produces, in culture, a powerful antibacterial substance ... (7) Penicillin is non-toxic to animals, even in massive doses, and is non-irritant ... (8) It is suggested that it may be an efficient antiseptic for application to, or injection into, areas infected with penicillin-sensitive microbes.'

This conclusion was the cause of the first, and perhaps the only, quarrel between Fleming and his master, Wright. When the latter read the paper, prior to authorizing its publication (his *imprimatur* was customary in the Department), he demanded the suppression of paragraph 8. Had he not said a hundred times that the natural defences of the body alone were effective? Had he not established, in conjunction with Fleming himself, the fact that antiseptics were the enemy? But Fleming, the ever cautious Fleming, who never used a word without weighing it well, and who, as the greatest possible compliment to another bacteriologist, Jules Bordet, was to say: 'Marvellous theories are sometimes promulgated — not always with sufficient scientific backing. Young Bordet set to work, not to invent theories, but to bring facts to light ...' — Fleming stuck to his guns, and paragraph 8 appeared, together with the rest of the paper, in June 1929.

While waiting for the doctors and surgeons of the hospital to provide him with patients on whom to test his penicillin (tests, the results of which he published in 1931-2), he finished his article on the staphylococci for *A System of Bacteriology*. A little later, he returned to the subject in connection with what was known as 'the Bundaberg catastrophe', when, in 1929, at Bundaberg, Queensland (Australia), a number of children had been inoculated against diphtheria, and twelve of them had died within thirty-four hours. The vaccine had been contaminated by a very virulent staphylococcus.

In the meantime, one of the best chemists in England, Professor Harold Raistrick, who taught biochemistry at the School of Tropical Medicine and Hygiene, had developed an interest in the products of moulds in general and especially in penicillin. A bacteriologist, Lovell, and a young chemist, Clutterbuck, joined forces with him. They obtained strains both from Fleming himself and from the Lister Institute. This team succeeded in cultivating penicillium, not, this time, in a broth, but in a synthetic medium containing some salts and a little glucose. Clutterbuck, Raistrick's assistant, studied the filtrate from the biochemical point of view; Lovell from the bacteriological.

Raistrick succeeded in isolating the yellow pigment which gave the juice its colour, and showed that it did *not* contain the anti-bacterial substance. The objective in view was, of course, to isolate this substance itself. Raistrick managed to extract it in ether and hoped that, by evaporating the ether, he would obtain penicillin in its pure state. In the course of this operation, how-ever, the penicillin, fugitive as ever, vanished. The activity of the filtrate, if it was kept, diminished in strength from day to day and very soon disappeared entirely.

In all research there is a human element. Raistrick wanted to continue his investigation of penicillin, but the mycologist of the team was killed in an accident. Clutterbuck, too, died while still quite young. Then the bacteriologist, Lovell, left the School to enter the Royal Veterinary College. 'But I did not go', he writes, 'until October 1933 and, so far as I was concerned, work on penicillin had stopped well before that date, though why, I do not know. I had intended to test penicillin by injecting it into the peritoneal cavity of mice infected by pneumococci. Having observed the astonishing activity of the substance on pneumococci *in vitro*, I wondered whether it would be equally effective *in vivo*. I was stimulated by some work done by Dubos on this, but my investigations remained in the planning stage, and never got farther.'[1]

'During all the time I was working on this subject', continues Professor Lovell, 'Fleming was very much interested in what we were doing, and gave us all the help he could. I constantly rang him up about the difficulties we were experiencing over the mutations which occurred with certain strains of penicillium. He was always ready to co-operate. He told me of the incorporation of a malt substance which he had obtained from the pharmacy at St Mary's, and I realized that he was treating the subject more as an artist than a chemist. It mattered little to him what the composition of the product was, so long as it gave good results. That was all he wanted to know. He offered to send me some.

'I think that our main contribution had been to show that the mould could be cultivated in a synthetic medium; that it was possible to keep it longer when the pH had been brought over on to the acid side, and that we could remove the penicillin by extraction with ether. It was a great misfortune that Clutterbuck died while still a young man. I feel quite sure that, had he lived, it would not have been long before he would have realized that by switching the pH over to the alkaline side he would have been able to recover the penicillin which was apparently lost when we treated the filtrate with ether — as became obvious when Chain took over from that point and succeeded in concentrating penicillin, which was the starting point of the work which he and Florey did.'

[1] The team of the School of Tropical Medicine and Hygiene published an account of its experiments, first in the *Journal of the Society of Chemical and Industrial Transactions* and later in the *Biochemical Journal*, in 1932.

It is only fair to admit that Raistrick and his assistants achieved useful results and were moving forward in the right direction. It is not surprising that they should have been brought up short, as Craddock and Ridley had been before them, by the baffling instability of the substance. 'We had realized', says Raistrick, 'that the effectiveness of penicillin was no less destroyed in an alkaline than in an acid medium, and that, when extracted with ether, it vanished. Such a thing had never happened to a chemist. It seemed incredible. Faced by difficulties of this kind, we had to abandon the work, and pass on to other experiments.'

Those who take a harsh view of the discontinuance of these attempts for the purification of penicillin forget that similar breaks are always occurring, either because the results obtained are disappointing, or because of the convergence of fortuitous circumstances. In the case of penicillin, all these factors played a part. The substance was more than usually unstable and, on two occasions, the investigating teams, which deserved to succeed, were dispersed by illness and death. Luck, bad as well as good, is always present in research. The man who is forced to stop short on the very threshold of discovery can have a clear conscience, provided he feels sure that he has done everything which was (for him) humanly possible. This was so with Raistrick and Lovell. 'I am only too glad', writes the latter, 'that I was able to contribute even a small amount towards the use of penicillin, and to the good it has done.'

The scientific research-worker finds his satisfaction in the knowledge that he has played his part in a great common task, without being influenced by either personal ambition or jealousy. 'No research is ever quite complete. It is the glory of a good bit of work that it opens the way for still better and thus rapidly leads to its own eclipse. The object of research is the advancement, not of the investigator, but of knowledge.'[1]

Meanwhile, Fleming was going ahead with his experimental local applications of penicillin at the hospital. The results were encouraging though not miraculous because, owing to its instability, penicillin had a way of giving out just when its use would have been most rewarding. 'I am convinced', said Fleming, 'that, before it can be used on a large scale, it must be concentrated.'

[1] Mervyn Gordon, *St Bartholomew's Hospital Journal*, June 1920.

Speaking at the Royal Dental Hospital in 1931, he reaffirmed his faith in the substance and, a year later in the *Journal of Pathology and Bacteriology*, published the results of his experiments on infected wounds. He had been bitterly disappointed by the ill-success of the chemists. It had never occurred to him that the extraction of a substance could present so many difficulties, and he had felt certain that, after the work done by Raistrick, the substance would at last be available for use in its pure state. All through the years to come, he obstinately retained a secret tenderness for 'his baby'. There is much evidence to show that, in spite of his habitual reserve, he frequently spoke of penicillin, and never despaired of one day seeing it purified.

Dr A. Compton, for a long time Director of the Laboratories of the Egyptian Department of Public Health, describes how in the summer of 1933 he paid a visit to Fleming who gave him a bottle containing a culture of *penicillium notatum* with a request that he should try it on his patients when he returned to Alexandria. But Compton at that time was hoping for great things from another bactericidal principle which he had himself discovered, with the result that the bottle remained in a corner of the laboratory at Alexandria and was never used. Fortune was not favourable.

Dr Rogers (who now works in Birmingham) was a student at St Mary's round about 1932 or 1933. Just before a shooting-match between the London hospitals in which he was due to figure, he was laid low with an attack of pneumococcal conjunctivitis. 'You'll be all right by Saturday,' Fleming told him, after treating his eye with a yellow liquid and remarking that, in any case, it couldn't do him any harm. On the day of the match, Rogers found that he was cured. Whether this cure was the result of penicillin, he never knew.

To Lord Iveagh, his neighbour in the country, who bred cows and was consequently brought face to face with the problem of mastitis, a streptococcal infection, Fleming spoke of a fungus which could arrest the development of certain microbes. 'Who knows?' said he. 'One of these days, perhaps, you'll be able to put it in the animals' feed, and be rid of your mastitis trouble for good and all.'

In 1934 Fleming took on as an assistant Dr Holt, a biochemist, for the purpose of preparing antitoxins. He went through the now classic experiments for his benefit: action of penicillin on a mixture of blood and microbes — microbes killed, leucocytes intact — which was the reverse of what happened with the known antiseptics. 'He was well aware', says Holt, 'of the therapeutic potentialities of penicillin, and was extremely keen that it should be purified, because, he said, it was "the only product capable of killing microbes with a high degree of resistance, such as the staphylococci, without injury to the white corpuscles" ...'

Holt was struck by the spectacular nature of these experiments and agreed to make an attempt at purification. He reached the same point as Raistrick had done, but could go no farther. He succeeded in passing penicillin into an acetate solution, but it disappeared with great suddenness. After numerous failures he gave up. Fleming was once again disappointed, 'but', says Holt, 'to those of us who lived with him in the lab. he said over and over again that penicillin had great potential therapeutic value. He continued to hope that some day somebody would come along and solve the chemical problem, and that he would then be able to make the appropriate clinical tests.'

In 1935, he copied into his diary — where he was in the habit of recording quotations to which he attached great importance — under the date December 20th, Friday, Ember Day, the following passage from a speech delivered by Lister in 1898 on the occasion of his having the Freedom of the City of Edinburgh presented to him: 'I must confess that highly, and very highly, as I esteem the honours which have been conferred upon me, I regard all worldly distinctions as nothing in comparison with the hope that I may have been the means of reducing, in however small a degree, the sum-total of human misery.' Such was his secret ambition. One day, it was going to be satisfied beyond his wildest dreams.

CHAPTER ELEVEN

A NEW MAGIC BULLET:
THE SULPHONAMIDES

The chemist gives birth to the drug, but the doctor supports its first steps.
FOURNEAU

THANKS to Lord Beaverbrook, Lord Iveagh and others, St Mary's Hospital was growing. In 1931, The Duchess of York (later Queen of England, and now Queen Mother) laid the foundation-stone of the new Medical School. In 1933 the School and the Institute of Pathology and Research were opened by King George V. The buildings were huge. There was a lecture theatre and a real library, but many there were who mourned the happy days when they were pressed for space. It was then, they thought, that their best work had been done. The famous teas, now held in the great library, no longer had the same charm as had been theirs in the congested little room used by the Inoculation Department, where few books were seen upon the shelves. 'When a man wants to read books,' Wright used to grumble, 'he'd jolly well better write 'em.' It was only a 'crack', for who, if not he, had read the great books of the world?

Fleming very soon managed to recreate in his new home the familiar state of 'ordered disorder'. String off parcels, elastic bands and empty cigarette boxes lay about everywhere. He hated to see his work-table neat and clean. All the things he needed — instruments, test-tubes and the rest — had to be exactly where he could lay his hands on them. 'The only chance I had of sweeping the place out and getting it a bit tidied up was when he was travelling or on holiday', says one of his old laboratory attendants. 'When he went away we did as much clearing up as we dared, and waited for the inevitable question as soon as he got back: "Who's been moving me?" One of his most frequent phrases was: "Just put that aside: it may come in useful." '

Games were now in high favour at St Mary's, as Wilson and

Fleming had always hoped they would be. After 1930 the hospital had as many as five Rugby fifteens which greatly distinguished themselves, more than once winning the Inter-Hospitals Cup and since then giving four captains to the All-England side. No matter how bad the weather, Fleming never missed a cup final, and shouted 'Mary's!' as loudly as any student.

The renovated Medical School had a magnificent swimming-bath. In 1935, 1937 and 1938, St Mary's won the Inter-Hospitals Swimming Cup and, in 1938, the Water-Polo Cup. This delighted the veteran swimmer who was now Professor of Bacteriology. Needless to say, the tradition of excellence remained very much alive in the rifle club. Every year there was a match between students and teaching staff and, with shots like Fleming and Freeman, the staff ran a very good chance of winning.

One year the professors found a student posted at the entrance to the range, who in tones of authority was asking each competitor his age and noting it down.

'What's age got to do with it?'

'For each year over forty we give you a handicap of one point,' said the student, condescendingly.

This annoyed Fleming and, when his own turn came, he said, without moving a muscle of his face: 'Ninety.' The student gave a start, but, not daring to go back on what he had said, wrote down 'Handicap, 50.'

Though Fleming was now a man in middle life, Wright still treated him like a Victorian father. 'This young fellow Fleming is doing a lot of good work,' he once said patronizingly to a visitor. In 1928 Fleming had been appointed Professor of Bacteriology in the University of London. At the Institute, salaries were still arbitrary, and settled entirely by Wright. The principal resources of the Institute came from the manufacture and sale of vaccines. But vaccines and serums did not, alas! solve all problems where infections were concerned. Fleming had had sad proof of this in the death of his brother, John. They had been together at a match one day when an icy south-west wind was whipping the stands. Next morning John Fleming went down with pneumonia. Two years before he had been saved from a similar attack by anti-pneumococcal serum. This second onset of pneumonia belonged to the same type, but this time the serum had no effect. The magic bullet for use against the pneumococcus had not yet been found. It existed in the penicillium juice, but could not be purified. Consequently it was impossible to use it.

Since the brilliant victory of salvarsan over the pale spirochaete, research in chemotherapy had continued. Ehrlich had demonstrated an affinity between the doubly nitrogenous dyes and the bacteria, and their bactericidal power, *in vitro*. Chemists in the employment of the Bayer company of Germany succeeded in synthesizing a large number of such products, and entrusted them to one of their colleagues, Domagk, to try on previously infected mice. In 1932, Domagk discovered that a certain red dye protected most of the infected mice against the streptococci. How was this? Probably one part of the dye, uniting with the substance of the microbes, was destroying its chemical equilibrium and so causing their death. These results had been obtained with doses very much inferior to what constituted a danger to the cells of the body. This seemed to be an important discovery.

Domagk gave the name 'prontosil' to this miraculous product. One of the first cases treated by him was that of his own daughter, who had become infected in the laboratory as the result of handling a culture of streptococci, and was saved by prontosil. For three years the tests continued in Germany without any publicity and almost in secret. Finally, in 1935, the discovery was solemnly announced to the scientific world. Domagk came to England and addressed the Royal Society of Medicine on the subject. Fleming was present on this occasion with Dr Young who was much impressed by the figures which Domagk had given. Fleming, on his way out, said to Holt: 'Yes, but penicillin can do better than that.' The quantity used by Domagk seemed large to him, and the results less dramatic than those he had himself obtained. All the same, he had been much interested.

Wright, even after Domagk's visit, remained sceptical. Chemotherapy still inspired him with an invincible repugnance. It so often happened that substances about which marvellous things had been promised had later proved to be ineffective or dangerous. How was it possible, said Wright, that bacterial infections could be cured so quickly with a drug administered by mouth. The German statistics? Wright did not believe in statistics.

Fleming, however, with the lessons of lysozyme and penicillin behind him, was more receptive where novelties were concerned. He had no preconceived ideas on the subject and was prepared to accept the evidence of experiments, provided those experiments had been faultlessly carried out. To a friend, Dr Breen, he said: 'I rather think that this time we really are on to something. It's called "prontosil", and is put out by the Bayer people.' Breen, ever a sceptic, asked: 'D'you think you could get me a little?' 'I'll do my best,' Fleming replied and, a week later, gave a small quantity of prontosil to Breen, who tried it on several cases of erysipelas and, much to his surprise, cured them completely. Yes, it *did* seem as though, this time, the medical profession had 'got on to' something new.

In France, four research-workers — Trefouël, Madame Trefouël, Bovet and Nitti — at the Pasteur Institute in the department presided over by the great scientist, Ernest Fourneau, made under his direction a careful study of prontosil. Their curiosity was aroused by an odd fact: the drug which was so active in the body did not kill microbes *in vitro*. This seemed to indicate that the product, when introduced into the human body, underwent some sort of transformation and that an element, toxic for bacteria, was in some way released. The same sort of thing had happened with atoxyl which, as Ehrlich had shown, was changed in the body into a substance containing arsenic and, therefore, fatal to the trypanosomes.

Systematic study of certain derivatives closely allied to prontosil revealed the fact that the bacteriostatic activity was in each case connected with one part only of the molecule: the para-amino-phenyl-sulphonamide. The researchers of the Pasteur Institute, when they resumed their tests on this particularly simple molecule, found that, in fact, it alone was active. The hypothesis formulated by them was that prontosil when in the body became split, and this was later confirmed by the presence of para-amino-phenyl-sulphonamide in the blood and urine of patients who had been injected with prontosil.

This discovery completely altered the conditions of its use. Prontonsil had been patented by the Bayer company, which meant that sick people all over the world would be dependent on them for supplies, whereas sulphonamide, being a known substance, could be manufactured freely by any makers of chemical products. It had been long in use for the making of dyes because the extremely stable molecule gave an added fastness to those which contained it. It 'clung' to the streptococci as it 'clung' to the material to be dyed.

The medical people in England and in France adopted this new weapon against infection. 'The chemist', Professor Fourneau has written, 'gives birth to the drug, but the doctor supports its first steps.' The successes achieved in France, at the Pasteur Hospital, by René Martin and Albert Delaunay deeply impressed the world of medicine. In England the new product was 'launched', with a very complete study of its effects in cases of puerperal fever made by two specialists at Queen Charlotte's Hospital, Leonard Cole-brook and Meave Kenny (it will be remembered that Dr Colebrook had left St Mary's in 1930). Though Lister, many years before this, had considerably ameliorated the condition of lying-in by asepsis, the serious ailments attendant on child-bearing were still fairly frequent in the London hospitals, where the mortality rate stood at about 20 per cent. In 1936, Colebrook and Kenny were able to announce that this rate, in over sixty-four cases treated with prontosil, had diminished to 4.7 per cent. The control was furnished by the other London maternity cases in which the rate of 20 per cent had not varied. This demonstration appeared to be irrefutable.

Very soon sulphonamide (1162F) was recognized in all countries as effective, not only against streptococci, but also against meningococci, gonococci and perhaps certain kinds of filterable virus. The field of research was widened. The chemists sought to perfect this magic bullet, on one side by diminishing still further the toxicity of the sulphonamides (some people did not tolerate them well), and, on the other, by creating different compounds which might be able to attack still other microbes.

Fourneau and his school supplied some remarkable directives to the investigators by showing clearly the nature of the group of atoms responsible for the therapeutic activity, the group, that is, which 'clung' to the bacteria. The sulphonamides multiplied and then, as always happens, became the object of an excessive craze. The miraculous element pleased the masses, but, discounting that, the positive effects were considerable. The mortality rate in cases of cerebrospinal meningitis fell from 70 per cent to less than 10 per cent. In blennorrhagia complete cure was achieved in ten days for 90 per cent of cases. It could be said that antibacterial chemotherapy, as a successor to Ehrlich's antiparasitic chemotherapy, had at last been born. On the other hand, in regard to certain microbes, the sulphonamides appeared to be powerless, and the clinician was still left weaponless.

Furthermore, there had been cases in which bacteria installed in dead tissues or in pus appeared to be immune to attack. They produced protective substances which inhibited the effects of the sulphonamides. Fleming, a bacteriologist of the old school, who, so to speak, lived with his microbes and knew their habits, had announced, when the sulphonamides were still in their infancy, that resistant strains would develop if, for example, the gonococci were exposed to doses of a strength insufficient to kill them, and, indeed, it was not long before the undaunted gonococci outfaced the sulphonamides. 'This may be due to one of two causes', said Fleming. 'Either the more sensitive organisms have been eliminated by the drug, while the naturally less sensitive have survived, and, in reproducing themselves, have engendered whole resistant generations: or as a result of insufficient treatment, a microbe, once vulnerable, has acquired the power to resist.'

Reticent he might be, and silent too, but he could not help thinking that one day *his* child, penicillin, would do better than anything so far found. He was still hunting for a chemist who might solve the problem of purification. Douglas MacLeod, the gynaecologist, tells how once, in 1935, when he and Fleming were lunching together in the canteen at St Mary's, they exchanged views on the astonishing results obtained, thanks to prontosil, in cases of puerperal fever. Fleming praised the new drug, but then, suddenly turning to his companion, said: 'You know, Mac, I've got something much better than prontosil, but no one'll listen to me, I can't get anyone to be interested in it, nor a chemist who will extract it for me.'

'I asked him what the substance was called. He said that he had given it the name "penicillin". I had to admit that I had never heard of it. He asked me to go with him to his laboratory, which I did. He showed me the mould, and actually gave me a specimen, which I still have. We discussed its possible use in gynaecology, and I suggested that it might be tried in certain cervical and vaginal infections. It was agreed between us that the experiment should be made of inserting the substance into the vagina, but the result was not satisfactory because the mould was quickly killed by the vaginal discharge.' MacLeod adds that Fleming asked him whether he knew any biochemist who might succeed, at long last, in extracting penicillin. 'I told him that I did know a very brilliant man, Dr Warren, but that he and I were trying just then, to find a way of determining sex during pregnancy. So nothing was done.'

Dr Breen tells how one Saturday at the Chelsea Arts Club he said to Fleming: 'I read somewhere that you've been talking about your discovery to a meeting of pharmacists ... that substance, you know ... what d'you call it?'

'I suppose you mean penicillin?'

'Yes,' said Breen. 'Does it really do all you say it can?'

Fleming immediately jumped down his throat: 'Of course. If it hadn't been true, I wouldn't have said it.'

Breen gave him a friendly tap on the shoulder: 'You know I didn't mean that. I just wanted you to tell me whether you think it will ever be possible to make practical use of the stuff. For instance, could *I* use it?'

Fleming stared into the distance for a moment and then said: 'I don't know. It's too unstable. It will have to be purified, and I can't do that by myself.'

The specialist in venereal diseases at St Mary's, Dr McElligott, though much younger than Fleming, was on very friendly terms with him. He often asked his advice not only on bacterial questions, but also on problems of diagnosis and administration of drugs. Fleming, after all, had been one of the first persons to use Ehrlich's 606 successfully in the treatment of syphilis at a time when the method was looked upon as revolutionary. He had followed the progress of some of his patients of those days and had seen with pride that the cure had been maintained.

Naturally he showed McElligott his famous culture which had been contaminated by the penicillium. 'This could do a power of good to your patients.'

They had a long discussion on the possibility of getting penicillin in contact with the gonococcus. But who would dare introduce a mould into the urethra at the risk of provoking a secondary fungus infection?

'From time to time', says McElligott, 'he would ask me to tea in the library of the Institute to meet Almroth Wright, and listen to that great oracle of Immunology. I remember describing the first results of treating gonorrhea with the sulphonamides, and Wright's incredulity at the successes we had had. In a way, he seemed annoyed that an antibacterial chemical agent should have proved to be so powerful.'

What was Fleming's attitude? He had his own well-proved methods for studying the effectiveness of an antibacterial drug and a firm belief in the importance of the natural powers of resistance in the body. He wanted to know to what extent leucocytes and sulphonamides could combine to destroy microbes. As opposed to the old-fashioned antiseptics which he had riddled with criticism during and after the war, the sulphonamides had no toxic effect upon the leucocytes, or only at concentrations very much in excess of those necessary for use against microbes. 'Such observations alone', he wrote, 'would make it practically certain that these chemicals would be effective in the treatment of pyogenic infections, and, of course, this has been clinically established. In the study of new chemicals designed to combat bacterial infections in the body, investigations of this kind should never be omitted, and if this were done we should have fewer extravagant claims and more truth in the advertisements of antiseptic chemicals.'

In a series of papers read to the Royal Society of Medicine, he showed: (1) That the sulphonamides are specific in their action (that is to say that they exercise a powerful action on some bacteria but are without effect on others). (2) That where large numbers of the microbes are present, the sulphonamides have little or no antibacterial action. (3) That their action is essentially bacteriostatic and the natural defence mechanism of the body has to complete the destruction of the bacteria.

The experiments had been carried out with his very simple equipment: slide-cells, Petri dishes, grooves made in agar. By hollowing out two parallel ditches, the one filled with a sulphona-

mide, the other with penicillin, and placing perpendicularly to
them cultures, more or less diluted, of streptococci, he noticed
that the penicillin proved active in all cases, whereas the sulphonamide, though very effective against weak microbial dilutions,
failed to inhibit the non-diluted cultures. Consequently, penicillin
was more valuable, but the sulphonamides had in their favour the
fact that they were stable and could exist in the pure state. For
the moment, therefore, they carried the day.

And what about the vaccines? The St Mary's team continued
to use them, not without success. In an article for the *British
Medical Journal*, Fleming drew attention to several remarkable
cures obtained with auto-vaccines. He was looking for a vaccine
against influenza and other respiratory infections. As to the
common cold, though admitting that, more often than not, it is
caused by a virus against which we have no weapon, he added that
in many cases the cold is aggravated by a bacterial infection.
Sometimes, even, the cold is purely bacterial and is due to the
temporary aggravation of a chronic infectious condition. In this
latter case the auto-vaccine could be of help.

Fleming advised a combination of vaccines and sulphonamides.
He reasoned as follows: 'The effect of the sulphonamides, such as
693 M&B, is bacteriostatic. It facilitates the action of the
leucocytes. But these are also reinforced by the presence of
antibodies. Why not, by means of a vaccine, provoke the formation of these antibodies? The sulphonamides would be the more
effective.' With his colleagues, Maclean and Rogers, he tried, by
means of an experiment with infected mice, to compare the
mortality rates of those which had been given 693 M&B without
vaccine, vaccine without M&B, and, finally, vaccine and 693
M&B combined. The answer was clear. With a combination of
the two substances, but *only* with that, *all* the mice were saved.

Experiments of this kind gave great pleasure to the Old Man.
There was still room for immunotherapy. Relations between the
Chief and Little Flem were excellent. Wright continued to pull
Fleming's leg. Fleming took it all in good part and acted in
precisely the way he knew was expected of him. In his turn, he
pulled the legs of the young, who were fond of him because they
knew that he was always ready to help them, and also because
he was full of original ideas, no matter how extravagant those

ideas might seem on the surface. Even in his gardening he advo-
cated the most startling methods. Once, on his way to The
Dhoon, he bought a great many bulbs of flowering plants, and
suggested to an aviator friend that the best way of planting them
would be by scattering from an aeroplane. In that way their
dispersion would be governed by chance, said he, and therefore
look more natural.

When he sketched unusual plans for his work in the lab.,
his colleagues used to say: 'What a *card* Flem is!' He never minded
their fun, but sat, with a look of feigned solemnity, at his work-
table, well aware that people always laugh at what is new.
'That'll be a success in the long run, you see if it isn't,' he would
say. In most cases he was proved right.

Though he was, above all, an *observer*, he loved rational explanations, provided they were inspired, and confirmed, by the facts.
He was entranced by a most 'attractive' theory put forward by
Fildes to explain the action of chemical medicaments. This theory
was that the chemotherapeutic products have a chemical structure so nearly analogous to that of one of the substances necessary
for the maintenance of the cells in a state of health that the microbial organism confuses them one with the other. The microbe,
therefore, absorbs the sulphonamides by mistake, and fills itself
so full of them that it cannot, then, take on an additional load of
the substances which it needs if it is to grow and multiply. This is
what leads to its death, or makes it an easy prey for the natural
defenders of the body. It was a brilliant piece of theorizing —
if rather surprising.

In 1936 the Second International Congress of Microbiology
was held. Fleming spoke of penicillin and demonstrated before an
audience of his colleagues the experiment of the groove in the agar
which the microbes had been unable to approach. Once again the
degree of interest aroused was very small. He was to recall the
occasion eleven years later, at the Fourth Congress. 'I spoke of
penicillin in 1936,' he said, 'but I was lacking in eloquence, and
nobody took any notice ... Here was something of extraordinary
importance, which was published in 1929, and demonstrated at
the Congress of 1936, but which was neglected by everyone
for years ... It may be that in *this* Congress there is something
like it. If there is, let us not miss it.'

Before his audience of 1936 he gave a number of other demonstrations, too, which, though less serious, amused him. Had any bacteriologist, previous to Fleming, had the idea of using the pigments of microbes for the purpose of painting? Probably not, but he certainly found this piece of professional relaxation great fun. Many microbes are brightly coloured: the staphylococcus is yellow, the *bacillus prodigiosus* red, the *bacillus violaceus* blue. With this living palette ready to his hand, he proceeded as follows. On a sheet of blotting-paper he drew his *motif* — a dancer, a mandarin, a Grenadier Guardsman or a flag. Then he laid the blotting-paper on the agar so that it might become nutritive, after which he coloured his design with broths of the appropriate cultures. All that remained was to put the blotting-paper into the incubator. As soon as the microbes developed, the picture showed up in colour. Sometimes, too, he constructed small rock gardens, on the soil of which penicillium laid a thick carpet of moss while the microbial colonies displayed a pattern of brilliantly coloured flowers.

One day, when Queen Mary paid an official visit to the hospital, he prepared a little exhibition of these bacterial fancies, dominated by a superb Union Jack, all in cultures. It appeared that the Queen was not amused, for she hurried past it. Perhaps she thought the game lacking in the seriousness appropriate to a learned institution, or maybe she considered that the microbes were unworthy of the Union Jack. But Fleming took a childlike pleasure in this strange art, and continued to produce gardens and ornamental borders which he mounted on cardboard, framed, and gave to his friends.

About this same time, he asked the Professor of Pharmacology (today, the Dean of the School of Pharmacy) to undertake the task of extracting penicillin. 'Unfortunately,' writes Professor Berry, 'and to my everlasting regret, I did not make an attempt to do so, nor did I see, as he did, its importance ... I remember the conversation very clearly. He seemed so completely convinced that his discovery had a great future. I recollect his prediction that, if only the substance could be purified, it would be possible to use it systematically in the human body.'

At a somewhat later date, in 1937, he spoke to Dr Laidlaw, a former worker in the laboratory, about penicillin. 'I have never forgotten the calm enthusiasm which he showed on that occasion.

"One day," he said, "someone will find a way of isolating the active principle, and of producing it on a large scale. Then we shall see it regularly used against the diseases caused by organisms which, I know, it can destroy." '

Such pieces of evidence could be multiplied indefinitely. We have only to think of Fleming's inflexible reserve to realize how firm his conviction must have been for him to have risked being snubbed so often, and that at a time when so many new experiments were demanding his attention. He returned again and again to the one he had carried out in 1928. There is something deeply moving in the spectacle of this shy man with his burning faith in the capital importance of a piece of research, trying, in vain, to persuade those who alone could have made its practical application possible, to see as he did. Not that they deserve blame. Every research-worker has his own problems which it is difficult for him to abandon in favour of the problems of others. Three times Fleming had seen a flicker of hope, and three times he had been disappointed.

As to his master, Almroth Wright, Fleming obviously could not turn to him for either money or staff. 'I have the feeling', writes Sir Henry Dale, 'that if Alexander Fleming had been working in an institute under a chief willing to accept, and even to find attractive, the possibility of antibacterial chemotherapy, things might have happened more quickly, and been taken farther. As Colebrook has made perfectly clear in his biography of Wright, the Old Man did not want to take an interest even in the sulphonamides. He just brushed them aside, and treated the discovery as though it had never been made.' All Wright's instincts were up in arms against penicillin. On the other hand, it is true that if Fleming had not been trained by Wright, he would not have devoted his whole life to waging war against the infections. Perhaps he would not have studied the antiseptics or the natural defences of the body, and perhaps he would not have discovered penicillin.

Even at the time of his worst disappointments, he never forgot what he owed to his old master. One day, when Dr J. Taylor said to him: 'It was easy for you to impose your ideas: you had a Wright to back you up,' Fleming replied, in a scarcely audible voice: 'No, on the contrary.' He said no more, and only smiled, fondly and indulgently. His capacity for silence was matched only by his capacity for waiting — and hanging on.

He did hang on, and he did wait. Tirelessly, and with the utmost clarity, he described again and again what should be done in order to make quite certain of the value of a chemotherapeutic drug. 'The testing of a chemotherapeutic drug', he said, 'somewhat resembles the testing which we all had to undergo as students to see whether we were safe to let loose on the public as medical practitioners. I suggest it should consist of three examinations, two pre-clinical, the final, clinical.

'The first examination consists of an investigation into the power of the chemical to kill, or interfere with the growth of, a microbe in human blood. The easiest way to do this is by the slide-cell method.

'The second examination consists of injecting or otherwise introducing into the body of an animal the chemical, and then testing the blood of the animal at intervals afterwards to see if it has an enhanced anti-bacterial power.

'The third or final examination is the cure of infections in men and in laboratory animals by means of the drug, and examination of its toxicity to the organism as a whole ...'[1]

Following the discovery of the sulphonamides, scientists the world over had been looking for a substance which would destroy certain microbes in the human body. At the Rockefeller Institute Dr Dubos was in charge of research work undertaken with the object of finding an antibiotic which would combat the pyogenic germs. His method, which was very ingenious, consisted in infecting soil with these bacteria in the hope that microorganisms, in acute competition with them, would develop by selection.

He made a culture from the infected soil and did, in fact, find there the *bacillus brevis* 3/4, which had an immensely powerful bactericidal effect on numerous and dangerous microbes. He was able to isolate the active substance, which he called 'tyrothricin', and established the fact that it was a mixture of two antibiotics: 'gramicid' and 'tyrocidin'. Unfortunately both were toxic for the kidneys, but they could effectively be used in local applications.

---

[1] *Transactions of the Medical Society of London*, vol. LXII, pp. 31-6, 1939.

And so the torch was passed from continent to continent. The seekers were on the right road.

By 1939 Fleming, now Professor of Bacteriology and Deputy Director of the Institute, had made for himself an important place in his speciality. But he was close on fifty-eight and it seemed unlikely that he would establish any extraordinary discovery before reaching the retiring age. Of course there was that penicillin of his about which he never stopped talking, but even he seemed to have given up hope of ever seeing it purified.

After the serious alarm of September 1938 all clear-sighted men were convinced that war could not be far off. Early in 1939 Fleming, happening to run into one of his assistants, Peter Flood, stopped him and said with a smile: 'D'you know what'll happen to the lab. if war breaks out?'

The question came as a surprise to Flood: 'No,' he said.

'Well then, I'll tell you ... Most of the staff will be attached to the First Aid Service; the rest, you and I among them, will stay on here. There will be very few of us, and our job will be to carry on with the work of the lab. until the bombs drive us away.' Flood nodded. 'Don't worry,' went on Fleming, 'we'll find somewhere to work, and we shall all be in the same boat.'

Flood replied that that would suit him down to the ground, and Fleming's face lit up: 'That's what I thought you'd say.'

He had been quite prepared to accept the prospect of ending his career quietly and silently in the laboratory where he had spent all his life and then, at sixty-five, retiring to cultivate his garden at Barton Mills in an atmosphere of esteem and friendship, but not aureoled with glory. Nevertheless, there are some (Dr Dyson among them) who say that he seemed to be suffering from some secret sorrow, and that his brevity of speech and dry humour masked a melancholy occasioned by his almost complete inability to express himself or to confide in others. The general opinion was that he was happy in his own odd way. To Professor Pryce he once said that he couldn't understand people who took their lab. troubles home with them. No worry of that kind had ever kept him awake. The only thing he regretted was that he could never really 'loosen up'. But he accepted with resignation what nature, Scotland and research had made of him.

Dr Craddock, who knew him well, describes his personal form

of happiness in the following words: 'He was something of a dilettante in his work, not at all the type of man who will go on, month in and month out, painfully slogging through hundreds of cultures, noting tiny differences, and then, after five years of extremely careful work, producing a classified table of variants in the same organism. He preferred something a bit more spectacular and exciting. He wanted to work at a task he enjoyed doing. Lysozyme had appealed to him enormously, and penicillin even more. It was an entirely new world, and he relished the flavour of it.

'In his daily life what he delighted in were the odd and interesting things. I remember one occasion when he was driving with me in the country and noticed a hand-cart of an unusual type, which had been made by a village blacksmith for the purpose of wheeling heavy churns from a farm to the road where they were loaded on to a milk-lorry. He asked me to stop, and, there and then, made a sketch of the object which had aroused his curiosity by reason of the ingenuity of its construction.

'My son, aged ten, made a metal crane with his Meccano set, and Flem insisted on taking a photograph of it, because he thought it a skilful job.

'He was fascinated by the clay ovens which are still used in our old farm-houses. A faggot of wood is set to burn in them. When the clay is white-hot, the ash is raked out, and the meat pushed in to cook. The whole operation is performed by the stored heat of the walls. The simplicity of the method and the economy in fuel appealed to him.

'When I say that he was a dilettante, I don't mean to imply that he was like a butterfly flitting from one bright flower to another, but only that he was selective in the type of work he did. Having made his choice, he went straight to the heart of the problem more quickly than any man I have ever known. All his work was most carefully done. There was nothing superfluous in it. He was remarkably neat with his hands. It is said that once at St Mary's, when blood-transfusions were a novelty, a surgeon failed to find the vein in a child, and sent for somebody to fetch Fleming and he, without the slightest difficulty, made the transfusion into the external jugular vein.

'He liked to work in the laboratory for six or seven hours a day, regularly, but he was not one of those who willingly put in twelve hours at a stretch. He had done it in his early years, at the time of the opsonic index, but now, fortunately, it was no longer necessary. He never idled, and got through more in six hours than others would in twelve. He adored his house and garden in the country and, in summer, would set off on Friday evenings with a light heart. But he was very glad, too, to start in again at the lab. on Monday morning, and go on with the work he loved.'

And so the years passed.

In August 1939 Fleming and his wife went to New York for the Third International Congress of Microbiology. There he met Dr Dubos whose work he much admired. Dubos asked him what had become of penicillin, which had seemed to be so full of promise. Fleming explained that he had given the product to one of the greatest chemists in London and had asked him to purify it; that the latter had said the body was too unstable, and that, from the chemical point of view, 'it looked as though it wasn't worth much.'

In America, a certain Dr Roger Reid, who worked at the Pennsylvania College of Agriculture, had read Fleming's papers and decided to make them the subject of a thesis. He had asked the college authorities for a hundred dollars with which to carry out some experiments (infecting mice with pneumococci and then injecting them with juice from the mould and, also, injecting penicillin into cows suffering from mastitis). This modest request had been turned down and, when one of the professors had offered to finance the experiments out of his own pocket, he had been threatened with dismissal! Fleming also met at the Congress an American doctor, Alvin F. Coburn, who took a lively interest in lysozyme and in the microbes of the pharynx which put up a resistance to it.

It was a great source of happiness to Fleming to know that the researches made so carefully in his tiny lab. at St Mary's, had crossed the ocean and aroused the interest of far-distant scientists. The month of August was, as is so often the case in New York, damp and overpoweringly hot. There were threats of storm. But the most violent was the human storm now piling up in central Europe. On September 3rd war was declared. Fleming and his wife immediately took passage for England on board the *Manhattan*.

CHAPTER TWELVE

THE OXFORD TEAM

It is the lone worker who makes the first advance in a subject but, as the world becomes more complicated, so we are less and less able to carry through anything to a successful conclusion without the collaboration of others. FLEMING

THE events and the stages leading to a great discovery are many and complex. Fleming had 'found' penicillin. He had demonstrated the bactericidal power and the non-toxicity of the substance in its crude state. He had suggested its use in the treatment of wounds infected by vulnerable microbes, and had published an account of the favourable results of his tests. He had tried to get the chemists to purify it. Obstacles and mishaps of every description had made it impossible for any of them to carry their attempts through to the end. Nevertheless, in 1935, the two men who together were to resolve the problem, were converging on Oxford from two points very far removed from each other on the earth's surface.

Dr Howard Florey, an Australian, was born in Adelaide in 1898. From childhood he showed a lively interest in science and, more especially, in chemistry. While still studying medicine, he married a fellow-student, Miss Ethel Reed. She wanted to be a practising physician, and he to give all his time to research. He was awarded a Rhodes Scholarship which took him to Oxford. There he studied physiology and later, at Cambridge, pathology. All the major subjects attracted him and in all branches of medicine he was successful, for he had a quick and vigorous mind combined with great force of character.

In 1925 the Rockefeller Foundation sent him to the United States where he worked in a variety of laboratories and made a number of friends, among them Dr A. N. Richards of the University of Pennsylvania who was destined to play a part in the story of penicillin. After his return to England in 1929 he learned about the work Fleming had been doing on lysozyme, and immediately showed interest in that astonishing substance which is present in human tears and human nails and can instantaneously dissolve certain microbes. The year 1935 saw him appointed to a Chair of Pathology at the Sir William Dunn School in Oxford. This institution was a model of its kind. It was situated at one side of the University Parks, was admirably equipped and employed far more research-workers than St Mary's Hospital, since there was a whole group of laboratories, all under one roof — pathological, biochemical and bacteriological. There Florey continued his researches into lysozyme. No one could have been better suited to direct and co-ordinate the work of a team of scientists, for he was competent in each of their special subjects. He entrusted Dr Roberts with the task of extracting pure lysozyme, which Roberts succeeded in doing in 1937, as did also another young chemist, Dr Abraham. Shortly after taking up his professorial appointment Florey invited Dr E. B. Chain to Oxford, there to direct the work of the biochemical department.

Chain was born in Berlin in 1906, of a Russian father and a German mother. Since his father was an industrialist dealing in chemical products, he had decided, while yet a boy, to make chemistry his profession. As a student at the University of Berlin he took an especial interest in the chemistry of the human body (biochemistry) and made physiology his second subject. He had already obtained his doctor's degree when the Nazis came to power in 1933. Chain was a Jew, and went to England where he worked first in London and then in Cambridge where the Director of the Institute of Biochemistry, Sir Frederick Gowland Hopkins, thought highly of him and took a great interest in his research-work. One day Sir Frederick turned up in the basement where Chain's laboratory was situated and asked him whether he would like to go to Oxford where the new Professor of Pathology, Florey, was looking for a biochemist.

Chain was delighted at the prospect. It had never occurred to him that he might get a post in England, and he was preparing to emigrate to Canada or Australia. He was at that time a young man of twenty-nine, with black hair, flashing eyes, and an exceptionally lively mind, very different from the English, who, however, got the impression that he was something of a genius — and not without reason. It was Sir Frederick Gowland Hopkins who, struck by his ability, had recommended him to Florey.

Chain went to see Florey, who explained to him the importance he attached in his department to biochemistry, since all pathological change rests upon a biochemical phenomenon. He promised Chain a perfectly free hand and the right to choose his own subject for research. At the same time, he suggested that he might do worse than investigate the behaviour of a bacteriolytic substance, lysozyme, which, said he, played a part in protecting the body against bacteria and, perhaps, gastric ulcers.

In 1936 Chain, in company with a Rhodes Scholar named Epstein, attacked this problem, together with another — the biochemical action of snake-venom. The first thing to be decided was whether lysozyme was really, as Fleming said it was, an enzyme, that is to say, an element capable by its presence of encouraging certain reactions and breaking down certain molecules. If the answer to that question should be 'yes', then it must follow that there must be in the bacterial cell a substrate on which the product acted, since enzyme and substrate are as closely related as a lock and its key, which explains the specificity of the enzymes. The result was positive. Chain was able to extract from the famous yellow coccus (*micrococcus lysodeikticus*) a substance (a polysaccharid which was broken up by lysozyme and, in this particular case, acted as the lock.

This piece of work having been carried through successfully, it seemed natural to go carefully through the 'literature of the subject', in other words, anything previously published, and to find out what had been done already in this field. Chain found close on two hundred papers dealing with antibacterial substances with a microbial origin, some of which had, like lysozyme, a lytic (or dissolving) action, while others killed this or that microbe in a different manner. Chain's attention was thus drawn to an immense field of study — microbial antagonism. Florey and he discussed the matter.

Of all the papers through which Chain had worked, the most interesting seemed to him to be the one written by Fleming in 1929 on penicillin. He learned from it of the existence of a substance 'with antibacterial properties rich in promise'.[1] It had this superiority over lysozyme, that it could destroy dangerous

[1] 'Penicillin as a Chemotherapeutic Agent', by Chain, Florey, Gardner, etc., *Lancet*, August 24th, 1940, p. 226.

microbes and in addition was, according to Fleming, completely lacking in toxicity. Continuing his reading, Chain found that a serious attempt had been made to extract and purify penicillin, which was more than could be said of the other substances, but that this had come to nothing.

He was ready to continue the attempt, but the necessary research would be pretty costly, and there was a shortage of funds. Walking one day with Florey through the lovely University Parks, he asked whether it might not be possible to get a few thousand dollars from the Rockefeller Foundation. The Medical Research Council had granted a few small sums, but these never amounted to more than fifty or a hundred pounds, which were almost worse than nothing. Florey forwarded the request and some time later informed Chain that if a programme of interesting biochemical research were submitted, the money would probably be forthcoming. Chain said that nothing would be easier and at once drew up for the Rockefeller Foundation a memorandum in which he suggested three subjects of study: snake-poison; the spreading factors;[1] and bacterial antagonism. There was enough material in these to provide work for ten years.

Florey approved the memorandum and after a delay of a few months went in high spirits to tell Chain that a subsidy of five thousand dollars had been granted by the Foundation. This was marvellous news. The biochemical laboratory would no longer be prevented for want of a ridiculously small sum of money from buying the necessary equipment. Chain began his experiments on penicillin at the beginning of 1939. Then he went to Belgium for a holiday and, when he got back, war was just about to be declared.

Why had he started with penicillin? Florey and Chain had decided that three types of substance should be studied: an enzyme, pyocyanase; the antibacterial substances produced by the actinomycetes (which were later to give birth to such powerful antibiotics as streptomycin, etc.); and penicillin. The latter had many advantages over the others. It had already been studied under several aspects: it was known to be non-toxic and finally,

---

[1] Principles, the nature of which was unknown, and which have the power to break down certain chemical constituents of the connective tissue. The most important was discovered by Chain in 1939.

though it could be neither conserved nor purified, it could at least be easily produced.

The Dunn School possessed a strain. How this came about must be explained. When Chain had arrived in Oxford in 1935, he had come across a colleague in one of the corridors carrying several Roux bottles containing a mould. At the time he had not paid much attention to this, but when he came to read Fleming's paper he realized that the culture he had seen in the hands of his colleague might perhaps have had something to do with penicillin.

He went and asked her whether this was so. She explained that she had been one of Dreyer's assistants: that Dreyer, Florey's predecessor, had been interested in the bacteriophages, forms of virus capable of destroying bacteria, and had thought that penicillin might be one of them. He had asked Fleming to send him a culture of penicillium and this Fleming, always pleased to find anyone interested in it, had done. Dreyer had soon seen that penicillin was not a *phage*, but had kept it with a view to further work. Chain, in his turn, asked for the culture.

At that time he knew nothing about moulds, and had to learn how to handle these extremely temperamental colonies. It seemed impossible to get any constant results. Sometimes the penicillium gave penicillin, sometimes it did not. The reason was that Fleming's strain had produced numerous mutations. Chain verified that the antibacterial substance was highly unstable, but this very instability aroused his curiosity. The chemists who before him had tried to extract pure penicillin had reached the conclusion that 'the substance vanished almost while you looked at it.' Chain set himself the task of finding the reason for this instability and attacked the problem by the very much gentler methods of the chemistry of enzymes, which he knew well.

It was agreed that Florey should carry out biological tests on the substance when Chain had managed to isolate it and to elucidate its structure. Chain himself undertook to work on penicillin, and asked one of his colleagues, Mrs Schoental, to proceed with the study of the pyocyanase.

Chain thought that penicillin must be an unstable enzyme. It is a known fact that the enzymes in solution often lose their activity when concentrated by evaporation, because the in-activating substances are concentrated at the same time as the enzyme and destroy it. But Chain had at his disposal a new method which had been developed since the time of the researches made by Ridley and Raistrick — lyophilization (freeze-drying), which was being much used in, for example, the conservation of blood-plasma.

The process is very simple and is based on the principle that when liquids become congealed in a vacuum they pass straight from the solid to the gaseous state. This phenomenon can be observed on the tops of high mountains, where ice is sublimated (transformed into vapour) without going through the intermediate stage of melting. Now if a liquid solution containing different substances becomes congealed, these substances, when solidified, cease to have any action on one another (*corpora non agunt nisi fluida*). If, therefore, the liquid is eliminated by sublimation, the solid substances which form the dry residue retain their activity almost indefinitely. Here was a way in which penicillin could be saved.

By freeze-drying the culture-liquid, Chain obtained a brown powder which contained, together with penicillin, several impurities (proteins, salts), and consequently could not be used for purposes of injection. Could one, as his predecessors had hoped, extract penicillin by dissolving it in pure alcohol? He tried the experiment, but without success. This did not surprise him, because he believed it to be an enzyme, and, therefore, not soluble in alcohol. All the same, so as to leave no stone unturned, he tried again, this time with methyl-alcohol (or methanol) and to his amazement succeeded. Some part of the impurities was thus eliminated. Unfortunately, however, the volatile penicillin, when dissolved in methanol, once again became unstable. The cure for this was to dilute the solution with water, and then have further recourse to freeze-drying.

Now that he had in his possession a partially purified penicillin, Chain was eager to test it. Since Florey was just then much occupied with other research-work, he turned to a great Spanish surgeon, Joseph Trueta, who happened to be working at the Dunn School on the floor above, with a young English assistant, John Barnes. At Chain's request, Barnes injected thirty milligrams of concentrated penicillin into the vein of a mouse. To the delight of Chain and to the surprise of Trueta, who was watching the experiment, no toxic reaction occurred.

Florey, much interested, at once repeated the experiment on another mouse, with a dose of twenty milligrams, and again there was no toxic effect. He, too, was so completely surprised, that he feared he might have missed the vein and said to Chain: 'Let me have another dose' — by no means an easy thing to do at that time. With the utmost difficulty Chain managed to get hold of the twenty milligrams required and once more Florey established the non-toxicity of the substance.

So, at last, the Oxford scientists had in their hands, in a concentrated state, stable and partially purified, a product which possessed the astonishing property of killing microbes but not the cells of the body. Florey asked Chain to enlist the help of Heatley, a young and inventive laboratory-worker who had just come back from Copenhagen, and together he and Chain perfected a practical method of purifying penicillin.

It would take too long to describe here the innumerable difficulties which they encountered. The essential points which emerged from their researches were the following: (1) the work must be done (*a*), at a low temperature, and (*b*) with a neutral pH; and (2) the neutral liquid solution must be freeze-dried in order to obtain a penicillin salt in powdered form. It is important to note that the method thus perfected was the one used by all the big industrial producers until 1946. Without freeze-drying it would have been impossible to manufacture penicillin on a large scale. Chain had been among the first to employ this process when he was studying the enzymes.

In order to measure the antibacterial power of penicillin, Heatley at first used Fleming's method (holes made in the agar of a Petri dish and filled with penicillin round which the vulnerable microbes disappeared). Then he substituted for the holes small glass or porcelain cylinders planted in the surface of the agar. His first experiments proved that the product, when partially purified, was a thousand times more active than the crude penicillin, and ten times more active than the most active of the sulphonamides. (When completely purified, penicillin turned out to be a thousand times more active than Chain's first samples and, therefore, a *million* times more so than Fleming's crude substance.)

Florey and his colleagues had tested the toxicity of penicillin given intravenously in a single injection. This Fleming had also done with his crude penicillin. But now, with most of the proteins removed and with the substance at last stable, the Oxford team could go farther. They proceeded to treat rats with an intra-muscular injection of ten milligrams every three hours over a period of fifty-six hours. Once again there was no accident. They tried the action of their substance on the arterial pressure and the respiration of cats. They repeated Fleming's experiments on the leucocytes. 'From all these tests', they tell us, 'it was clear that this substance possessed qualities which made it suitable for trial as a chemotherapeutic agent.'

The moment had now come for the crucial test. It was made on May 25th, 1940, on three groups of mice infected, respectively, with staphylococci, streptococci and *clostridium septicum*. Heatley remembers with emotion the night he spent in the laboratory observing the reactions of the animals, and his joy when he saw the controls die one after the other, while the treated mice sur-vived. Next morning Florey and Chain went to ascertain the results. Chain's eyes still sparkle when he speaks of the occasion.

June 1940 — it was the time of the great German offensive ... and Dunkirk. Was England going to be invaded? The Oxford team had decided that, should there be an invasion, they must at all costs save the miraculous mould the importance of which could no longer be doubted. They soaked the linings of their clothes in the brown liquid. It would be enough if only one of them escaped, for he would have on his person spores enough with which to start new cultures. By the end of the month they had enough penicillin for a decisive experiment. This was carried out on July 1st, on fifty white mice. All of them were given a more than lethal injection of virulent streptococci — ½ c.c. Twenty-five served as controls. The other twenty-five were treated with penicillin every three hours over a period of two days and two nights. Florey and his assistant, Kent, slept in the laboratory and were aroused by an alarm-clock every two hours. At the end of sixteen hours the twenty-five control mice were dead. Twenty-four of the treated mice survived the experiment.

The results smacked of the miraculous. They were set down in sober black and white in a note published by the *Lancet*.[1] The signatories were Florey, Chain and Heatley who had done the

[1] 'Penicillin as a Chemotherapeutic Agent', August 24th, 1940.

extracting and conducted the first tests on animals. To their names were added those of Jennings, Orr-Ewing, Sanders and Gardner, whose help Florey had enlisted for the purpose of studying the miraculous substance more thoroughly. Gardner supplied the bacteriological study, confirmed Fleming's results and added some microbes to the list of those on which penicillin had an effect, in particular, that of gas-gangrene which in time of war was of paramount importance.

These names accounted for all but one of the Oxford team. Fleming had never had so large a group of specialists working with him. For this discovery to come about, first and foremost the solitary worker had been necessary, and only after him, following on his heels, the team. 'The work of a team', Chain has written, 'is important for the development of an idea already formulated, but I do not believe that a team has ever produced a new idea.' And Fleming: 'For the birth of something new, there has to be a happening. Newton saw an apple fall; James Watt watched a kettle boil; Roentgen fogged some photographic plates. And these people knew enough to translate ordinary happenings into something new ...'

When Fleming read in the *Lancet* the first communication made by the Oxford team, he had the happiest surprise of his life. He had always known, and had never tired of saying, that a day would come when penicillin would be concentrated and purified, and that then it would be possible to use it in the treatment of generalized infections. He had but one thought — to see his darling substance in its pure state.

He therefore went to Oxford to see Florey and Chain. The latter was taken completely by surprise: he had thought that Fleming was dead! 'He struck me', he says, 'as a man who had difficulty in expressing himself, though he gave the impression of being somebody with a very warm heart doing all he could to appear cold and distant.' The truth was that he was making a great effort to conceal his joy, for he had always made it a rule never to show his feelings. 'You have made something of my substance,' was all he said to Chain. Craddock who saw him on his return relates that, speaking of the Oxford team, he said: 'They have turned out to be the successful chemists I should have liked to have with me in 1929.'

Fleming to Florey, November 15th, 1940

Dear Florey,

I am sorry to have been so long in sending you cultures of the penicillium which did not produce much yellow colour. When I got back from visiting you, I planted out a large number of my old cultures in broth, and I have selected from these a number which, while producing a good yield of penicillin, did not appreciably colour the broth yellow. I am sending these on to you, and I hope you will find them useful.

I have been comparing the solid penicillin which I got from you with the sulphonamides and it seems to be, weight for weight, a great deal more potent than the most powerful of those on the ordinary septic microbes.

It only remains for your chemical colleagues to purify the active principle, and then synthesize it, and the sulphonamides will be completely beaten.

Yours sincerely
ALEXANDER FLEMING

Dr E. W. Todd to Fleming, August 23rd, 1940

London County Council,
Public Health Dept,
Belmont Laboratories,
Stanley Road, Sutton, Surrey

My Dear Flem,

I was delighted to read in the *Lancet* this morning about penicillin. When can we start production? I am laboriously making *gas-gangrene anti-toxin*, and *penicillin* sounds much simpler.

I can claim to have been in the same room when you made the great discovery. Do you think that there is any chance that I might get a knighthood on that claim when you are raised to the Peerage?

Are you producing penicillin for therapeutic use?

Congratulations,
Yours ever
E. W. T.

The time had now come to try penicillin on human patients, but that would need great quantities of penicillin in as pure a state as possible. The substance to be dealt with was a madly temperamental mould and it was essential to move quickly. Heatley gave himself to the problem of extracting the product; Chain and Abraham concentrated on its purification. To describe here all their difficulties and disappointments would involve too many technical explanations. But it can and should be said that they showed admirable qualities of ingenuity and tenacity. The group met every day at tea-time, recorded their failures, deplored them, but never showed discouragement. The stake was well worth the trouble taken.

After innumerable washings, manipulations and filterings, they at last obtained a yellow powder which was a salt of barium containing about five hundred units of penicillin per milligram.[1] At first, the percentage of penicillin, for the same weight, had been half a unit. This was an excellent result. Next, the yellow pigment had to be precipitated. The final stage of the operation, the evaporation of the water in order to obtain a dry powder, still presented difficulties. The normal method of turning water into steam is to make it boil: but heat destroys penicillin. They had to have recourse to the other method, which consists of reducing the pressure above the water and so lowering the boiling-point. The use of a vacuum pump made it possible to evaporate the water at a very low temperature. The precious yellow powder remained at the bottom of the jar. It felt to the touch like cornflour. This penicillin was still only half pure. Nevertheless, when Florey made his bacteriological tests, he found that a thirty-millionth solution of this powder was enough to inhibit the development of the staphylococci.

The most convincing case would have been one of septicaemia. But this presented certain difficulties. On the one hand, the quantity of penicillin available did not permit the injection of a massive dose; on the other, the rapid excretion of the product would mean that it would remain in the body for an insufficient length of time. It was very quickly eliminated by the kidneys. No

[1] This Oxford unit is the smallest quantity of the product which, dissolved in a cubic centimetre of water, can inhibit the golden staphylococci in a circle having a diameter of 2.5 centimetres.

doubt it would be found in the urine and could be extracted and used again. But these operations would be lengthy, and the patient would have plenty of time in which to die. Giving the product by the mouth would be ineffective, because the gastric juices would destroy the penicillin as soon as it reached the stomach. What appeared to be desirable was the maintenance in the blood stream, by successive injections, of a quantity of the substance sufficient to allow the natural defence mechanisms of the body to destroy the microbes which, thanks to the penicillin, would have become far less numerous. The best method, therefore, would be frequent injections, or perhaps, even, intravenous drip.

The inadequate quantities on hand increased the natural anxiety always aroused by any brand-new experiment on a patient. There was the risk that a treatment might be begun which could not be continued. Florey went to see the directors of a great industry specializing in chemical products, told them that he had in his hands a substance which looked as though it would turn out to be a miraculous remedy, and asked, without concealing from them the difficulties of the enterprise, whether they were prepared to undertake its production on a large scale. After thinking the suggestion over, these industrial chemists refused. They are not to be blamed. Their factories were fully occupied by Government orders for war-material; the methods perfected, with the greatest difficulty, by the Oxford team, would have involved an enormous amount of work; and, last but not least, the concern would have run the risk, after equipping their factories at great expense, of seeing some research-worker suddenly solve the problem of making synthetic pencillin and so drastically reducing the cost of production.

The only thing left for the Oxford chemists to do was once again to work with such means as they could find ready to hand. The task given by Florey to Heatley was to produce a hundred litres of culture a week and to extract the penicillin. A small quantity of the yellow powder was put aside in a refrigerator for emergencies at the beginning of February 1941. At that very moment a case turned up which, because it seemed desperate, justified the carrying through of a daring experiment. A policeman in Oxford was dying of septicaemia. It had started with a small infected scratch at the corner of the mouth. Then the whole blood-content of the body had been poisoned. The microbe in question was the *staphylococcus aureus*, which is vulnerable to penicillin. The patient had been treated unsuccessfully with sulphonamides. There were abscesses all over his body and his lungs had been affected. The doctors regarded his condition as hopeless. If penicillin resulted in a cure, it would be a shattering proof of its power.

On February 12th, 1941, an intravenous injection of 200 mg. of penicillin was given to the dying man and, thereafter, an injection of 100 mg. every three hours. At the end of twenty-four hours the improvement in his condition was startling. The wounds had ceased to suppurate. It was obvious that the patient, only the day before at the point of death, was now well on the way to recovery. While continuing the penicillin injections, the doctors gave him a blood-transfusion. Unfortunately, the tiny reserve of yellow powder was dwindling in a tragic fashion. It was possible to recover a certain amount from the man's urine and the improvement became still more marked. The patient felt better. He was eating. His temperature had dropped. Two facts in painful contrast to each other were now only too obvious. The penicillin treatment, if it could be maintained, would undoubtedly save his life, but it could not be continued long enough because there would not be sufficient penicillin available. Heatley worked devotedly, but he could only wait until the cultures had produced a fresh crop. He very soon had to stop the injections. The patient managed to hold on for a few days. But the microbes, being no longer attacked, got the upper hand and, on March 15th, the policeman died.

Florey now *knew* that if he had had enough penicillin, the man could have been saved. But he could not *prove* a hypothetical success. A transfusion had been given and it was open to sceptical critics to say that the improvement had been due to that. The first test, therefore, had partially failed. The yellow powder, fruit of so much hard work, had been used in vain. The Oxford team was saddened but not discouraged. When a new supply of penicillin was ready, three other cases were treated. All of them gave evidence of the immediately beneficial and spectacular action of the substance. Two of the cases were completely cured. The third, that of a child who had been brought out of a coma by penicillin, was getting much better, when death supervened as the result of the accidental rupture of a blood-vessel. But even severe judges could no longer doubt that medicine now possessed a new chemotherapeutic product of unparalleled strength, which was non-toxic. The first patient, when injected, had had a sharp rise in temperature and a rigor, but this was due to certain impurities still remaining in the drug, and was not repeated when penicillin had been completely purified.

Was it possible that on the strength of these first results the British Government would set on foot an immense effort to manufacture the miraculous remedy on an industrial scale? Florey very quickly realized that the answer to that question would be in the negative. England in 1941 was suffering under incessant bombing raids. It was conducting, or preparing, a war on all fronts. Urgent day-to-day necessities took priority over everything else. The men and women who were living under the constant threat of seeing their homes reduced to ruins on top of them could scarcely be expected to regard the war against microbes as a matter of essential importance. But Florey could measure the effects of a massive employment of penicillin and envisage the consequences for the wounded and for the war-effort as a whole.

The Oxford scientists approached nearly all the major manufacturers of chemical products. The reply in almost every case was the same: 'Yes, Doctor, you have made a most important discovery, but the production of your substance on a commercial scale is impossible because your output is too small.' The treatment of a single case needed thousands of litres of cultures. The proposition was not a practical one. The obvious remedy for this state of affairs was an increase in output and the financing of a vast research programme. But the English factories, under the harsh conditions of war, were in no state to make the necessary effort. The only alternative was to turn to America.

Florey and Heatley left for the United States via Lisbon in June 1941, taking with them some strains of penicillium. The heat was intense and they were in a condition of the most extreme anxiety throughout the voyage, since the precious moulds could not stand high temperatures. In New York, Florey renewed acquaintance with an American friend who at once put him on the track of the man who could get things moving, Charles Thom, who had identified the *penicillium notatum*, and was now Head of the Mycological Section of the Northern Regional Research Laboratory at Peoria, Illinois. This laboratory had been created to make research into the utilization of the organic by-products of agriculture which were polluting the rivers of the Middle West. The intention was to convert these waste products into usable fermentations, and the chemists there had been concentrating their efforts on producing gluconic acid by using the fermentation powers of moulds of the *penicillium chrysogenum* type. In this work they had been using, as their source of nitrogen, corn steep liquor, a by-product of the manufacture of starch from maize. This liquor had accumulated in the region to an embarrassing extent. The chemists had succeeded in making the gluconic acid production work by using a method of submerged fermentation.

Florey passed from scientist to scientist and finally reached Dr Coghill, who was Chief of the Division of Fermentation at Peoria. To him he explained his problem. It should be mentioned that the English scientists (and this is as true of Fleming as of Florey, of Chain as of Heatley) had done nothing to protect their discoveries by taking out a patent. In their eyes a substance which could render such services to mankind ought not to become a source of private profit. So extreme a degree of disinterestedness deserves to be stressed and applauded. They gave to the Americans all the results of their prolonged researches and all their methods of manufacture, asking in return only for penicillin so as to be able to continue their medical experiments.

Heatley stayed on in Peoria to take part in the work. The first objective was to increase output, which meant finding a favourable medium for the penicillium culture. The Americans suggested corn steep liquor with which they were familiar and which they had used as a medium for similar cultures. They quickly obtained an output twenty times higher than that of Oxford and this brought them within sight of a practical solution of the problem. It would be possible, at least for war purposes, to produce penicillin in quantity. The substitution of lactose for glucose still further improved the output.

Once again we are left wondering at the curious operations of Chance. If the Americans had not been embarrassed by an excessive accumulation of their steeping liquor, they would not have set up a laboratory at Peoria. Had it not existed, no one would have hit upon that particular culture medium — maize-liquor + lactose — and the commercial production of penicillin might have been indefinitely postponed. On the other hand, the arrival of the scientists from England had alone made it possible for this laboratory to do the work for which it had been set up, since the making of gluconic acid would not of itself have absorbed the immense quantities of corn steep liquor available, whereas the manufacture of penicillin would very soon make it extremely precious and increase its value a hundred times.

The new culture medium was not the only contribution made by Peoria. The mycologists attached to the laboratory were looking for mould-strains which would give a larger yield of penicillin, for it is a curious fact that all the cultures so far made in England and America were descended from the same spore, the one which had landed on Fleming's work-bench. Up till 1943, nothing better had been found, though a great many strains had been tried. It was most unlikely that this particular strain, which had not been deliberately chosen, should turn out to be the best. The American research-workers had enlisted the help of the Army authorities in getting specimens of moulds from all over the world, but none had proved to be usable. But the laboratory had also taken on a young woman whose function it was to go to market and buy every variety of mould she could find. She was very soon known as 'Mouldy Mary'. One day she returned from market with a mould of the *penicillium chrysogenum* type which she had found growing in a cantaloup melon which had gone bad. It showed itself to be remarkably productive. The application of genetic methods improved its yield still further, and most of the strains used today (after mutations) come from the rotten Peoria melon. The scientists, as so often happens, had on their doorstep what they had been searching for in vain all over the world.

While Heatley was working with the chemists at Peoria, Florey started on a pilgrimage which was to take him all over America and Canada, visiting numerous factories turning out chemical products and trying to interest industrialists in the production of penicillin on a really great scale. The situation in America seemed to be less difficult than it was in England. In early 1941 the country was still not yet at war. But it was receiving a considerable number of orders, and most of the industrial leaders whom Florey saw showed only moderate enthusiasm for an enterprise which they regarded as both uncertain and difficult. All the same, many of them expressed their good will and, when Florey left for England, he took with him promises from two firms, each of which had undertaken to produce ten thousand litres and to send the penicillin to Oxford for purposes of medical research. His last visit was to his friend Dr A. N. Richards whom he had known formerly at the University of Pennsylvania. Dr Richards had just been appointed President of the Committee of Medical Research. This important post would give him considerable influence and make it possible for him to interest the American Government in penicillin. The journey had been productive of great results.

CHAPTER THIRTEEN

WAR AND GLORY

If you can meet with Triumph and Disaster
And treat those two impostors just the same. RUDYARD KIPLIN

It is good to know that honours can find their way to the quiet scientist, too.
K. A. JENSEN

IN September 1939 when coming back on the *Manhattan*, Fleming had had as a fellow traveller another bacteriologist, Allan W. Downie of Liverpool. The two men had spent almost every evening together in the smoking-room with glasses of beer before them, talking about their work, the war, wounds and infections. Downie found that, contrary to what some people said, Fleming, when he fell in with somebody who was interested in the same things as he was, could be very good company. Far from St Mary's and the colleagues who expected him to be always the same, he was a different man. Mrs Fleming and Mrs Downie complained that their husbands spent the whole night talking.

When he got back Fleming learned that he had been appointed a Regional Pathologist, with headquarters at Harefield in Middlesex. This did not prevent him from going on with his work at St Mary's. He thought that he would be most useful there by sticking to the subject which he had studied with such good results from 1914 to 1918: infections consequent on war-wounds. The young had forgotten, if they had ever known, what Wright and Fleming had established at that time with so much difficulty. Whenever there were wounded at St Mary's, after every surgical operation on purulent injuries, he had samples of tissue sent to him. These he examined under the microscope and gave a great deal of valuable advice. Thanks to the sulphonamides, the surgeons were now better equipped than they had been in the first war. All the same, Fleming frequently spoke to his students about penicillin which, in their eyes, was little more than a laboratory curio. 'Just you wait,' he said to Dr Reginald Hudson, 'one of these days you'll find that penicillin can beat all the sulphonamides when it comes to the treatment of wounds.'

From time to time he went to Harefield to have a look at his Regional laboratories, accompanied by his assistant who is, today, Professor Newcomb. There was a fine avenue of trees which Fleming the gardener much admired. Professor D. M. Pryce, who was working under his orders, says that Fleming had a way of turning up unexpectedly and that they were always glad to see him. He was anxious to help, efficient and never discouraged. Going from laboratory to laboratory, as he was obliged to do as Regional Chief, he had to remember the many requests made to him. His method was to scribble brief notes on odds and ends of paper which he then stuffed into his trouser pockets, hoping that they would turn up again some day, and that he would be able to decipher them — which was all very much in the Wright tradition.

At the beginning of the war he was living in Chelsea with his family. In September 1940 bombs fell near by and broke some of the windows. Then, in November, incendiaries scored several hits on the house. Robert was away at school. Alec and Sareen, who had been dining with friends, returned home to find their flat flooded, the firemen still at work, and themselves refused right of entry. They went to lodge with Professor Pryce at Rickmansworth.

In March 1941 they tried to go back, but one night in the following month, a land-mine fell between the famous Chelsea Old Church — which stands at the corner of Old Church Street and Cheyne Walk — and the house. The shock was tremendous. Alec, Sareen, Robert and his cousin, as well as Sareen's twin sister, who were all sleeping there, suddenly saw doors and windows moving in on them, and ceilings collapsing over their heads. One door was flung on to the bed in which Alec was lying, and would have killed him, had it not been stopped by the wooden framework. It hung suspended above him.

Next morning he brought one of his laboratory attendants, Dan Stratful, to Chelsea to help him rescue the most necessary objects. 'We got there,' says Dan Stratful, 'and things looked pretty grim. The damage all round us was bad. Inside the flat everything was covered in dust and plaster from the ceiling. In the bedrooms it was worse. The ceilings were down and the window-frames awry.

It was a shambles. I said to him: "It must have been grim when the mine went up."

'He nodded, and then said, with a grin: "When I saw the entire window-frame moving towards me, I decided to get out of bed."

'We took a lot of stuff to the Institute and I rigged up a bed for him in the dark-room. He bought a radio and settled down there, at nights, quite happily.'

The family first went to live with Robert Fleming, Alec's brother, at Radlett. Then Dr Allison, who had been moved to another Region, offered them his house at Highgate. It had a garden, and there the green-fingered couple grew vegetables, fruit and flowers. When Allison returned after the war, he found flowers and fruit growing everywhere, sometimes in the most unexpected places. Fleming's horticultural 'experiments' had been successful. He spent most nights at the hospital. During the raids someone had to do duty as a fire-watcher on the roof. Generally, it was arranged that only one man at a time should take this risk, but Fleming, always attracted by the spectacular, could not resist going up there when he heard the alert.

Many of the doctors and students slept in a dormitory which had been arranged in the basement, with hot-water pipes round them, and their clothes hanging all over the place. They took their meals in the school canteen. Professor Fleming shared this life, not without a certain sense of satisfaction. 'There was a good deal of the bachelor in him, and he enjoyed the company of men. Sometimes, when a research-worker was kept late in the laboratory, the door would open, and in would walk the professor with his neat little bow-tie, and a cigarette dangling from his lips. With an eager and expectant look, he would say: "What about a pot of beer?" The worker would abandon his microscope and the two of them would go off together to the near-by pub, the Fountains, where they would find other St Mary's men.'

Fleming loved this atmosphere of youth where he was treated with affection and respect. The constant banging of the slot-machines and the cascade of coins when somebody struck lucky made the bar-parlour a lively place. Sometimes he ordered beer, sometimes an M&B, which was a play on words for the bacteriologists, because the two initials stood for both 'mild and bitter' and 'May & Baker'. He would spend a happy hour of relaxation there and then go back either to the hospital or to Highgate with Allison, who had kept a *pied-à-terre* in the house which he had lent to the Flemings.

Meanwhile at Oxford, while Florey was absent on his successful trip to America, the team under Chain's direction had been doing a great deal of work. The method of extraction had been perfected. What amounted to a factory was springing up, with Dr Sanders in charge. Several young women, known as the 'Penicillin Girls', worked in the bitterly cold room, muffled in woollen comforters and wearing warm gloves. The most serious problem was the contamination of the cultures. In vain did the 'Penicillin Girls' watch their every step so as not to stir up dust or create a draught. In vain were the floor and the benches painted with oil. In vain did the young women wear protective masks over their mouths. In vain was a curtain hung in front of the door and gone over every day with a vacuum cleaner. One single germ was enough to spoil a whole 'batch'.

Nevertheless, a small stock of the precious powder was being built up in the refrigerator against the day when it should be needed for a case. Florey was waiting for his ten thousand litres from America, but time was passing, and nothing came. He did not fail, however, to give part of his store for the treating of infected wounds. The first patients on whom it was used were some R.A.F. pilots who had been seriously burned during the Battle of Britain. Then the Oxford team sent a small parcel of penicillin to Professor (at that time, Lieutenant-Colonel) Pulvertaft, a bacteriologist working in Egypt, for the use of the Desert Army.

'We had an enormous number of infected wounded,' says Pulvertaft, 'terrible burn cases among the crews of the naval armoured cars, and fractures infected with streptococci. The medical journals told us that the sulphonamides would get the better of any infection. My own experience was that the sulphonamides, like other new products sent us from America, had absolutely no effect on these cases. The last thing I tried was penicillin. I had very little of it, something like ten thousand units, maybe less. The first man I tried it on was a young New Zealand officer called Newton. He had been in bed for six months with compound fractures in both legs. His sheets were saturated with pus and the heat in Cairo made the smell intolerable. He was little more than skin and bone and was running a high temperature. Normally, he would have died in a very short while, as did all our wounded when infection was prolonged. We introduced small rubber tubes into the sinuses of the left leg and injected with a very weak solution of penicillin (a few hundred units per cubic centimetre), because we had so little. I gave three injections a day and studied the effects under the microscope. I noticed, much to my surprise, that after the first treatment the streptococci were *inside* the leucocytes. That was a tremendous moment. Out there in Cairo, I knew nothing of what was being done in England, and the thing seemed like a miracle. In ten days the left leg was cured, and in a month's time the young fellow was back on his feet. I had enough penicillin left for ten cases. Nine of them were complete cures. We at the hospital were now convinced that a new and important therapeutic had been found. We even got a culture sent out from England, so's we might produce the stuff ourselves. A sort of factory was set up in the Old Citadel. But, of course, we hadn't the means to concentrate the substance ...'

Between 1940 and 1942 very little was said about Alexander Fleming. His publications had been forgotten. Several research-workers, in perfect good faith, published as original discoveries facts which had already been described in his early papers. In August 1942 he was led in dramatic circumstances to carry out his first therapeutic test with purified penicillin, on a patient whose condition appeared to be hopeless. The patient was a friend of his, a man of fifty-two. He was one of the directors of Robert Fleming's firm (which made optical instruments) and had been admitted to St Mary's in a dying state about the middle of June. The diagnosis was difficult. The patient showed symptoms of meningitis, but examination of the cerebro-spinal fluid did not reveal the presence of the expected microbe. Fleming worked tooth and nail on this rebellious case and finally succeeded in disclosing the presence of a streptococcus. He tested its sensitivity to sulpho-namides but without success, and then to penicillin, in the only form he had (an impure filtrate). The penicillin worked and, on the agar, eliminated the germs within a radius of eleven millimetres. But the only reserve of *pure* penicillin then to be found in England, and a very small reserve at that, was at Oxford.

On the 6th he telephoned Florey and explained matters to him: 'If you could possibly spare a little penicillin, I should like to try it.' Florey gave him the penicillin with full instructions how to use it, on condition that his case formed one of the series of cases which were being treated in Oxford.

'He was good enough', wrote Fleming, 'to place his whole stock at my disposal. On the night of the 5/6 the patient was drowsy, comatose, with bouts of extreme restlessness, during which he was wandering and rambling: he had been suffering from uncontrollable hiccough for 10 days. On the evening of August 6, three-hourly intramuscular injections of penicillin (15,000 units) were begun. Some improvement was almost immediately manifest. In 24 hours the patient was mentally clearer, the hiccough had disappeared, and head-retraction was less marked. The temperature had fallen to 97° F. But when the spinal fluid was examined it was found that little or no penicillin was present.

'I consulted Florey on the telephone about the possibility of injecting penicillin into the spinal theca. He had never done it, but as the case was desperate, and from what I knew about the innocuity of penicillin to human cells, I injected 5000 units by lumbar puncture. Later in the day Florey rang me up on the telephone and told me he had injected penicillin into the spinal theca of a cat and that the cat had promptly died. However, the man did not die. The injection of penicillin into his spinal canal did not upset him at all and he made a rapid recovery. On Aug 28th he got up. His temperature had been normal for two weeks and he had no sign of meningitis. On Sept 9th he left the hospital, completely cured.

'Here was a man who seemed to be dying, but who, in a few days, with penicillin treatment, was out of danger. Such a case makes a great impression on one.'

This miraculous cure was tremendously talked about, both at St Mary's and in medical circles everywhere. On August 27th, 1942, *The Times* published a leading article entitled 'Penicillium', laying stress on the hopes which this substance, a hundred times more active than the sulphonamides, must arouse. At the moment, said the article, it was not easy to obtain a synthetic product, but that did not much matter, since the mould was easily accessible. 'There will', it went on, be general agreement with the plea of the *Lancet* that "in view of its potentialities" methods of producing penicillin on a large scale should be developed as quickly as possible.'

This was more than advice given to the British Government: it was tantamount to an order.

The article mentioned neither Fleming nor the research-workers at Oxford, but on August 31st, *The Times* printed a letter from Sir Almroth Wright:

TO THE EDITOR OF THE TIMES

Sir,—In the leading article on penicillin in your issue yesterday, you refrained from putting the laurel-wreath for this discovery round anybody's brow. I would, with your permission, supplement your article by pointing out that, on the principle of *palmam qui meruit ferat*, it should be decreed to Professor Alexander Fleming of this research laboratory. For he is the discoverer of penicillin and was the author also of the original suggestion that this substance might prove to have important applications in medicine.

I am, Sir, yours faithfully,

ALMROTH WRIGHT

Inoculation Department,
St Mary's Hospital,
Paddington, W.2   Aug. 28

Thus did the old master proclaim the merits of his disciple. It must have cost him a great effort of intellectual honesty — which he made with perfect loyalty — publicly to sing the praises of chemotherapy. He continued to believe, or at least to hope, that in the last analysis immunization would prevail — as was only natural.

Wright, now 81, had left London and was living in the country (at Farnham Common). But he still came up, three times a week, to spend a few hours in the laboratory. His train was often delayed by air-raids. He might have made the journey by car, but that would have meant, he said, being driven by women (the only available chauffeurs in war-time) 'and they would have talked all the way.' He preferred the fatigue and danger of the railway.

About Wright and Fleming we have a good deal of first-hand evidence from a secretary, the first Fleming had ever had — Mrs Buckley. 'What struck me', she says, 'was the extraordinary difference between the two men: between the great master and the great pupil: between Sir Almroth, a creature of intellect, urbane, academic; and Professor Fleming, also with a powerful brain, but much more like a child in his manner of dealing with everything, even with his work. He had an astonishing simplicity of approach, and it was this, I imagine, which so often led him to the right solution of a problem. Yes, they saw things with very different eyes, but the Professor was always the most loyal of disciples.'

Wright had by no means lost his love of argument. 'I remember', says Professor Pulvertaft, 'one occasion in particular when I had gone to tea with him. We talked, or rather, he talked, about Shakespeare, of whom he had a somewhat poor opinion. He said that Shakespeare did not doubt enough, that no one could be an artist who was too certain. None of Shakespeare's characters had doubts. I murmured, rather treacherously: "To be or not to be; that is the question." He gave a loud sniff and changed the subject.'

During and after the miraculous cure of 1942, Fleming and Florey corresponded. Both of them thought that the time had come to start mass-production of a substance capable of achieving such marvels. In August, Fleming said to his host and friend, Dr Allison: 'Things look promising ... I am going to see Sir Andrew Duncan, the Minister of Supply. He is a Scot and a friend. Will you, on your side, make the Ministry of Health people get a move on and press for the industrial manufacture of penicillin?' He duly went to see Sir Andrew who, much impressed by the miraculous effects of the substance, replied: 'I am going to give you a committee, and a very active man who will get things moving.'

Sir Andrew sent for Sir Cecil Weir, the Director-General of Equipment, and a remarkable organizer. 'Fleming', said the Minister, 'has been talking to me about penicillin. He believes, and so do I, that it offers immense possibilities for the treatment of wounds and of numerous diseases. I want you to do everything you can to organize its production on a great scale.'

On September 25th, 1942, Sir Cecil Weir summoned to a conference at Portland House, Fleming, Florey, Raistrick, Arthur Mortimer (his assistant) and representatives of the chemical and pharmaceutical industries; in short, all those interested in the manufacture of penicillin.

Five big firms — May & Baker, Glaxo, Burroughs Wellcome, British Drug Houses, and Boots — had formed, in 1941, the 'Therapeutic Research Corporation', to which all had pledged themselves to communicate what they could find out on the subject of penicillin. Other large concerns, I.C.I. and Kemball, Bishop, were in direct contact with the Oxford team, and the latter had even made a free delivery of penicillin to Florey's Institute a few days before the committee met.

Sir Cecil Weir said that all information about the substance and its production must be shared. Research-workers and industrialists must keep one single goal before their eyes: rapid and abundant production. The reaction was unanimous, enthusiastic and favourable. All undertook to share their secrets and to enlist their knowledge and their talents in the service of the community. Florey told how he had passed on the results obtained at Oxford to the American concerns. He added that reciprocity ought to be complete and expressed some uneasiness about patents taken out by American research-workers to protect the manufacturing processes. The Therapeutic Research Corporation promised that all information received from America should be made available to the English scientists.

It was, however, agreed that the work of the different laboratories should *not* be centralized. A single research centre would, in view of air-raids, be too vulnerable. As to the quantities to be produced, it seemed premature to discuss that question there and then. Florey informed the conference that, though enormous doses had been necessary for the treatment of a single case of septicaemia or of meningitis, that would not be so in the treatment of local infections. Experiments made, for example, on burns showed that ten grams a month would suffice for *all* infected burns in the Middle East Forces. Dr Maxwell announced that the Therapeutic Research Corporation was thinking of putting up a factory capable of delivering a million litres every year. I.C.I. also had a plan. As to the distribution of the finished product,

Florey hoped that it would be made under the control of biologists, as a safeguard against the improper and harmful use so often made of new remedies.

At the end of the conference, Arthur Mortimer whispered in his chief's ear: 'I don't know whether you realize it, but this will rank as an historic meeting, not only in the annals of medicine, but probably in the history of the world. For the first time, all those concerned in the production of a remedy, are going to *give* their knowledge and their work without any ulterior motive of gain or ambition.'

Manufacture got under way very soon. A 'General Committee of Penicillin', at first presided over by Arthur Mortimer, and later by Sir Henry Dale, directed the operation. Professor Raistrick was its technical adviser and rendered immense services. He went to America, as did the engineers belonging to the great manufacturing chemists, to study the progress already made.

In the United States the large-scale production of penicillin had got off to a slow start.[1] The chemists wanted fermentation in depth, but penicillium prefers to live on the surface. In addition, the struggle against contamination remained difficult. One of the firms which made a great effort was Charles Pfizer Inc. It was not a factory specializing in pharmaceutical products, but its staff had a great experience of fermentations. One of the directors, John L. Smith, a little man with grey hair and a poker face, who with his technical advisers, had tried, so far without success, to industrialize the production of penicillin, happened to witness the resurrection of a little girl smitten with an infection which every doctor had, so far, despaired of curing.

She was suffering from infective endocarditis and was going to die. In June 1943 one of the hospital doctors, a Jew from Brooklyn, Loewe by name, came to Smith and asked him for some penicillin with which to treat her. Smith objected on the ground that the National Research Council reserved to itself the allocation of this rare product, and was of the opinion that it had no effect on endocarditis. Loewe said that, provided it were used in conjunction with heparin, penicillin would be effective. Smith went to

[1] Paul de Kruif, *Life Among the Doctors* (Harcourt Brace, 1949).

185

see the little girl — an action which, for the overworked head of a big firm, was both praiseworthy and surprising. He was deeply moved by what he saw, broke the regulations, and gave Loewe some penicillin. For three days the golden liquid flowed, drop by drop, into one of the young sufferer's veins. Every day, after long hours of work, Smith went to her bedside. When she was getting better, Loewe was satisfied with intra-muscular injections. One month later, the girl was out of danger.

Loewe then undertook the treatment of other obstinate cases and Smith continued to help him. The doctor was by that time administering up to 200,000 units a day. What did it matter, seeing that penicillin was non-toxic? But the National Research Council insisted on the regulations being observed. Endocarditis was still excluded since, according to the Council, the statistics were not 'convincing'. The patients, however, continued to take on a new lease of life, and Smith, in spite of the risk, went on supplying Loewe with penicillin. In October 1943 the Council sent a representative to Brooklyn to take a look at those sick folk who had walked out of their coffins. 'Take an eyeful of me,' said one old woman. 'I'm alive amn't I?' Her eyes were shining. 'All the same, statistically, I'm dead.'

After his visits to the hospital, Smith returned to the factory a changed man. 'You've saved another life,' he said to his engineers, bacteriologists and mycologists. All, thrilled by the grandeur of the struggle, spared neither time nor trouble. By sheer determination they succeeded, by sterilizing the air, in producing deep fermentation in huge vats. Bacteriology for giants. In all the rooms there were notices: '*Exercise scrupulous care ... contamination of penicillin may cause death ... Penicillin must be absolutely sterile. Are you doing everything you can to see that it is? The sick are relying upon your vigilance to protect them.*' In America this sort of appeal never fails. Very soon a torrent of penicillin was cleansing infected bodies.

Arthur Mortimer tells how certain persons in the United States suggested that they had a right to royalties on the new processes discovered by them. 'Our answer', says Mortimer, 'was that they were free to demand as high a sum in royalties as they liked. They began to wonder and asked us why we were being so generous. We replied that the moment they began to claim royalties, we should demand the like on the total production of penicillin, since the substance had been discovered in England, and that the amount would be exactly twice that asked by them for the use of their processes. After that, nothing further was heard about royalties.' Not unnaturally, when the war was over, patents were taken out — and respected — for the new processes. But penicillin itself remained unpatented and free of all royalties.

There were certain difficulties connected with the word 'penicillin', which a number of firms claimed they could use as their trade-mark. Fleming had to intervene in person. In 1929 he had made of 'penicillin' a scientific term which was common property. No one had a right to monopolize it. The governments of the different countries gave their support to this view and the question was settled without friction. It did, however, become necessary, even in England, to keep a sharp look-out on the way in which the word was used. As soon as it got about that a miraculous remedy had been discovered, the market was flooded with penicillin ointments, penicillin lotions for the eyes, penicillin pills and penicillin beauty preparations. Fleming, much amused, said to Arthur Mortimer: 'I wonder what they're going to invent next? I shouldn't wonder if somebody produces a penicillin lipstick.' 'That's more than possible,' answered Mortimer, 'and it wouldn't be difficult to float: *Kiss whom you like, where you like, how you like. You need fear no tiresome consequences (except marriage) if you use our Penicillin Rouge.*' Fleming responded with a barely perceptible smile, and said it was a good idea, though it would be necessary to apply the Therapeutic Substances Act so as to make sure that no improper use was made of it.

In 1943 the factories began to produce on a big scale, and relatively large quantities became available for the armies. Major-General Poole, Director of Pathology at the War Office, sent two specialists to North Africa. They arrived in Algiers immediately after the Allied victory at Cap Bon. They at once embarked on a whole series of treatments. The wounds in this campaign had been worse than ever and the Tunisian flies had done as much damage as the enemy. There was no end to them, and, proof even against D.D.T., they infected wounds with every type of bacillus, and laid their eggs in them, which produced worms. The treatment of such wounds required enormous quantities of penicillin.

It was not long before Florey arrived in Algeria. His experience enabled him to give much useful advice to the surgeons. The first results had made a tremendous impression on the medical world, and there was reason to fear that penicillin would be used for every kind of wound and every type of illness. Florey set himself energetically to point out that penicillin was not a universal panacea. Certain microbes are susceptible to it, others not. The first thing to be done in every case was to make a culture of the infecting germs and to carry out a test which would show the degree of their sensitivity to penicillin. Where the experiment showed that the germs were vulnerable, then penicillin could be administered and the wound stitched up. The surgeons had to reconsider much of their earlier knowledge and methods. Most of them took an objective view, but others grew indignant. There was still pus in some of the wounds, they said. Some bacteria, the pyocyaneus for instance, were not, it is true, affected by penicillin, but the phagocytes, freed from the other microbes, were strong enough to digest these ultimate assailants.

Meanwhile, small quantities of penicillin were finding their way into the war-factories. Dr Ethel Florey and her colleagues of the Birmingham Accident Hospital demonstrated the effectiveness of penicillin dressings for hand injuries, which were of such frequent occurrence in those surroundings. More than usually spectacular were the results obtained in the fight against gonorrhoea, which penicillin mastered in twelve hours. This was of capital importance in the armies, for the military hospitals were filled with venereal cases.

All of a sudden Glory, that goddess whose movements are unpredictable and violent, laid hold of the silent Scot. He was overwhelmed by a mounting tide of letters. His telephone rang from morning till night. Ministers, generals, newspapers of every country, were continually asking for him. He was a bit surprised, at times amused, but on the whole enjoyed it all, and made a point of insisting on the part played by Florey and Chain.

The public and the Press were fascinated by so original and modest a character. There was something romantic about the story of penicillin: the spore drifting in through a window and settling on a culture; the discovery brought to completion at the very height of the war just when it would be most useful; the marvellous reports pouring in from the armies — all these things helped to create a legend, most of which was true. Honours began to rain down on Fleming. In 1943 he was elected a Fellow of the Royal Society (F.R.S.), the oldest and most highly respected of all the scientific societies in Great Britain. It had emerged, in 1660, from an 'invisible Oxford College' where the philosophers held their meetings. Newton had been its President from 1703 to 1727. Wright belonged to it. To be made a member of it was for a scientist the highest honour which could be conferred upon him by his peers.

His friends at St Mary's, colleagues and students, gave him an eighteenth-century silver salver. Handfield-Jones, one of the hospital's most eminent surgeons, delivered the speech, which accompanied the presentation, in the presence of Sir Almroth Wright. 'There is no member of this community', he said, 'whom it values more highly than Professor Fleming. He has always entered into the spirit of this house, even so whole-heartedly as, sometimes, to come down from the heights and drink a glass of beer at the Fountains.'

Fleming, in reply, said: 'In the course of my life I have had a few small successes which have given me pleasure. But I can quite honestly say that this is the greatest moment of my life, for you, my master, my contemporaries and my pupils, have come together to do me honour.' He confessed that he found it difficult to speak intelligently in his present profoundly emotional state. 'I could tell you a lot about staphylococci, spirochaetes, and, even, penicillin, but the situation is very different when I am, myself, the subject under discussion.'

He had, indeed, been terrified all that day at the prospect of having to reply to the eloquent Handfield-Jones. While lunching with MacLeod, he had told him how frightened he was, and MacLeod had reminded him of two famous lines by their compatriot, Robert Burns, which would give expression to the modesty appropriate to the occasion, and might well serve as a peroration.

Fleming decided to make use of the quotation, and to say: 'What do we really know about ourselves? I am a Scot from

Ayrshire. One hundred and fifty years ago, a famous Ayrshire man, Robert Burns, wrote:

> O wad some Pow'r the giftie gie us
> To see oursels as others see us!

If others see me as I have just been described by Handfield-Jones, then I must have seriously underestimated myself. But my Scottish upbringing has taught me prudence, and I know that on occasions like this, as in obituary notices, flattery is permitted.'

But when he came to speak he was so nervous that he used the Burns quotation at the wrong moment. While he was speaking, it occurred to him that there were three students of St Mary's who had become Fellows of the Royal Society, and he was one of them. He made an impromptu reference to this. 'Many years ago,' he said, 'there were three students here at St Mary's. All three are today Fellows of the Royal Society. Would you ever have thought such a thing possible?' He then immediately quoted Burns's lines, with the result that he appeared to be using the lines to imply that the others had not seen how clever he, and the other two Fellows, really were. However, those present could, for once, see on Fleming's face the emotion he was feeling, and this charming mix-up in his speech was received with affectionate laughter.

Alexander Fleming to Ronald Gray: They had their meeting at the hospital and presented me with a very beautiful silver salver. That was pleasant, but it was not so nice to have to sit on a platform and then have to make a speech. I hope I did not disgrace myself, but in that matter I am not a good judge ...

The papers seem to have been busy with penicillin. I actually had a request from somebody in America for an autograph, and I had a letter of congratulations from the Council of my native village, Darvel. The provost of the town had read about penicillin when he was in Cairo. On Thursday week I am supposed to be broadcasting to Sweden ... Nothing startling happening here. We all just go on.

To another friend, the bacteriologist Compton, who at that time was director of a laboratory in Alexandria, he wrote on July 3rd, 1943:

> I was naturally pleased at being elected to the Royal Society, and it is nice to think that my friends were pleased also ... I am very busy at present, trying out my chemotherapeutic baby. It seems to be extraordinarily powerful stuff and, when enough of it is available, some of the sulphonamides will have to take a back seat. In the last week or two we have had two staphylococcal septicaemias snatched from the jaws of death, a gonorrhea in which the infection disappeared in twenty-four hours, and some rather wonderful 'cures' by local application. I can see it keeping me very busy for the next six months or more.
>
> We are all just waiting for something big to happen, but we know just as much or as little as you do about what is to happen. Maybe, before you get this, the whole Mediterranean business will be cleared up ...
>
> The Missus is well and busy and Robert is at St Mary's as a student. We all send our best wishes to you and your family and look forward to seeing you when Hitler is finished.
>
> Yours sincerely
ALEXANDER FLEMING

Meanwhile, in the United States, as in England, the spore carried by the wind was giving birth to an industry which grew with every day that passed. In May 1943 the American Army had put in an order for twenty million units. England was preparing to spend three million pounds on the production of penicillin.

In 1944 Dr Coghill, of the Peoria laboratory, presented to the American Chemical Society a brilliant report which revealed the extraordinary rapidity with which the industrial production of penicillin in the United States had been developing:

> Seldom within our memory has any topic so taken the interest of the scientific and lay world as has penicillin. For the past two years or more it has played Cinderella to the mycologists, chemists and engineers of the whole English-speaking world.

Product of the humble moulds, which until comparatively recent years have been something to control rather than to cultivate, it has miraculously been clothed with the raiment of $20,000,000 worth of plants, and is now attended upon by hundreds of footmen, and the party is proceeding with fanfares galore. Penicillin is very patently taking the limelight from its older sulfa sisters. Two years ago, those of us who were concerned with promoting the party used to wake up in the middle of the night and wonder whether at the stroke of 12.00 this lovely vision would flee, leaving us clutching at an empty glass slipper — the work and strife we had been through, and the plants we had built. However, the stroke of 12.00 is now upon us, and we find the two stories are digressing, for the few dozens of spectacular cases upon which we had originally built our hopes have now been augmented by hundreds more like them ...

This scientist wrote well, and the myth of Cinderella could be truly applied to Fleming's adventure.

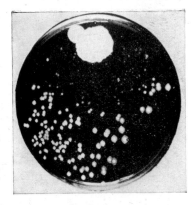

The original mould growth of *penicillium notatum*, and Fleming's drawing and notes on its antibacterial action on staphylococci

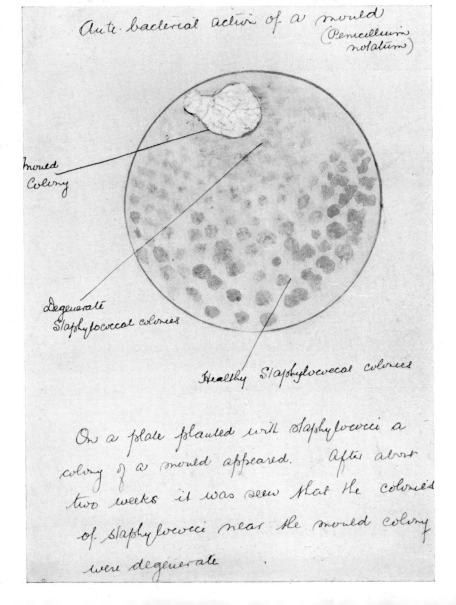

Anti-bacterial action of a mould
(Penicillium notatum)

Mould
Colony

Degenerate
Staphylococcal colonies

Healthy Staphylococcal colonies

On a plate planted with Staphylococci a colony of a mould appeared. After about two weeks it was seen that the colonies of Staphylococci near the mould colony were degenerate

Left: A typical photograph of a colony of penicillium and its inhibiting effect on the growth various micro-organisms

Below: Fleming printing photographs of similar bacterial plates in the darkroom of the Wright Fleming Institute

CHAPTER FOURTEEN

SIR ALEXANDER FLEMING

In recent years life for me has become a little difficult. FLEMING

THE summer of 1944 in London was the time of the flying-bombs. These objects, fired from the Continent, travelled with a terrifying rumble, and slowly enough to be seen with the naked eye before they reached the end of their trajectory. At St Mary's as soon as the sirens sounded, a watcher went up on to the roof, ready to give the alarm if he saw any 'doodle-bug' making towards the hospital. This he did by setting off a bell. A second and a third shrilling meant 'Danger imminent' and 'Go down to the shelter'.

Often at the first warning Fleming and his friend, Professor Pannett, would rush up to the roof to watch the 'doodle-bug' through their glasses and compare notes on where they thought it would fall. One day when Clayden was on watch-duty, he said to Fleming: 'Look sir, this is becoming a bloody farce. You send me up here to keep people away, and then you come up yourself. You and Professor Pannett are important men and can't easily be spared.'

'That's all right,' replied Fleming, 'just say we're carrying out an inspection.'

Sometimes it happened that if he was in the laboratory engaged on an interesting piece of work, he did not hear the siren. His secretary, Mrs Helen Buckley, describes how, one morning, he was dictating a difficult letter when the alert went.

'I just looked up, a bit nervously,' she says, 'hoping for the best, and then presently the second warning rang and I could hear the wretched flying-bomb grumbling away in the distance getting louder, and then the third warning rang, and there was the horrible thing coming straight at us. I could see it from my window, and the sweat began to drip off my face on to my block. I could hardly hold on to my pencil, and I looked at him out of the corner of my eye — not a move! Finally, the thing rattled overhead, the whole building shook, and the objects on the desk tinkled. When it was gone, and the fourth bell rang for "All clear", suddenly the Professor came to, out of his deep thought, looked at me, and said "Duck!" He had not heard either of the first three warning bells, nor the flying-bomb.'

The military authorities were beginning to permit the use of penicillin for civilian patients. Bernard Shaw's play, *The Doctor's Dilemma* thus became a reality. Each case had to be considered on its merits, for if the still far from abundant penicillin were used for a sick person who could be cured by other means, there was always the risk that there wouldn't be enough available when it was a matter of life and death.

Sometimes the identity of the patient had an influence on the decision. Philip Guedalla, the author, for instance, received privileged treatment. 'I am,' he said later, 'one of the animals into which the life-saving substance has been injected. I am afraid that in my case it was applied as a corpse-reviver at a very late stage, but it revived the corpse. If it had not been for the investigation which Professor Fleming carried out so brilliantly, I should not be here this afternoon. I wish to testify with all humility and thankfulness to the treatment which in six weeks can bring a man out of the shadow into a state in which he is able to resist the efforts of three Government Departments to amend the text of his book.'

From all sides the relatives of sick persons wrote to Fleming begging him to help in the cure of all kinds of diseases. He always did his best to see whether anything could be done, and never failed to answer these hundreds of letters in his own tiny, elegant and readable hand. But the simple-mindedness of some of these requests saddened him. 'I have never said that penicillin can cure *everything*. It is the newspapers that have said that. It does have an extraordinary effect in certain cases of illness, but none in others ...' The publicity which he had not sought showed him no mercy and, say what he might, it was firmly fixed in the lay mind that penicillin was a 'miraculous panacea'. He knew that, like other remedies, it was specific, that is to say that it acted on certain microbes and had no action on others.

'That makes things much more difficult for the doctor. No doubt he would prefer to have a chemical substance which he could use for all cases of infection. But, since that is impossible, he should not waste his time, or his patient's, by using the wrong drug on the wrong microbe. This means that, from now on, every doctor will have to pay a great deal more attention to bacteriology than in the past. Penicillin was born in the laboratory, and has grown up in close association with the laboratory. Penicillin treatment can only satisfactorily be carried out in association with a bacteriological laboratory.'

He insisted on certain essential ideas. In the first place, penicillin could act on the microbes only if it were in contact with them, either locally or in the blood stream. 'Put the champion in the ring face to face with his opponent, and he will do the rest.' But it was not treating a boil with penicillin merely to give it a surface application of penicillin ointment, for that did not establish contact with the centre of infection. Next, care should be taken not to use penicillin for minor affections — a sore throat, for instance — because that only encouraged among the microbes the development of resistant strains. For the same reason Fleming advised doctors not to hesitate, when dealing with severe cases, to use very strong doses. There could be no danger, seeing that the product was non-toxic, and in this way they could avoid the risk of leaving resistant strains in the organism. It was necessary to wage a blitzkrieg against microbes.

Honours were now showering down thick and fast on this man who had neither sought nor wanted them, though he felt the same pleasure in receiving them as formerly in carrying through some experiment better than anybody else or, at shooting, handing in a better target. Fame could not spoil him. He was still the same simple, approachable individual about whom, very often, celebrated foreigners who had come to congratulate him at the Institute would say: 'What! is *that* the celebrated Fleming?' A young American army doctor, who sat next to him at a football match, spent the whole afternoon trying to find out the name of the friendly little man with the spotted bow-tie, who had solemnly explained the rules of Rugby to him. He felt sure he had seen him somewhere. Could it have been at the Royal Society of Medicine? Driving back to London through the ruins of the bombed city, he kept thinking of the smiling professor who in these agonizing days could get so excited over a game. To his friend, who was at the wheel, he said: 'Tell me, Dave, who was that prof. I was next to? I've forgotten his name.'

'Why, that's Fleming, the bacteriologist at St Mary's — the guy who discovered penicillin!'

For the young American scientist, who had seen penicillin make hay of virulent cases of septicaemia, it was as though a door had opened, and a legendary figure appeared suddenly on the threshold. 'I went on thinking about that friendly professor, but not as formerly. So *that*, jostled by the crowd, unrecognized and not wanting to be recognized, cordial and human, was the man I had met, whose name, for the good he had done, would rank higher at the Judgment Throne than Hitler would be low for the evils he had committed. In the most bitter hour of the war, I had watched the English at play, and had felt their greatness.'

In July 1944 the newspapers published the new Honours List. The 'bacteriologist at St Mary's' had become Sir Alexander Fleming, and his wife, Lady Fleming. She showed her pleasure more visibly than he did, not that he wasn't pleased, but he was still incapable of showing his feelings. 'I am almost sorry,' he said, 'that I'm not Irish, because then I could *really* have enjoyed it all.' For many years now, Sareen had shown him how completely the Irish can accept the most ordinary compliments, to say nothing of well-deserved honours ... Of course he enjoyed his honours — everyone could see that: what he meant was, give himself up entirely to enjoyment.

The day before the new Knight Bachelor was to receive the accolade from the King at Buckingham Palace, he said to Clayden: 'How about a party tomorrow evening?'

'What about the doings? It's difficult to get stuff these days.'

'Next door,' said Fleming, with a jerk of his cigarette, 'there are five bottles of gin. Lay in some beer, and all the usual what-nots, and we'll have a party when I get back.'

The investiture took place in the Palace basement, for security reasons, and Sareen was disappointed. When Fleming returned to the Institute for tea, he found only eight persons in the library. Many of the doctors were absent on duty. It happened to be one of the days when Wright came to London for a few hours, and he was presiding over the gathering as he had done for the last forty years. But he seemed to be in one of his bad moods, slumped heavily into an armchair, and did not utter a word until Fleming turned up. The total, the lowering, silence continued for a few minutes, then, deliberately turning his back on Fleming, Wright launched out into a tremendous discourse on the merits of immunization, and the demerits of chemotherapy which, he declared, was a heresy bristling with danger for all genuine medical research.

Dr Hughes, who was sitting opposite Fleming, expected to see some sign of amusement or anger on his face. But it remained completely impassive. Finally the Old Man had to stop talking from sheer lack of breath. Craxton, the secretary of the Institute, thinking to ease the tension, asked Sir Almroth to decide a few administrative questions. The answer came like a thunderclap:

'Don't bother me with such trivial things! *Doctor* Fleming will deal with them!'

Professor Sir Alexander Fleming held out his hand for the papers, got up and left the table without a word.

Wright returned to the country and the evening was a great success. The headquarters staff of the hospital was present in full force. Many toasts were drunk to Sir Alexander, and Sir Zachary Cope, the great surgeon, who had been a student with 'Flem', read a poem of his own composition:

To Alexander Fleming, Knight

To achieve an outstanding success
  In one's chosen career
To become a world-famous F.R.S.
  With a merit so clear;

On a pedestal high to be raised,
  With no fear of fall;
By the Commons and Lords to be praised,
  To be talked of by all;

Just to take in a leisurely stride
   The physician's top rank,
And to dream that Americans vied
   To put cash in one's bank;

To be praised by the authors who write
   And the poets who sing;
To be given the title of Knight
   By our Most Gracious King;

To know well that while still in one's prime
   One has not lived in vain,
And that none has done more in his time
   To alleviate pain;

To imagine these Castles in Spain
   Is a dream of one's youth,
But for you — one need hardly explain —
   It is less than the truth.

When all had left, Sir Alexander went up to Clayden, his companion in two wars, and the organizer of this party. Clayden shook his hand, and said: 'I'm damned glad about all this, sir.'

Fleming answered: 'That's the nicest thing I've heard this evening.'

There was still some beer left, and the two men spent an hour together, talking over old times at Boulogne and Wimereux. It had been a memorable occasion.

Paris was liberated in August 1944. In September it was the turn of Brussels. Fleming wrote to his friend, Bordet:

Inoculation Department,
St Mary's Hospital, London, W.2
Sept. 4, 44

My Dear Professor Bordet,

It is indeed great news we have heard today, that once more the Germans have left Brussels and that you are free of Nazi domination.

Every bacteriologist in England hopes that you — one of the fathers of this science — have come through the years of sadness with a stout heart and that you will still have years of fruitful work in front of you. We rejoice in your long deferred freedom.

With all good wishes
Yours sincerely
ALEXANDER FLEMING

Innumerable invitations poured in upon him, not only from his own country but from America and the continent of Europe. He was presented with the Freedom of Paddington, in which district of London he had spent all his medical life, and in 1946 of Darvel, the small Scottish town in which he had been at school. Early in 1945 he was elected President of the newly founded Society of General Microbiology. In his inaugural address, he said:

> Other and more distinguished members were asked to assume this presidency, but they were sufficiently strong-minded to refuse it. But, true to Scottish tradition never to refuse anything, when it came to my turn, I accepted, and I was very pleased until the time came when I received a note from your Secretary saying that I had to deliver the inaugural address ...

He continued in the same half-serious, half-humorous tone. This Society, he said, would not, like many others, be a platform from which its members would read papers 'designed to advance their own honour and glory', but a place of meeting where bacteriologists, doctors, industrialists, agricultural specialists, mycologists and biochemists could come together to exchange information. A discovery of capital importance might well be born of a simple conversation.

'I have the impression', writes Dr Clegg, 'that few people realize what a magnificent ambassador for Britain Fleming was when he went abroad. Modest to the point of shyness, by no means an orator on public occasions, he impressed those he met with his simplicity and essential humility. With it all, there was a naive schoolboy delight in simple pleasures.

199

' "I hear you are going to the U.S.A.," I said to him when I saw him one evening at the Athenaeum.

' "Yes," he said, "isn't it great? I am going to see the Brooklyn Dodgers!" '

This baseball side interested him as much as all the marvels of that gigantic country.

Before leaving for America, he was, as befitted his new eminence, interviewed for the B.B.C. by Bebe Daniels. 'I had asked the B.B.C.', she says, 'whether I could have Sir Alexander Fleming. Their answer was: "Oh, no! Sir Alexander will never consent to speak on the radio!"

' "All the same, I'm going to give him a ring."

' "Sir Alexander never answers the telephone."

'I thought that rather odd, so I wrote him a letter, and had it delivered at the hospital by my secretary, Joan Murray, with strict orders to give it to Sir Alexander in person. When she came back I asked her: "Well, what happened?"

' "I was shown in to Sir Alexander, and he said: 'Why all this fuss? Who sent you? Mr Churchill?' 'No,' I answered, 'Bebe Daniels.' " She left my letter with him, and half an hour later Sir Alexander himself rang me up. "Come and see me tomorrow, at one o'clock, at St Mary's."

'I was punctual to the minute. I had expected to find twenty-four secretaries, eight guards and I don't know what else. Actually, the only person I saw was a technician in a white overall in one of the corridors. I asked him: "Where shall I find Sir Alexander Fleming?"

' "At the end of the passage: he's making tea."

'I found him with his sleeves rolled up, making tea over a Bunsen burner. "Would you like a cup?" he asked me, and, before I could say yes or no, I had a cup in my hand. Then he said: "It would interest me to talk on the radio ... Would you like to see the original culture?"

' "That'd be marvellous!"

'He vanished behind a pile of dishes, found the precious culture, and showed it me. Then he asked: "What's the programme? What d'you want me to say?"

' "You will be free to say exactly what you like, sir."

' "I thought that'd be your answer ... Here's what I've prepared." He read it to me, and it was perfect. Sir Alexander was marvellous, and had a delicious sense of humour.'

In June, July and August 1945 Fleming made a triumphal progress through the United States. 'It is clear to me', he said in his report, 'that they attach a great deal more importance to penicillin in America than in England.' John Cameron, of the British Mission, was his guide, and asked him to give press conferences, radio interviews and public lectures at the various universities, because it would be excellent propaganda for Great Britain. Fleming acquired a taste for this sort of thing and did it very well.

He visited the factories which were turning out penicillin, and the laboratory at Peoria which had made success possible. He was amazed by the tremendous resources available to the Americans. At Peoria, where he stayed with Dr Robert D. Coghill, he found a veritable museum where all the varieties of penicillium were displayed. In his lectures he reminded his audiences that it was English scientists who had set this immense industry going, that Florey had brought the methods of production to Peoria, and that America had then perfected the technique of manufacture, and had provided England with penicillin. It was, he pointed out, a fine example of mutual aid.

In New York, the producers of penicillin gave a banquet at the Waldorf, 'to do honour,' said the president, 'and to express gratitude to the one chosen by Providence to discover and to reveal to the world the existence and the properties of the most potent weapon yet known to man to aid him in his war against disease ... We have the closest approximation yet attained to the fulfilment of the dream of chemotherapy, a substance incredibly powerful against a multitude of bacterial invaders, and incredibly innocuous to the tissues of the invaded host.' When he called upon Fleming to reply, he quoted from the Gospel according to Saint John:

' "Now there is at Jerusalem by the sheep market a pool which is called in the Hebrew tongue Bethesda, having five porches.

' "In these lay a great multitude of impotent folk, of blind, halt, withered, waiting for the moving of the water.

' "For an angel went down at a certain season into the pool and troubled the water: whosoever then first after the troubling of the water stepped in was made whole of whatsoever disease he had.''

'Certainly,' concluded the president, 'it was an angel who first moved the spirit of Sir Alexander Fleming when he saw, for the first time, the effect produced on a bacterial culture by a wandering mould, for the pool thus troubled has cured not *one* sick man but myriads of sick men.'

Sometimes the questions put to him after his lectures were rather too personal. On one occasion at Brooklyn, John Smith, the head of Pfizer Inc., and at that time the biggest producer of penicillin in the world, asked: 'Why have you never touched the royalties which would have enabled you and yours to live as a man should who has rendered such services to humanity?'

Fleming's reply was: 'It never occurred to me.'

His visit to the Pfizer laboratories had been well publicized in advance and the benches had all been scrubbed and the instruments polished in readiness for his arrival. Looking round him at the vast and gleaming surfaces, on which there was not so much as a grain of dust, he said: 'If I had been working in these conditions, I should never have found penicillin.'

At one of the universities, a professor of chemistry asked him: 'Why didn't you complete your work and purify the product?'

'Why didn't you do it yourselves?' answered Fleming. 'All the necessary information was in the literature.'

At Washington, the press conference irritated this least irritable of men. 'Were you a boxer when you were a kid? ... If not why have you gotten a broken nose? ... Who found the dough for your studies in London?'

Nothing, as a rule, ever ruffled him. His gift of silence stood him in good stead at such moments. When he did not want to answer, he grunted and stared into the distance. But on this particular day, he suddenly said to Cameron: 'I've had about enough of this ... let's go.' And he got up.

One morning he found two newspaper men waiting on his landing at the Biltmore Hotel just as he was going downstairs to the coffee-room for breakfast.

'What are you thinking about at this moment? We'd like to know what a great scientist thinks about when he's going in to breakfast.'

Fleming looked at them with a somewhat solemn expression.

'It's curious you should ask me that. It so happens that I am thinking about something rather special.'

'What?' asked the two journalists in great excitement.

'Well, I was wondering whether I should have one egg or two.'

John Cameron, himself a Scot, was proud of his companion. He liked his quiet, dry humour and his kind heart (at Yale, hearing his hostess say that her maid, a Scots girl, was feeling homesick, he said to Cameron: 'Why shouldn't we go and cheer her up a bit?' and they did), and his utter lack of self-seeking.

The great American chemical firms, during his stay in the country, collected a hundred thousand dollars which they gave him as a token of their gratitude. Fleming said that he could not possibly accept it, but that it would make him very happy if that enormous sum might be presented to their laboratories at St Mary's, to be used for scientific research. This was done, and an Alexander Fleming Fund set up, capital and interest being put at the disposal of the research-workers.

The high-spot of his American trip was Commencement-Day at Harvard, on which occasion he was given the high honour of a Doctor's degree. He had a close bond with this university, which was very dear to him: the memory of Boulogne where in 1916 and 1917 he had a group of Harvard men working with him: Dr Roger Lee, Dr Harvey Cushing, and several others. Six thousand people had gathered in the court where the ceremony was held. When Dr Conant, the then President of Harvard, said: 'It is a great honour for me to present Sir Alexander Fleming, the discoverer of penicillin,' the whole audience rose as one man and the ovation lasted for three minutes during which time Fleming stood quietly before the microphone, his head slightly bent, stealthily smiling at Cameron. When at last it was possible for him to make himself heard, he said in his quiet voice:

'I had proposed to tell you a story in which Destiny plays a large part. It is perfectly wonderful what a part chance or fate or fortune or destiny — whatever you like to call it — plays in our lives. Decisions which we make for no particular reason, or for totally inadequate reasons, or decisions which others make, may have a profound influence on our own career. Perhaps we are merely pawns moved about on the board of life, thinking foolishly that we are deciding our own fate ... Let me take my own career. I was born and brought up on a Scottish farm ...'

He went on to explain that he might well have been a farmer, had not others — his mother and his brothers — sent him to London: that he might have remained a simple clerk had not a small inheritance enabled him to study medicine: that he would never have chosen St Mary's had he not been a good swimmer: that St Mary's would have turned him out as a simple general practitioner like many others but for the fact that Almroth Wright had asked him to work in his laboratory. 'Almroth Wright,' he added, 'one of the great men of this world, whose work as a pioneer has never been sufficiently recognized ...' Then followed the story, first of lysozyme, then of penicillin. He paid homage to Raistrick, 'a great chemist', to Florey, to Chain and to their collaborators in Oxford, who had made penicillin possible.

'I have been trying to point out that in our lives chance or fortune may have an astonishing influence, and, if I might offer advice to the young laboratory worker, it would be this — never to neglect an extraordinary appearance or happening. It may be — usually is, in fact — a false alarm which leads to nothing, but it may on the other hand be the clue provided by fate to lead you to some important advance. But I warn you of the danger of first sitting and waiting till chance offers something. We must work, and work hard. We must know our subject. We must master all the technicalities of our craft. Pasteur's often quoted dictum that Fortune favours the prepared mind is undoubtedly true, for the unprepared mind cannot see the outstretched hand of opportunity.

'There is, then, nothing new in my advice to the young. Work hard, work well, do not clutter up the mind too much with precedents, and be prepared to accept such good fortune as the gods offer ...'

When he had finished, he was loudly cheered. An old Harvard man, then President of Smith College, hurried up to Roger Lee and said: 'Roger, Fleming's from Ayrshire: I'm an Ayrshire man: introduce me.'

Roger Lee did as he was asked.

Professor Neilson said: 'I'm from Ayrshire, you're from Ayrshire.'

'Aye,' said Fleming.

They shook hands, and that was all. The Scots are a laconic race, even when they have crossed the ocean.

What useful knowledge had he acquired in the course of this journey?

(*a*) That scientific research in the United States was advancing more rapidly than in Europe, because of the status it enjoyed and of the resources at its disposal. 'The cost of laboratories', he said in his report, 'is insignificant when compared with the results for both industry and medicine.'

(*b*) That an American, Captain Romansky, had perfected a form of delayed-action penicillin (a mixture of salt, calcium and penicillin with beeswax and peanut oil). This was of great value, since it made possible the presence of a constant quantity of penicillin in the patient's body without the necessity of injecting every three hours.

(*c*) That an extended series of researches was paving the way to the discovery of new antibiotics. One of these, streptomycin, would quite certainly prove effective.

John Cameron, who had not left his side during these two months, has written: 'I was completely under the spell of his charm, and our friendship has become for me one of the things that make life worth living ... I have learned to know Alec really well, and to respect him.'

CHAPTER FIFTEEN

THE NOBEL PRIZE

If it be true to say that a great life is a dream of youth realized later, then
Fleming will be known to history as the happy man who realized his dream.

DR GRATIA

In September 1945 Fleming went to France as the guest of the
French Government. It was his first European visit since the
war had ended. French doctors and research-workers were all
agog to meet him. Penicillin had reached France during the war
by way of Spain and Holland. When a French scientist went to
Madrid in 1942, a Spanish colleague gave him a copy of the
British Medical Journal containing an article on the extraordinary
cures it had worked, and a culture. Another culture had come
through Holland. With these the Army had done its best, but the
output was too weak to make production on a large scale possible.
In 1944, after the liberation, the English had provided better
strains, and under the direction of three officers of the French
Medical Service — Major Broch, Captain Koch and Captain
Netchk — the Military Research Centre had started work.

The intention had been to give him an impressive welcome.
He flew from London on September 3rd, and landed at Le Bourget
at fifteen minutes after noon. Professors Pasteur Vallery-Radot
and Jacques Trefouël (Director of the Pasteur Institute), as well as
representatives of the Ministry of Public Health and of the Army,
were waiting for him on the airfield.

When he left the aeroplane he saw about fifty journalists armed
with cameras, and as was his custom, kept well behind the other
passengers. Suddenly, one of the reporters approached him and
asked a question. All he could understand was his name and
nodded his head, thinking he was being asked whether he was he.
At once, the photographers rushed forward and 'shot' a gentle-
man with an impressive beard who, wrote Fleming, 'looked a great
deal more like a scientist than I did'. When the officials had
identified the illustrious traveller the journalists were surprised

and indignant, for the question which he had answered with an uncomprehending nod had been: 'Is that man with the beard really Fleming?' Having recovered from their astonishment, however, they photographed the genuine Fleming and had a good laugh over the incident.

Fleming's diary, September 3rd: Left 10.30. Crossed French coast 11.30. Arrived 12.15. Enormous reception. Had to broadcast. Driven to Ritz. Lunch. Sacré-Cœur. Panthéon. Notre Dame ... made up speech.

Tuesday, September 4th: Finished speech. Breakfast (no coupons so no butter) ... Gobelins. Saw methods of weaving tapestry and carpets ... Presented with small piece of tapestry. Lunch with Kaminker (interpreter). Reception at Académie de Médecine. (All stood up.) President and Oldest Member made speeches. Then champagne and cakes (like wedding). When came away cheering crowd.

At the Academy of Medicine, he said that it gave him great pleasure to think that he was going to belong to that august body. 'I have been accused of having invented penicillin. No man could *invent* penicillin, for it has been produced from time immemorial by a certain mould. No, I did not invent the substance penicillin, but I drew people's attention to it, and gave it its name.'

Diary, Wednesday, September 5th: In France only 10,000 Roux bottles a day making penicillin. Great chance for England to organize at small cost a larger bottle plant or to help with advice. Send Raistrick and someone from Boots, Glaxo (who can talk French and who is quite familiar with actual bottle production) ... Interesting planting device, but growth does not cover surface quickly ... Presented with 100,000 units.

Was to have seen de Gaulle at 11.30 but postponed till 4.30. Went to Louvre ... received by Director who showed me round. Pictures, Sculptures, long gallery, etc.

1.30. Lunch at Foreign Office. Sat on right of Foreign Minister ... Very good lunch. Melon, Sole, Chicken, Salad, Cheese, Sweet and Coffee — Chablis, Claret, Champagne,

Brandy. Speeches. Foreign Minister, Minister of Health, Pres. of Academy of Med. Then I had to reply. 1066 — hundreds of years of war-history. My life-time peace and Allies in 2 wars. Scars. Penicillin. Thanks.

4.30. Went to gen. de Gaulle at 14 Rue St Dominique. Trefouël, Vallery-Radot and about 12 others in antechamber. Introduced immediately. Conversation 10 min. Then others introduced and de Gaulle presented me with Commander of the L. of H. (Hung round neck and kissed both cheeks.) Said thank you and retired. *5 p.m.* Went to Centre de la Pénicilline de l'armée (near Invalides). On the way Kaminker went to shop in Palais Royal and bought Commander of L. of H. button ...

8.15. Dinner with Duhamel at Café at end of Boulevard St Michel. About 40 people, doctors, literary, political, head of trade-unions. Good dinner ... Then had to reply (all translated by interpreter wonderfully). Got home early midnight.

At this dinner, at which Georges Duhamel presided, many doctors were present, as well as Julien Benda, Paul Éluard, Claude Morgan, Albert Bayet, Le Corbusier. Duhamel relates that when in the course of his speech he said to Fleming: 'You, sir, have gone a step farther than Pasteur,' the British scientist exclaimed: 'But for Pasteur I should be nothing!'

Diary, September 6th: 10, Reception Pasteur Institute ... *12.15* lunch Vallery-Radot opposite Duff-Cooper, Billoux and about 40 (sat next Mme Trefouël). Speech by Vallery-Radot (English), Billoux and another. Replied (1) Eulogy of Pasteur. (2) Eulogy of Wright. (3) Penicillin. Rules for use. Production. Fastness. Thanks. Presented Pasteur Medal. *2.30.* Visited Pasteur Hospital. Dr Martin ... Has nice wife, speaks English ... Saw local treatment of carbuncle — very painful. Then to Garches. Ramon there but apparently only researching — not directing. Bearded man does micro-cinema only. Saw good one of phagocytosis. Tea at Golf-Club at St Cloud.

Friday, September 7th: 9 a.m. Hospital for Sick Children.

ve: Florey, Chain and Fleming at the presentation of the Nobel Prize by the King of Sweden

w: Fleming and Sir Almroth Wright

The little lab. at The Dhoon. Below is the photograph which Sir Alexander inscribed for Am Voureka

The Little Lab which you were fond of. and which liked you as the only one that kept it clean

Alexander Fleming

Met by Prof. Debré. He gives address and I reply. See
n° of pen. cases. Meningitis good. Pneumo one of 4 died.
Osteomyelitis good. If abscess opens and evacuates then sewn
up with needle left in, through which pen. given ... *11*.
Claude Bernard. Dr Laporte (Lemierre away). Lung abscesses treated by injection locally ... Endocarditis few ...
5.30. Reception Hôtel de Ville ... Pres. of Academy of Science
said going to be a member. Speeches and Reply.

Saturday, September 8th: ... Delay at aerodrome. Debré
there to meet me with inhalation apparatus and book on
painting ... Off at 2 p.m. Home.

It is interesting to know the impression made by this visit on a
French doctor, Professor Debré. 'What struck me in Fleming was
an extreme intellectual caution. It would not be exactly true to say
that he was modest. He was fully aware of his fame, and enjoyed
it. But, more than anything else, he feared going too far in his
conclusions. He limited the extent of phenomena to what he had
seen. When we showed him the results obtained in France, thanks
to penicillin, he paid more attention to the failures than to the
miracles. "Tell me some more," he said, "about that osteomyelitis which you didn't succeed in curing." He wanted to keep his
feet firmly planted on the ground.'

To Mrs Davis, who had been one of the friends of his youth and
was now living in France, he wrote: 'My week in Paris was indeed
extraordinary ... What a difference from the innocent youth you
helped to educate – and yet I do not believe there is any difference.
I now meet all sorts of high-ups, but it is not really more interesting than meeting ordinary people – they are just ordinary folk,
except that some of them are a bit conceited.'

The formal reception he had had in Paris was repeated, with
variations, in Italy, Denmark and Sweden. He became an itin-
erant ambassador of British science.

To Roger Lee: I am sorry that I can't get used to all this fuss,
but I suppose I have to put up with it. It is very nice to look
back on when it is all finished, but at the time I cannot get
rid of the scared rabbit feeling.

If he was scared, he managed to conceal the fact, and took this deluge of honours with tranquil dignity. It pleased him to think that he was passing, not unsuccessfully, the last and stiffest test of all — the test of fame. It seemed a far step from the Scottish farm and the little lab. to the academic and royal platforms which he must now ascend. But all this noise, a bit wearisome though it might be, he looked on as part of the day's work. He knew that he had given of his best, that all his life long he had laboured hard and conscientiously. It seemed to him but natural that the reward should have come at last, and he adapted himself to the new routine conscientiously, contentedly, resignedly.

Among the endless letters which piled in upon him at this time none gave him greater pleasure than that written by the mistress of his 'wee school'. It came from Durban, Natal, was signed Marion Stirling, and began with these words:

Dear little Alex,
    Please forgive me — but you were about 8 or 9 years of age at most when I knew you, a dear little boy with dreamy blue eyes … This little letter is just to congratulate my dear little friend of many moons ago and to tell him that I have been following his career and rejoicing in all his wonderful successes. I just have been reading the marvellous story of Penicillin — and almost feel proprietor. By the way, your wonderful injections cured a very delicate little grand-niece of mine — by name Hazel Stirling.
    Kindest regards to you and *just go on as you are doing*. I see that you were honoured by France — a really fine people I found them …

In Belgium (November 1945), he beat his own record: three honorary degrees in two days, at Brussels, Louvain and Liège. At Louvain he delivered a charming speech. The University had conferred, after the war, degrees on three British subjects — Churchill, Montgomery and Fleming. 'I did hope that we could all three come together. Then I should have been able to listen to a politician and a general, both orators, both leaders of men, both the idols of their country — and deservedly so — give addresses, and you would have expected little of me, a simple laboratory worker who sits at a bench in a white coat playing with test-tubes and microbes.

'But it was not to be. Winston Churchill has come and gone. Montgomery has yet to come and I am here alone ... My occupation is a simple one. I play with microbes. There are, of course, many rules in this play, and a certain amount of knowledge is required before you can fully enjoy the game, but, when you have acquired knowledge and experience, it is very pleasant to break the rules and to be able to find something that nobody had thought of ...'

To John Cameron [his guide in the United States]: I had better tell you about my adventures ... At the end of November I went to Belgium — apparently as a guest of the Belgian Government for the [*sic*] paid my fare and put me up. The evening I arrived I dined with our ambassador. The next day I lunched with the Prince Regent and then went on to the University to receive an Honorary M.D. This was a solo performance. There was a crowded auditorium. Then a solitary chair in front where Queen Elisabeth sat. Then, on one side there was a throne with two seats where the ambassador and myself had to sit. You can imagine me in that predicament.

On October 25th a telegram from Stockholm announced that the Nobel Prize for Medicine had been awarded to him, together with Chain and Florey. The Nobel Scientific Committee had at first suggested that one half should go to Fleming, the remaining half to be divided between Sir Howard Florey and Chain. But the General Committee decided that a division into three equal parts would be fairer.

On December 6th he flew to Stockholm.

To John Cameron. Isle of Arran: Arrived 10.30 p.m. ... Bed. Off at 8 a.m. to Upsala, and back after dark ... Then official engagements with a small break for shopping. (You could buy as many Parker 51s as you like in Stockholm and Nylon stockings.) Then we had dinner with the British Ambassador (I am getting used to that now). Next day the prizegiving. Full evening dress with decorations. (I had great difficulty in tying the Legion of Honour round my neck but it got there and it was the only one.) This was at 4.30 p.m. Then with fanfares of trumpets we were ushered on to a platform and sitting before us were the whole of the Royal Family and thousands of audience. Then trumpets, orchestra, singing, speeches and receiving our awards from the King. After the reward a banquet of about 700 where I sat beside the Crown Princess. We all had to say a few words (I talked about Fortune), then after the banquet we adjourned to a students' sing-song and dance. Home at 3 a.m. ... Next day the official lecture and then dinner with the King in the Palace. Early to bed it should have been, but when we got back to our hotel we adjourned to the bar and drank Swedish beer for a long time. Among us there was an Argentine woman poet who got a Nobel Prize but could not stand up to the drink.

Another honour which delighted him was being given the Freedom of Darvel, the small Scottish town where he had been at school. Nothing is more pleasant or more rare than to be acclaimed as a prophet in one's own country. Fleming had travelled by rail from London to Glasgow with his wife, his son Robert, his brother Bob, and his sister-in-law. He had invented a new card-game to while away the time. Flags were out in the streets of Darvel. The Provost and the Councillors were waiting at the town gate, with reporters and camera-men. 'Prayers. Speeches. Numerous autographs. A great number of people said they had been at school with me ...' He could not resist the temptation to have a sly dig at his fellow citizens, and said that the mayor of Darvel would never have heard of him if he had not happened to go to Cairo. 'Your Provost had visited Cairo and he had found there that I had achieved a certain amount of notoriety, so when he came back he proposed to the Burgh Council that they send me a letter of congratulation. This gave me very great pleasure, and it was the first time I knew that I had been noticed since I left Darvel ...'

All the enthusiasm with which he had been greeted in the course of his far-flung travels, all this universal glory, though it had failed to change his character, had made his manner not so much more affable (he had always been naturally polite), as less brusque.

The necessity of speaking often in public had given him a greater ease of manner. His friend Sir Zachary Cope, after hearing him deliver a short but witty speech, said to him on the way out: 'That was quite a brilliant effort.' 'Yes,' replied Fleming, 'I know it was.'

He spoke very well, too, on the day when Lord Webb-Johnson, President of the Royal College of Surgeons, presented him with the College's Gold Medal, a high and rare distinction which had been conferred only twenty times in one hundred and forty-four years. The ceremony took place at a dinner attended by members of the Royal Family, the Prime Minister and the Lord Chancellor. When the speeches were over, his old colleague, Dr Breen, offered him his congratulations. 'To my surprise,' writes Breen, 'he brushed them aside: "Come on, for heaven's sake! Let's go and have a game of snooker."

' "What? Have they got a table here?" I asked.

' "No, no," said Fleming, "I meant let's go to the Club."

'There was only one club, so far as he was concerned, the Chelsea Arts, and, accordingly, we set off in our cars to Old Church Street. This was shortly after the war, when formality in evening wear had not generally returned. The irruption of Fleming in full rig, with the ribbon of the Legion of Honour round his neck, and a multitude of decorations flapping from his coat, into the club had the effect of a bombshell. That, however, did not prevent us from having our game, and it was the small hours of the morning before we left.'

He was still devoted to this club, with its great room painted in light green, the two billiard-tables, the bar, and the free and easy manners of the painters and sculptors. He went there every evening about six, looked happily round the familiar scene, and played snooker, as he played all games, inventing all sorts of extraordinary strokes. Sometimes, to oblige one of the painters, he agreed to 'sit', but never said a word in praise of the portrait. To have done so would have run counter to the unwritten code of all 'Lowlanders'. The club members had been staggered when their silent fellow-member had become a great man. When honours came to him, several of them offered their congratulations.

'Oh, that's nothing,' he said, and changed the subject.

At St Mary's, where for some years the question of Wright's successor had been a live issue, Fleming's Nobel Prize settled the question once and for all. In 1946 Wright retired and Fleming, unopposed, became Principal of the Institute (this title had superseded that of Director). But during one of his absences, Wright took the opportunity to announce the various heads of the services, as chosen by him, with the result that Fleming never had *his* team, and found himself in an awkward position. He felt this deeply, but did not complain. All he said was: 'That's the way the world is made.'

He had always loved the communal life of a laboratory. Collective work had made it possible for him at any moment to draw one of his neighbours' attention to the odd appearance of some culture or other, and say: 'Have a look at this: I'll tell you the line your research ought to take.' Only with great difficulty was he persuaded that, as head man, he must, from now on, live in a room apart where he could conduct important and confidential conversations. 'Now that you're the Principal, Sir Alexander,' Craxton told him, 'you must have a lab. to yourself.' He gave in, but stubbornly set his face against the room ever being allowed to look like an office. 'No!' he said. 'It shall be a laboratory, and nothing but a laboratory.'

For all who were actively engaged in research, he was an admirable chief. No matter what the work he was doing, a colleague had only to knock at his door, which always stood wide open, for him to say at once: 'Yes, come along in!' — and to give his full attention to the tale of difficulties or discovery. One of his most precious qualities was this ability to detach his mind in a split second from what had been occupying it, and to go straight to the heart of the new problem submitted to him. In three words or so he would sort out the tangle and indicate the line to be taken, after which he would return to his microscope. A few minutes later there would be another knock at the door and another young man would immediately receive the same attention. Sometimes he would follow it up with: 'Now you've told me about *your* headache, tell me, what d'you think of this?' and he would point to something that had aroused his interest. He never made his colleagues, whether seniors or juniors, feel that they were working under him: they were doing a job with him, guided by his experience. Dr Ogilvie relates how one day Sir Alexander took him into his brother Robert's factory to vaccinate two hundred workmen who had been laid low with influenza. 'Though I was only a very young assistant,' says Ogilvie, 'he insisted on doing exactly half of the work himself, sterilizing his own syringes and giving the inoculations.'

He rarely praised a piece of work. His greatest compliment was something like: 'I suppose it's not bad.' His approval more often took the form of help and support. He would lend a colleague a hand in writing up a paper, or would arrange that at a meeting of the Pathological Society — or some other learned body — some piece of apparatus invented by one of his young men should be demonstrated. When he thought an idea good, he became its champion, prepared to fight for it through thick and thin. If he thought it bad, he demolished it with one word: 'Rotten!' — and that was the last anyone heard of it.

Many found conversation with him more than difficult. His interlocutor would wait for an answer to his question, often only to get 'Hmm!' or a groan, or complete silence. 'There you stood with your mouth open, with the conversation suspended between heaven and earth, not knowing whether you ought to say something more or make yourself scarce. At other times he could be charming, and always in the most unexpected fashion.' He was invariably more friendly in his dealings with simple folk than with the 'big-wigs'. To a young nurse, who had gone by mistake into his office and been terrified by suddenly finding herself face to face with the Great Chief, the showed the most exquisite kindness, went back with her into the corridor, chatting all the while, showed her the way to the laboratory she wanted, and left her in a state of adoration. These courtesies were never premeditated, but were wholly spontaneous.

He loved brevity and precision. 'I was always very enthusiastic over donations to our research funds', writes Craxton (the secretary of the Institute). 'I once reported the receipt of one particular gift, and showed him a copy of my proposed acknowledgment, which amounted to about 100 words. He glanced at it and with a quiet smile, remarked: "That's a nice effort, Craxton, but the gist of it is that we are very grateful for his thoughtful donation." "Yes," said I, feeling rather pleased. "Then why not keep it at that," he said, "and save yourself labour?" '

★

He had a very special admiration for neat-handed technicians. 'Bacteriologists nowadays,' he said, 'are becoming incapable of doing the simplest technical jobs for themselves.' All his life long he had done them better even than the experts and for this reason had gained their respect. He came down like a ton of bricks on any research-worker who was too full of his own importance to undertake an occasional bit of manual labour.

Much of the research-work done at the Institute was inspired or directed by him. He was extraordinarily generous in his attitude towards it and refused to put his name to papers which, but for him, would have lost the greater part of their value. On occasions when he did consent to add his signature, he said: 'Put my name last, then they'll have to mention all of you. If you put it first, they'll say, "Fleming and others," and I don't need that.' Having succeeded beyond all his expectations, he made a point of leaving the limelight to his colleagues.

Both as scientist and master he was admired by those who worked with him. As an administrator he came in for a certain amount of criticism. There were some who said that he had a horror of wrangling and always chose the line of least resistance. Craxton, however, who as secretary of the Institute knew what went on behind the scenes, did not share this view. 'I remember one occasion when, to satisfy the majority, he took a decision which was contrary to his own personal feelings. This worried him very considerably, and he was an unhappy man for weeks. He was not himself again until, at last, he decided to act according to the dictates of his own conscience, and reversed the original decision.'

Says Dr Brooks: 'If he held views different from your own, he could be a formidable opponent. He never budged once he felt quite sure that his course of action was the right one.' When he was up against too strong an opposition, he reserved judgment. 'If you leave a problem alone for long enough,' he said, 'it will solve itself.'

He was never in a hurry. He kept a tight rein on his impulsiveness and refused to let himself be influenced by the impulsiveness of others. He was careful not to become involved in the quarrels and meannesses which inevitably arise when a lot of men are working together. 'You know', says his secretary, Helen Buckley, 'how jealous and quarrelsome men of the same profession can be when they are all herded under the same roof. But I never saw the faintest trace of jealousy in Professor Fleming. It prowled all round the place, but never had the slightest effect on him. He was by nature noble and by temperament bigger and better than the greater part of mankind. Mediocrity in all its forms, all pettiness and all the small dishonesties of thought and conduct, had no place in him.'

She gives us a glimpse of how he dealt with administrative matters. 'Someone with a grievance would come in and sit down beside him. With a cigarette in one corner of his mouth, he would grunt out: "Go on." The visitor would say what he had to say. The Professor would listen with the greatest attention, all the while going on with his own work. Then somebody else would sit down on his other side, and put *his* case. He could do two or three things at the same time, and do them well. When the two men had had their say, he would sit for a while turning over in his mind what he had heard, and then give a reasoned reply to each.'

'He was a man', writes Dr Bob May, 'with whom one could discuss personal problems without the slightest hesitation. One knew that he would listen sympathetically, and do his level best to help.' He once insisted that a scientist who had recently been suffering from nervous depression should be put on a certain committee. 'It'll do a lot to get him on his feet again. He will see that people still have confidence in him.' But he concealed this kind of helpfulness as though it were something to be ashamed of, and from sheer shyness made more than ever a show of being dour, reticent and abrupt.

One reason why he was so little known by those who did not work with him was the queer pleasure he took in deliberately allowing a distorted picture of himself to be put forward. His 'legend' amused him. Every piece of baseless information about him published in the newspapers was as carefully pasted up and filed as though it were strictly true. His secretary and Dr Hughes kept up to date, at his orders, a whole dossier entitled 'The Fleming Myth'. He repeated these various imaginary stories more frequently than anybody else, and saw to it that they did not go out of circulation.

At the Institute he never ceased to insist on the fruitfulness of free research. 'The research-worker must be at liberty to follow wherever a new discovery may lead him ... Every research-worker should have a certain amount of time to himself, so as to be able to work out his own ideas without having to give an account of them (unless he wants to) to anybody. Momentous things may happen in a man's free time.' He had an ironical little story, which he loved telling, about a small firm of chemical manufacturers the directors of which had taken the momentous step of adding a genuine research-worker to the staff. A laboratory was arranged for him, divided by a glass partition from the board-room. For a whole morning the directors watched, with the utmost curiosity, the white-coated newcomer at work. Round about midday they could contain themselves no longer, but went into the laboratory and asked: 'Well, have you discovered anything?'

'This thirst for immediate results', said Fleming, 'is by no means uncommon, but it is extremely harmful. Really valuable research is a long-term affair. It may well be that nothing of practical utility will emerge from a laboratory for years on end. Then, all of a sudden, something will turn up — very different, perhaps, from what was being looked for — which will cover the costs of the laboratory for a hundred years.' He quoted the example of Pasteur: 'People said, why all this fuss about a little dissymmetry of crystals? — to which one might have answered, like Franklin, what does a new-born child amount to?'

He went back to France in November 1946 for the fiftieth anniversary of Pasteur's death. All the invited scientists were taken by special train to Dôle. 'In the train', writes Dr van Heyningen, 'we were joined by a company of young students who had been sent, they said, to act as guides and interpreters. They kneeled — literally kneeled — at Fleming's feet, and spoke of him as one of the greatest scientists of all time. Heavens! — I thought: how terribly embarrassing this must be for poor Flem! — an ordeal if ever there was one — let's see how he comes through it! ... Well, he came through it with flying colours, and the way in which he did so gives, I think, the measure of the man. He was not in the least pompous, but just his usual self, and spoke in the truculent manner which he sometimes assumed.' He described to the students the research-work on which he was then engaged and in which he was a great deal more interested than he was in his previous discoveries. He enjoyed their attitude of veneration, but without the least hint of pride. He collected decorations as a schoolboy collects stamps, delighted whenever an especially rare specimen came his way.

In the course of the press conference, he reminded his listeners how Pasteur, in 1876, had observed that a mould from one of his cultures destroyed the anthrax bacillus and had intuitively foreseen that a substance of the penicillin type might one day be used in the treatment of infectious diseases. 'I have been in France for a week,' he said, 'making a pilgrimage to all the places where the spirit of Louis Pasteur still reigns: Dôle, where he was born; Arbois, where he spent his youth; Paris, where he is buried. His body lies in the Pasteur Institute, but his spirit is everywhere throughout the world where serious work is being done in that field of microbiology in which he was one of the earliest pioneers.

'He laid the foundations, and laid them so well that they now, in the short space of the fifty years since he died, support a superstructure more vast and glorious than even the wonderful genius of Pasteur could have foreseen.'

And yet, while all the peoples of the earth were inviting him and showering honours on his head, he knew no truer pleasure than living with his family in his Suffolk garden. He had the love of family in the highest degree. 'He was never in better form than when they were all together, which happened often', says Mrs MacMillan. He adored his son, a doctor to be. His wife, now Lady Fleming, was the same simple person she had always been — faithful to her old friends and not in the least intoxicated by success. She knew him so well that his silences, surprising though they might sometimes be, no longer worried her. 'I remember', writes Professor Cruickshank, 'a story told about his return home after one of his triumphal progresses: how he entered the house, put down his suitcase on the floor, and said ... nothing at all! His wife announced dinner. He sat down and ate in silence. There was no conversation. No doubt he wanted to talk about his trip, but a curious feeling of reserve made it impossible for him to do so.'

Sareen was still running the two houses with almost no help, though they were usually overflowing with friends. Life at The Dhoon was never lacking in those picturesque and unforeseen incidents which were so dear to Fleming's heart. One Monday morning, when he was taking his guests to the station in his car after a week-end, he realized that they were late and that his friends had missed their train. 'It'll be all right!' he shouted and began a mad race with the locomotive to the next station on the line. His wretched passengers, flung from side to side, clinging to their seats, but fully entering into the fun, urged him forward: 'Go on, Flem! Go on!' The car pulled up with a shriek of tyres and a scream of brakes in the yard of the next station just as the train was running into it. All joined in a cry of 'Well done, Flem! Well done!' and made a dash for the nearest carriage.

These old friendships and these country pleasures were his only happiness. He wanted nothing else. When a friend said to him: 'It's a crying scandal that the nation has not recognized what penicillin has done for humanity by making you some tangible recognition, a hundred thousand pounds, for instance, as was done at the end of the war to the victorious generals,' he replied: 'What should I do with a hundred thousand pounds? I've got everything I want.'

Never was a man so little spoiled by success. 'I have often been struck', writes Dr Stewart, 'by the fact that Flem was the living incarnation of what, in our day, is a very rare thing — a thoroughbred human-being. There was nothing in him of the mongrel, nor of the artificial. Until the very end, in spite of so much travelling, in spite of so many solemn receptions, in spite of everything, he remained in every way the same young man who, long ago, came to London from his native Scotland.

'One day, I made the acquaintance of a French lady who was very knowledgeable in the breeding of dogs. When she heard that I was a Scot, she told me that she had a great friend who was a Scot, too — Alexander Fleming. She had met him several years earlier, and had liked him, as a man, long before she had known that he was an eminent scientist. My reply to this, stupid perhaps, but spontaneous, was: "That's because you are fond of thoroughbred dogs." She looked startled for a moment or two and then said: "Do you know, you are perfectly right." '

CHAPTER SIXTEEN

ENVOY EXTRAORDINARY

There is no such thing as a national science, as there is no such thing as a national multiplication-table. TCHEKHOV

IN 1946 the British Council offered, as it had done before the war, a number of bursaries to foreign research-workers. Among the candidates was a young Greek woman, Dr Amalia Cout-souris-Voureka. Her father, a physician who had studied in Paris and in Athens, was established in Constantinople up to the time of the outbreak of war in 1914. Then he had to flee to Athens leaving behind all his belongings, which were confiscated. His daughter, Amalia, when herself a medical student, married her brother's friend and colleague the architect Manoli Voureka. During the Second World War, husband and wife, both of them active members of the Greek Resistance, were imprisoned by the occupying power. By the time the war ended, their house, the architect's studio and his young wife's laboratory had been reduced to ruins. Amalia, cut off as she had been because of the war from all recent scientific developments, thought of trying to go to England for a period of study. She was free from family ties. Already for ten years she had to all intents and purposes been separated from her husband, though she still had a feeling of affection for him.

The bursaries of the British Council were not awarded by competitive examination. The candidates were asked to produce diplomas in science and to offer evidence of their studies and their war-time record. Those whose names found their way into the final list had an interview with the Director (then Steven Runciman, the historian). A clear and simple answer to the question 'Why do you wish to take up scientific research?' resulted in the young Greek woman being given an excellent report. Since, furthermore, her teachers recommended her strongly, she found herself at the top of all the candidates. After completing her medical studies, she had specialized in bacteriology.

Until Greece was liberated, nothing had been known in that country about penicillin. A number of extravagant rumours were current and that was all. It was said that the English were making use of a small jelly-fish which had marvellous therapeutic powers. The story went round that sick persons were made to swallow it, and that, before being digested, it produced a substance which had the effect of curing septicaemias. After the war, this new myth had been replaced by information of a more serious nature. Alivisatos, Amalia's Greek professor, who had himself discovered a phenomenon of antibiosis, was well acquainted with, and a great admirer of, Fleming's work. He advised the young woman to apply for a position in the department presided over by the Scottish scientist. Fleming was approached and agreed to take her on for a period of six months. On the strength of this, Amalia Voureka left for London.

She appeared for the first time at St Mary's on October 1st, 1946, and was received by Fleming in a tiny office. He asked her what subject she wanted to work at. 'The viruses,' she said. He replied that he had no vacancy in the virus section. Would she be interested in allergy? His voice was low, his accent Scottish, and the words came through closed lips from one corner of which a cigarette depended. The young Greek woman, who did not know English very well, failed to understand the word 'allergy' (as pronounced by him without its 'r').

He noticed her embarrassment, and took it to mean that she did not want to study allergy. His face lit up with a kindly smile and, in the tone of a man asking a favour, he inquired whether she would like to work with him. She at once said 'Yes,' partly to put an end to this terrifying interview, but also because she had been struck by the radiant smile and the sudden gleam in his eyes. It seemed to her as though a mask which at first had appeared to be impenetrable had, all of a sudden, been dropped, revealing an infinite kindliness. Why the mask? she wondered. Was it due to reserve, modesty, prudence or shrewdness?

She realized that, seeing her a little put out, he had wanted to help, and was the more grateful because she felt terribly alone in a country which was so different from her own. When she had come into the room, she had seen a man of small stature with a cold, austere expression. But there had been a surprising change.

She saw him now as somebody not at all like that — as a person whose extraordinary eyes seemed to radiate vitality, intelligence and humanity. Was he really, perhaps, two men — the genuine and the pretended? At this, their very first meeting, she found fascination in that double personality.

As soon as she had begun to work with him, Fleming introduced her to Sir Almroth Wright, who still came occasionally from the country to breathe again the laboratory air. Upon the young foreign student the impression he made was almost that of some prehistoric mammoth, as much by reason of his size as from the fact that she remembered having seen his name in scientific text-books quoted side by side with those of the giants of the past — Pasteur, Koch, Ehrlich. She was the first woman to be admitted to an organization which was still dominated by Wright's anti-feminism. It was not until after the Old Man's death that she was allowed to take her meals at the hospital or to be present at the famous library teas. Fleming entrusted one of the younger doctors with the duty of instructing the 'new girl' in the special technical processes used in the laboratory. These were delicate and demanded, as we know, a high degree of dexterity. It was a matter of pride with Fleming to show that he was 'handier' than anybody else. She came to the conclusion, not without reason, that there was a good deal of the small boy in him.

He frequently called her into the technicians' room, and showed her how to make micro-pipettes over a Bunsen burner. She found this difficult, and he laughed delightedly at her failures.

It was not long before he suggested that Dr Voureka, Robert May and he should embark upon a piece of joint research. He stated the subject (a titration of streptomycin), laid down the programme of experiments, and himself drew up the report on results, insisting, as he almost always did, that his name should come last on the list: 'That'll do you a lot of good, and me no harm.' This attitude, combined with his simple manners, his kindness, his refusal to take himself seriously, the extraordinary quality of his intelligence, and his silences, soon made him a hero in the eyes of the Greek student.

It was marvellous to have a master the door of whose room stood always open, whom she could see without any difficulty whenever she wanted to, no matter what time of day it was. He would swing round in his desk-chair and look at one with an expression of lively interest and eager expectation. If one asked whether one was being a nuisance, 'No, no,' he would say, 'I've nothing to do.' Then one would tell him about some problem on which one had been chewing in vain for days, and back would come the answer, without a moment's hesitation, to throw immediate light upon the subject. 'He could always be relied upon', says Dr Ogilvie, 'to suggest some aspect which had never occurred to you, and an entirely new series of experiments' — very often on matters which were far removed from his habitual preoccupations.

One day Amalia Voureka heard him discussing with a colleague the respective merits of Koch and Pasteur. The colleague preferred Koch.

'Pasteur,' he said, 'did not carry out a sufficient number of adequately controlled experiments.'

'Pasteur,' replied Fleming, 'was a genius. He could observe things and, what's more, could measure their value and see their implications. Any one of Pasteur's experiments was so decisive that it was worth a hundred of anybody else's. The proof of that is that he could always repeat it successfully.'

'He, too, I thought,' writes Amalia, 'possesses, like Pasteur, and in the highest degree, the art of choosing the crucial experiment and of grasping the capital importance of a chance observation. The glint in his eyes when he said that showed me that he knew very well how close, in this respect, he was to Pasteur. But I reflected, also, that the two men were wholly different in their attitude to themselves. Pasteur, conscious of his genius, was wholly absorbed in his research. To interrupt him when he was working was looked upon as a crime. For Fleming there was a wide world lying beyond the confines of his laboratory. The appearance of a new flower in his garden was as interesting to him as the work he might be engaged on. Everything was important, but nothing *too* important. There was the same wonder in his eyes as there must have been when, as a child, he had looked at the vast stretches of the moors, the beauty of the hills, the valleys and the rivers round Lochfield. In those days he had felt himself to be an infinitesimal part of nature, and from that feeling was born his refusal to indulge in self-importance and his dislike of big words. It was almost possible to say that he was a genius in spite of himself, and reluctantly.'

He was for ever starting off on one of those enormous journeys in the course of which he collected degrees, medals and decorations. When he got back he would tell Bob May and Amalia Voureka, with a twinkle in his eyes, about the comic incidents of the tour. The affection and eager attention with which they listened had the effect of melting his shyness. When he arrived each morning in the laboratory, Amalia loved to hear the sound of his young and lively footstep in the passage. His presence gave her a sense of serenity, security and happiness.

Sir Almroth Wright died, after a short illness, on April 30th, 1947. His going was the source of profound grief to Fleming. Never had there been men so different. 'Fleming', says Dr Philip H. Willcox, 'was an easy man to get on with, and to me he always seemed to be unruffled and utterly lacking in fussiness or strained nerves. He was calm, easy-going, docile, never detached from the world around him or over-engrossed in his work. In this respect he was more "worldly" than Sir Almroth Wright, who gave one the feeling that he was a man with a gigantic brain, concentrated on the world of bacteria, and caring little for sport or gaiety.' That is true. Wright was at once an ascetic and an aesthete, an austere, self-torturing philosopher who despised luxury in any form, and found his only real pleasure in talking with his intellectual equals about music, science and poetry. Colebrook in an obituary notice recalled that, to his disciples, Wright had been not only a scientist, but a friend and a great man.

'We remember his quiet entry into the laboratory for the day's work, and his greeting: "Well, friend, what have you won from Mother Science today?" We remember the simple austerity of his way of life; his great kindliness and generosity shown to many, known only to a few; we see him wandering round his garden at the week-end, hoe in hand; the characteristic twinkle in his eye as he told us of some new discovery about the short-comings of the female intellect, or of some new word he had coined; we remember, too, his wonderful gift for conversation, and the great store of poetry which enriched his mind throughout a long life.'[1]

For Fleming, Wright's death marked the end of an epoch. His master had sometimes caused him pain, but he remembered only

[1] *Obituary Notices of F.R.S.*, vol. VI, p. 309, November 1948.

the immense debt he owed him. He loved to display to newcomers certain technical processes, explaining that they had been invented by Wright, with whose memory they would always be closely linked. No doubt, realizing that he was now in isolated splendour at the summit of the Institute, he felt much as a son may feel when, his father having died, it is suddenly borne in on him that he is the head of a family and standing at the water-shed of the generations.

When the moment came for Dr Voureka's bursary to be renewed, the British Council sent Fleming a long questionnaire which greatly amused him. He enjoyed teasing the young woman and kept on coming into the laboratory to ask her: 'How ought I to answer this? *Are* you good at that? I wonder.' True to form he said these things with a perfectly serious face. It was impossible to know whether he was joking or not. But he sent in a eulogistic report and the bursary was duly renewed.

It was at about this time that he received a letter from an American (Alsatian by birth), who with remarkable generosity acted as a patron of scientific research not only in his own country, but in England and France as well. The name of this excellent man was Ben May. He had started life working for three dollars a week, but later had founded a timber business in Alabama which had made him a fortune. He devoted a very large part of his profits to helping medical research-workers in America and Europe. In November 1947 he wrote to Fleming as follows:

'You do not know me, but I am one of the many who feels himself indebted to you, and I should like to show my appreciation in something more than words ...

'If you ever have a few minutes to spare, you might tell me if you think there are many *good* research-workers in England who are hampered by lack of funds. Likewise, in France ... For instance, I am not even sure that the Pasteur Institute in Paris has all the money it needs ... Tell me, please, if you have a phase-contrast microscope. Please do not hesitate about telling me what you want. In doing so, you will be helping me ... I have not found any way of taking my money with me, nor do I feel at all certain that I shall be able to use it on the other side of the Styx. I shall get more fun out of it if I can employ it in the service of things that are worth while ...' He concluded by offering a scholarship for research, the choice of recipient, of course, to be left to Fleming.

Fleming replied that a phase-contrast microscope would be of the greatest use to him, and then, without asking Dr Voureka for her views and without even telling her what he was doing, put her name forward for the scholarship. Only when everything was settled did he let her know, advising her to refuse the British Council grant in favour of Ben May's offer, which would last for a longer time.

She was now being frequently invited to the Flemings' house in Chelsea. This quarter of London, so rich in literary associations, as well as the charming house, delighted her. She loved its beautiful furniture, the rare china, old glass, and odds and ends collected with taste, which were displayed in cabinets. Above all, she found never-ending amusement in the improvisations contrived by Fleming, who equipped his home, as he did his laboratory, with anything that came to hand. If, for example, he wanted an electric lamp on his desk, he attached it to the ceiling-light in the bedroom with a long flex which hung down to the floor and was then, without any attempt at concealment, led under the door to where he planned to use it. People were always tripping over it. An interior-decorator would have thought it hideous, intolerable and a scandal. But Fleming was inordinately proud of it, and Amalia found the arrangement quite irresistible because no one but he in all the world would have thought out, or put up with, so primitive a contrivance.

She sometimes acted as interpreter between the Flemings and their numerous foreign visitors. That anyone should have a fluent command of three languages seemed to Alec nothing less than a miracle. One evening, when she was translating the remarks of a Greek from Spain, the latter asked whether he might have a signed photograph of Fleming to take home with him. She took this opportunity to ask for one for herself. Fleming pretended not to have heard. His wife intervened: 'Give her one of your photos, Alec.' He said nothing. Sareen leaned across to Amalia and, with great sweetness, said that her husband had often spoken about her. He looked embarrassed, but she insisted: 'Tell her what you have told me.' He grunted, then abruptly took a photograph, signed it and gave it to Amalia. This portrait she kept beside her bed. Her friends used to pull her leg about him. 'Is that that great Viking with the curly golden hair?' But the jokes glanced off her: she had as much affection as admiration for her master.

Meanwhile, invitations kept on coming from all over the world. In 1948 he returned to Paris to be made a member of the Académie Septentrionale, of which Georges Huisman was President.

Fleming's diary, Friday, April 23rd, 1948: No troubles, customs or other, at Le Bourget. Met by Monseigneur Detrez and wife of President of Acad. Sept. By car to *Lutetia* ... Went for walk along the river ... A lot of nice things in the shops, especially antiques, but prices very high ... Taxi to Restaurant Louis XIV in Place des Victoires. Driver could not find restaurant which is a small one on a corner ... Went upstairs and found about 15 of the Academy folk: churchmen, literary lights, but no doctors. Excellent dinner ... Had to make short speech ... Managed to put a dramatist in his place: he had read one of my speeches and pretended he knew all about me. I told him he was flattering himself, because even my wife, after 30 years, hadn't managed to do that.

Saturday, April 24th: Walked for an hour in Luxembourg Gardens. Very gay. Wall-flowers, alyssum and pansies. Chestnuts in full bloom. Taken to Études Carmélitaines, Rue Scheffer. Academicians and Carmelites. Paul Claudel — old and deaf. Admiral d'Argenlieu, head of French Navy in England, and now a monk. Sat between Huisman (President) and the admiral, who spoke English. Enormous lunch. Began 1.15, ended 5 o'clock. Speeches galore. Many nice things about me, but did not understand most of them ...

During his stay in Paris he sat for a sculptor, Baron, who was to do a medal of him for the French Mint. Some days later he received a letter from Baron enclosing some photographs of the medal.

Showed to (1) Hughes: remark — tough.
           (2) MacMillan: remark — prize-fighter.
           (3) Mme Voureka: remark — wild.
           (4) Jennings: remark — very good.
           (5) S. M. F. [Sarah Marion Fleming]: remark — very good.

Also letter from Director of Mint asking permission to issue the medal. Replied 'yes'.

At the end of May 1948 Fleming and his wife set off for Madrid, as the result of a very warm invitation. Two great scientists, Bustinza (of Madrid) and Trias (of Barcelona), had arranged the tour, which took on the appearance of an apotheosis. Everywhere the deluge of honours which now formed part of his daily life descended upon him: university degrees, honorary membership of academies — in Barcelona no less than in Madrid, decorations and receptions. Never before had he aroused so much popular enthusiasm, nor so much gratitude from sick persons who had owed their lives to penicillin. They knelt before him, kissed his hands, gave him presents. If his wife Sareen had not been taken so ill in Madrid that she had to have a nurse, the memory of this trip would have been enchanting. Fleming's diary shows him, as always, interested in everything, and happy.

Barcelona: Thursday, May 27th, 1948: To the flower-market where we walked about 300 yards. Recognized. Much clapping. Stall-keepers gave us roses and carnations ... To Town Hall to see Corpus Christi procession. Mayor and Councillors in evening-dress. Balcony reserved for us, and, when we appeared, cheering and clapping — most embarrassing ... After procession more clapping and cheering all the way back to hotel. Impression that I was Winston or Princess Elizabeth. New experience. In our rooms enormous wreathes of flowers ... Consul-General says he is very pleased I came as it will do a great deal to help relations. It seems to me I am more an ambassador than a lecturer on medicine ... Vizconde de Guëll, art patron (looks like Edward VII).

May 29th: Interviewed by important newspaper. Had to answer questions like — 'Is Bogomoletz's serum any good?' ... 'Will there be another war?' ... 'Why is Spanish science backward?' ... If I were a more talkative person I should soon be in trouble. At 11, started for Montserrat ... Meal served by monks in silence, except for a voice chanting something in Latin the whole time. Prior introduced an old monk to me who had been cured by penicillin (of septicaemia) ... Sherry, coffee, benedictine. This benedictine made at the monastery: slightly different from the ordinary. Happened to have in my pocket a culture of penicillin mounted in a locket. Gave it to the Prior. He was delighted and put it among the monastery treasures (with a description which I had to write) ... For dinner to a small restaurant across the road. Proprietor refused any payment. I seem to be a hero in Spain.

May 30th: Bull-fight. Photographed with three toreadors. On taking my seat received another ovation from all round arena — 20,000 people (mass hysteria) ... Back to bed about 3 a.m.

The number of presents increased. A bootmaker, saved by penicillin, gave two pairs of shoes, one in crocodile for Fleming, the other in black and gold for Lady Fleming; a tailor, two suits; a Spanish woman, miraculously cured, a sable stole; a grateful optician, a pair of gold-rimmed spectacles. For a hunter of junk-shops it was a marvellous opportunity. But he had to give thousands of autographs, make a great many speeches (which an interpreter translated into Spanish), lecture at the hospital on the use of penicillin, and dine in the open air at La Rosalid, where Queen Marie-José of Italy had expressed the wish to meet him.

Seville: Reception by the Mayor. A swarm of beautiful young girls did some Andalusian dances very gracefully. Curious throaty chants of oriental type. Elected Honorary President of Medical Society of Seville. In evening-dress at 11.30 a.m. for Academy ceremony. Crowd. *God Save the King.* Presidential speech. Gold Medal. Then my lecture on the story of penicillin read in Spanish. Lasted three-quarters of an hour ... I went to sleep, or almost.

At Seville, he was given, among other things, a sombrero which was too small for him. A larger one had to be found.

Toledo: Greco. Goya ... By car to the Maranon house. View over Toledo. Magnificent house and charming family. Lunch outside. Very pleasant. Today's presents: a paper-knife (Toledo steel): a doll: an enormous cigar: some books, including Scott's Poems.

At last, after Cordoba and Xeres, back to Madrid. The capital had obviously set itself to go one better than Barcelona. Many flowers. Royal suite at the Ritz Hotel. Dinner at the golf club, with the Duke of Alba, 'who was charming, and claimed to have dined with me in Oxford — but he's wrong about that'.

He was decorated with the Grand Cross of Alphonso the Wise, and given a Doctor's degree by the University of Madrid, where he had to put on a blue hood and gown, the whole topped by a curious blue cap. A ring was placed on his finger, and he was given a pair of white gloves. He mounted the rostrum, preceded by the senior student, and delivered a speech which his friend Bustinza translated into Spanish. When, after his return, Dr Hughes asked him which of all his Doctor's degrees had pleased him most, he replied, without a moment's hesitation: 'Madrid ... they *gave* me my hood and gown.'

Taken all in all, it had been an Arabian Nights' journey, but very exhausting. Neither of them had had a moment's respite. His wife, already a sick woman when they started, had had to take to her bed in Madrid. They returned to England by air on June 14th, and in the course of the next few months Sareen's condition became increasingly serious. She could no longer go with her husband on the journeys he still had to make as a result of promises already given.

One very great pleasure for him at this time was the presentation of the Freedom of Chelsea. In his speech, he spoke of Whistler, Turner and his beloved Arts Club: 'It would be impossible to imagine Chelsea without its artists ... Art, using that word in its widest sense, is one of the genuinely important things. Prime Ministers and Chancellors of the Exchequer may be prominent figures for a while, but when they pass from the stage, they are, nearly all of them, forgotten. Only the artist is immortal.' Fleming was worried at that time about the future of Chelsea artists. He feared that in the post-war building schemes for Chelsea the need for studios would be neglected. He therefore took this opportunity of reminding Chelsea what it owed to the artists.

In 1949 he was made a member of the Pontifical Academy of Sciences and went to Rome, where he was received in audience by the Pope. Scarcely was he home again than he sailed in the *Queen Elizabeth* for the United States where he had promised to be present at the inauguration of the 'Oklahoma Foundation' for medical research. He had thought at first of refusing this invitation, pleading his increasing age and the distance of Oklahoma City, but on further consideration decided that it was his duty to go. He did not regret having done so, for he met 'his old penicillin friends', was dubbed *kiowa* by an Indian chief in full regalia, and made to the Foundation one of his best speeches:

> The research-worker is familiar with disappointment — the weary months spent in following the wrong road, the many failures. But even failures have their uses, for, properly analysed, they may lead him to success. For the man engaged in research there is no joy equal to that of discovery, no matter how unimportant it may be. That is what keeps him going ...

He spoke of the excessive material perfection sometimes to be found in scientific establishments. This was not the first time he had expressed his disdain of unnecessary adornments and marble palaces.

> If a worker who has been used to an ordinary laboratory is transplanted to a marble palace, one of two things will happen: either he will conquer the marble palace, or the marble palace will conquer him. If he wins, the palace becomes a workshop and takes on the appearance of an ordinary laboratory. If the palace wins, then he is lost.

> We have only to think of the marvellous work done by Pasteur as a young man, in a Paris attic which was so hot in summer that he could not stay in it. I, myself, witnessed what, in the early years of this century, was done by Almroth Wright and his team in two small rooms at St Mary's Hospital — work which drew to his tiny laboratory bacteriologists from New York and Colorado, from California, from Oregon, from Canada. My own laboratory has been described in an American paper as looking like 'the back-room of an old-fashioned drug-store' — but I would not have exchanged it for the largest and most luxurious of installations ... I have known research-workers reduced to impotence by apparatus so fine and elaborate that they spent all their time playing with a plethora of ingenious mechanical devices. The machine

conquered the man, instead of the man conquering the machine.

In other words, what the research-worker needs is equipment which is effective rather than splendid. 'But I should hate you to think', he added, 'that I decry good equipment. The different pieces of laboratory apparatus are, for the research-worker, the tools of his trade, and a good worker should have good tools.'

As an orator he had made great progress and now his speeches, simple and solidly constructed, were very effective. They sparkled with little flashes of the true Fleming humour. 'One sometimes finds', he said on one occasion, 'what one is not looking for. For instance, the technician who set out to find a way to synchronize the rate of fire of a machine-gun with the revolutions of an air-screw discovered an excellent way of imitating the lowing of a cow.' And again: 'During my forty-eight years at St Mary's Hospital, I had built up the useful reputation of being the world's worst after-dinner speaker, so I was never asked to talk. A year or two ago, the *Observer* made me the subject of a "Profile" in which they said that I was too fond of the truth to be a good after-dinner speaker. I commend this statement to some of the brilliant speakers here.'

There is a story current in Oklahoma to the effect that an old lady, who had contributed generously to the Foundation, asked him to what he attributed his success. He is said to have replied: 'I can only suppose that God wanted penicillin, and that that was His reason for creating Alexander Fleming.' When this story was told him, he made no comment, but, since he did not include it in the 'Fleming Myth' dossier, it is probably true.

On his way home he visited several laboratories and was introduced to aureomycin and chloromycetin. The family of antibiotics was growing.

When he reached London, he found his wife more seriously ill than when he had left. To his friends at the hospital he said sadly: 'She's not going to recover.' When Mrs MacMillan called for news, he opened the door to her. 'I shall never forget', she writes, 'the look on his face when he said, "And the most horrible thing about it is that penicillin can do nothing for her ... When John died it had not been perfected: now it has, but it is useless in Sareen's case." ' He showed the utmost devotion in nursing his wife. She died on October 29th, 1949. Her death was a terrible shock to him. To his old and dear friend, Dr Young, he said: 'My life is broken.' Sareen had been his companion for thirty-four years. She had been his support in difficult times, she had helped with all his projects in their country home, and she was his mainstay in success when, at long last, fame had come to him.

Immediately after the funeral he went to the hospital and, as usual, took his accustomed place at the head of the table when tea-time came. He did not speak of his grief, but looked twenty years older. His eyes were red. For several weeks he was just a pathetic old man with trembling hands. He worked longer hours than ever at the laboratory, and kept his door shut, an unusual thing with him.

He still went every evening to the Chelsea Arts Club and stayed there later than had been his custom. At home in the empty house he felt solitary and at a loss. His son was finishing his hospital training in London. Sareen's twin sister Elizabeth, John Fleming's widow, had a flat on the upper floor. The two women had been much alike in appearance, but very different in temperament. Sareen, before her illness, was gay, exuberant and full of life. Elizabeth, since the death of her husband, had become melancholic. After the loss of her twin sister, she had long spells of depression. The loyal Fleming asked her to take her meals with him. For some time, he often had the company of his son Robert, who lived at home, and of a young cousin, Harold Montgomery, also a student at St Mary's. But later Robert left home to live in the hospital where he worked and, in 1951, went with the Army overseas. Then Sir Alexander became very lonely. At week-ends, he visited Radlett where his brother Robert and his sister-in-law welcomed him. Yet he spent many evenings in the company of an old and ailing woman. Fortunately for him, there was Alice Marshall, young, intelligent and devoted, who had kept house for him since Sareen's illness. She did everything in her power to lighten the atmosphere and to make life for him at home as smooth and as tolerable as possible.

Work was his only refuge. For some time now he had been studying, with Dr Voureka, Dr Hughes and Dr Kramer, the action of penicillin on a certain microbe, *proteus vulgaris*. This *proteus*, when cultivated in a medium containing a small quantity of penicillin, went through the most curious changes and assumed fantastic forms. It is equipped with *flagella* or wing-like filaments which seem to enable it to move about. In the normal *proteus* these filaments cannot be seen, but in the 'monstrous forms', and under the phase-contrast microscope, they were clearly visible. Fleming studied their movements with an interest the more lively because a well-known bacteriologist, Pijper, thought he had proved that these filaments were *not* a means of locomotion, but threads of mucus which came from the creatures' bodies as *a result of* movement.

One day he showed Dr Voureka, under the microscope, a remarkable variant of the *proteus* which seemed to be furnished with large, spread wings, which it agitated violently in an attempt to get out of a corner in which it had become wedged. After a few seconds the movement stopped. Fleming, annoyed by this cessation, exhorted the *proteus* to move: 'Get a move on, can't you!' Naturally, there was no response. At that moment someone called him from a near-by room, and he went out of the laboratory, saying: 'Make it move!'

It suddenly occurred to her to agitate the mirror which served to refract the light on to the preparation. To her great joy, as soon as the *proteus* was touched by the light-ray, it immediately responded to the stimulus. By passing her hand up and down between the mirror and the source of illumination, she could make it beat its wings, or stop it, at will.

When Fleming came back, he was delighted by this small observation. For weeks he played with the new phenomenon, noting the length of time occupied by the movements and the period of rest after exhaustion. Somebody had given him a tape-recorder, which he used in place of an assistant. He counted out loud, described what he saw, and his words were recorded by the apparatus. After Sareen's death, during the first forlorn months of his loneliness, when he used to shut himself away in his laboratory, people passing the door could hear his hoarse, tired voice counting. For those who knew him well and loved him, there was something disturbing in the sound.

But soon he began once more to feel the need to share his observations with his colleagues. One day, Dr Stewart, a newcomer to the Institute, suddenly saw his chief's face looking at him through a chink of the half-open door.

'Are you doing anything you can't leave for a moment?'

'No, sir; certainly not, sir.'

'D'you know anything about *proteus*?'

'Not much, sir.'

'Well, come into the laboratory.'

Stewart did so and saw three microscopes set up, with filters between them and the several sources of illumination. Fleming passed rapidly from one microscope to another, moving the filters, observing the effect, and dictating his comments to the tape-recorder. He asked Stewart to help him, but very soon the 'whole business', writes the doctor, 'had turned into something like a clown-act in a circus. We jumped from microscope to microscope, often colliding. The bacilli moved and stopped, went up and down, while we said "*Start! — Stop! — In! — Out! — Up! — Down!*" and so absorbed were we that we did not even notice the appearance of a distinguished visitor, who, opening the door and seeing two men running round and shouting, must have thought that Fleming and his assistant were both a bit "touched" ...'

> *Fleming to Todd:* For the last six months, what little work I have been able to do has been with a phase-contrast microscope, watching little slide-cultures of *proteus* in penicillin agar. They roll themselves up like watch-springs, and go round and round like Catherine-wheels all day long in the same field of the microscope. We can time their movements, stop them, start them, and observe how their flagella move. They respond beautifully to stimuli, and I am beginning to believe that even a lowly bacterium has some primitive nervous system.

In September 1949 the generous American, Ben May, presented the Institute with two marvellous pieces of apparatus, so as to help Dr Voureka to complete the work she was engaged upon — a micromanipulator and a microforge, devised by a French scientist, Dr de Fonbrune. These made it possible to handle single microbes with instruments invisible to the naked eye. Dr Voureka spoke French perfectly, and Fleming sent her to take a course in their use at the Pasteur Institute.

Dr Voureka to Ben May, September 14th, 1949: I quite understand your enthusiasm for the French micromanipulator. It is just marvellous. Sometimes I find it hard to believe that we can really make these little instruments and perform these operations. Monsieur de Fonbrune is being very helpful. He deals with me from 2 till 7 every day, showing me how to use his fantastic machinery, and isolating my bacteria. When I think of the time when I used to say 'if only I could pick this one up' — and now I see this happening, in no time, I think I am dreaming ... I agree with you that the range and delicacy of the operations one can do with the French equipment is far beyond the possibilities other equipments offer ...

Ben May to Sir Alexander Fleming: Dr Fonbrune told me that Dr Voureka was different from any other woman scientist he had met: besides being a scientist, he says, she is a person and a personality.

Dr Voureka to Ben May, November 5th, 1949: I don't know whether you heard of Lady Fleming's death. The whole story has been most distressing to Sir Alexander. So much sorrow should certainly not come to a man who has given so much of value to humanity. He is being very brave, working as always. Yesterday, at long last, the equipment arrived. To my very great delight Sir Alexander *en est émerveillé*! He thinks it a very ingenious and marvellous machine. I am glad in a way that it arrived now, because it gave him a distraction from his worries ...

Fortunately, he still retained his taste for lovely toys. In spite of his profession of faith at Oklahoma City, the phase-contrast microscope, the micromanipulator and the tape-recorder gave him great joy.

In addition to his research-work, travelling did much to help him to recover from the grievous shock he had had. He spent quite a considerable part of his life at that time in aeroplanes and liners. *January 1950:* Dublin. *February:* Leeds, to receive the Addingham Medal. *March:* To the United States in the *Queen Mary*. *June:* Milan, to give a lecture on the new antibiotics. *August:* Brazil. *September:* Rome. *November:* Brussels, where he had to make a speech in the name of the foreign scientists on the occasion of the eightieth birthday of the Belgian bacteriologist, Jules Bordet, for whom he felt a great affection. To give pleasure to Bordet, he wished to speak in French. At his request, Amalia translated and recorded the speech, and this busy man spent hours in learning it by heart, and trying to pronounce each word in an intelligible manner. At the University of Brussels, in the presence of Queen Elisabeth, he delivered his oration, and praised in Bordet the qualities he most admired:

> The essence of Bordet's work is simplicity — simplicity of attitude and simplicity of technique ... He has always shown himself to be very sceptical of fancy theories insufficiently supported by experimental facts. He has worked away and produced new facts which have helped us all. It is not given to everybody to be world-famous in science for so long. But it has not made any difference to Jules Bordet. He is still the simple investigator he always was. Bordet is, by nationality, a Belgian, but medicine is not national. There is, fortunately, a free exchange of medical knowledge, and Jules Bordet is international.

Sometimes, when he was in London, he invited his 'little G'eek f'iend' to go with him to the Royal Academy banquet, or to other dinners and receptions. Since the house in which she was living was on the way from the laboratory to Danvers Street, he took her home every evening in his car. He left St Mary's at half-past five, dropped her, and went on to the Chelsea Arts Club. They both felt happy when they were together, and talked of everything under the sun with complete mutual understanding, as they drove through Hyde Park.

In mid-summer 1950 he took her to a dinner given by the Worshipful Company of Dyers in the City. This very ancient company owns one-third of the swans on the Thames, one-third belonging to the Crown, and the remaining third to the Vintners' Company. Each year, at a solemn banquet, a number of young cygnets are presented on a silver dish. Amalia saw, with him, for the first time, at the mid-summer ladies' night dinner, the ceremony of the loving-cup which is passed up and down the tables. She found it all very novel and charming. It was long since she had seen Fleming so gay. He seemed to be happy at having her for partner.

In December, while Fleming was away in Stockholm for a meeting of the Nobel Institute, she went back to Greece for the Christmas holidays.

Dr Voureka to Ben May: My only regret is that I shall be parted from my very dear laboratory at St Mary's.

During this holiday absence she was asked whether she would accept the post of head of the laboratory at the Evangelismos Hospital in Athens. This was the most important hospital in the city and the one in which she had done part of her training. The idea of returning to it as the head of a department was tempting. She wrote to Fleming to tell him of the proposal. He replied as follows:

January 23rd, 1951

Dear Dr Voureka,

I was very glad to get your letter and to hear of your adventures. Congratulations on your new research Institute. I knew that you would find a research job one day, but a whole Institute is much better.

You will have got the *Lancet* by this time. They have done you well. I have sent a copy to Ben May to show him that he is getting his money's worth.

Your bench still awaits you.

Yours sincerely,
ALEXANDER FLEMING

The *Lancet* had just published a report on the work done by Dr Amalia Voureka on the mutations of certain microbes. This also formed the subject of the editorial. She was faintly disappointed by this letter. Not a word of advice. She thought she could detect a note of irony in his reference to 'a whole Institute'. She had spoken only of a laboratory. And why 'your *bench* still awaits you'? Was it an expression of regret, or a desire to keep her? She thought so for a moment, then reproached herself for an excess of imagination. In any case, the final appointment depended, in Greece, on the decision of the council, which would not be in session for some time. While waiting for it, she returned to London and went on with her work.

In April 1951 a UNESCO congress took him to Pakistan. In Karachi, as always, he was asked to speak in public. The subject was given to him: 'How the children of Pakistan can become the research-workers of tomorrow'. He rapidly jotted down a few notes:

All of us, in our ordinary pursuits, can do research, and valuable research, by continual and critical observation. If something unusual happens, we should think about it and try to find out what it means ... There can be little doubt that the future of humanity depends greatly on the freedom of the researcher to pursue his own line of thought. It is not an unreasonable ambition in a research-worker that he should become famous, but the man who undertakes research with the ultimate aim of wealth or power is in the wrong place ... Not all Pakistan children can become research-workers, but, with care, especially in their early youth, many can reach that proud dignity.

He visited mosques and rose-gardens; he flew as far as the Afghan frontier. Garlands of flowers were hung round his neck. He was photographed riding on a camel. But his greatest pleasure was dining with old comrades of the London Scottish, and being accompanied to the airport, when he left, by pipers.

CHAPTER SEVENTEEN

THE SILENCES OF PROFESSOR FLEMING

We spoke to each other about each other
Though neither of us spoke. EMILY DICKINSON

ON his return in June 1951 he invited Amalia Voureka, for the first time, to spend a week-end at Barton Mills. She was enchanted by the beauty of the old village, by the flowers, the river and the peace of the countryside. He showed her the garden-room which he had turned into a laboratory and furnished with dilapidated cupboards and seatless chairs picked up for two or three shillings at local fairs. Superb and costly pieces of apparatus, presented to him by admirers, stood on an assortment of old tables cheek by jowl with other odds and ends of equipment which he had constructed from old biscuit-tins and lengths of wire. On the wooden walls prints of birds had been glued and covered with varnish. In one corner a number of fishing-rods stood with their tops leaning against one of the rafters of the ceiling. There was a pile of goloshes and gum-boots by the door. The sterilizer was heated by means of an electric flex from the house. Through the large windows one could see the multi-coloured garden of The Dhoon. The whole place presented a faithful picture of the man who had conceived and made it.

His visitor immediately fell in love with the quiet and charming house. She told Fleming that, should he ever decide to retire there, she would apply for the position of lab.-boy-cum-cook. He teased her about the far more brilliant post which she had just obtained (a unanimous vote of the Council of Management had just confirmed her appointment to the Evangelismos Hospital) and said: 'I'm afraid that would be beneath your dignity.' But she, secretly to herself, was thinking that she would willingly give up any post to work here, in this tiny laboratory in a garden, with a man on whom she felt she could rely in any circumstances. The peace of it all seemed to her like Paradise.

He had planned to spend the whole of August at The Dhoon,

and suggested that she should stay for a week. She said she had a number of experiments on hand. 'Then, bring your cultures down here,' he replied, 'you can work in my laboratory.' She set off with him in the car and had seven marvellous days. She cleaned the little lab. — something nobody had ever done before — and helped him to cut the nettles and long grass with a new machine of which he was very proud. She fished in the river, she made acquaintance with the little summer-house, an Eastern pagoda built by a local builder from the Willow pattern on a Wedgwood plate, and the garage-workshop where, on rainy days, he pottered about with electric saws and other tools. She went with him to village sales where old iron lay higgledy-piggledy with fine china. When she was working in the laboratory, he kept on coming in to see how she was getting along, or to show her something. Sometimes, not looking at her but into the distance with a curiously detached air, he said: 'Why not stay here for the whole month?' But she did not think he really meant it, and left, after a day of brilliant sunshine, under a full moon.

A few days later she received the following letter:

My dear Amalie,

I hope that is the way to spell your name, but am not sure ... we are all lonely since you left — you cheered us all up — and I have no one to help me with my nettle-cutting.

You found that the little laboratory suited you, so you had better collect some cultures and bring them down.

Be good to the mice.

Yours, A. F.

She replied with a gay and friendly letter. Far from being good to the mice, she had massacred eighteen of them! Her experiments had been held up.

My heart is broken, and, for the time being, I have abandoned my enterococcus ... Are you coming to London at all before the end of your holiday?

Kind regards,
Yours, A. VOUREKA

My name is spelt Amalia.

She felt that she ought not to accept his invitation to return. It had seemed to her vague, and she thought that it was probably just a piece of good manners. But by return of post came another letter:

My dear Amalia,

I have just got your letter — thanks. The lab. is empty and needs a lab.-boy to clean it. I have got a boat — it came last night, and I was on the river this morning ... There is a sale at Bury St Edmunds on Tuesday — I enclose catalogue and you will see that there are plenty of antiques. Does it appeal to you? If so, come down and we can spend another day hunting for bargains. If you are coming, ring me up this evening, and we can make arrangements. If you cannot come, send the catalogue back.

On Monday evening we are having some people in for cocktails, so if you come you can join the party.

We still miss you.

Yours, A. F.

This time there could be no doubt: he wanted her to go back. She arrived at The Dhoon on the evening of the cocktail party.

While Fleming was giving drinks to his friends and neighbours, the housekeeper, Mrs Marshall, told Amalia how much Sir Alexander had missed her. 'All the time you were here he was a totally different person.' Then, abruptly, she added: 'That's what he needs, a young woman in his home.' It suddenly dawned on Amalia, through her confusion, what it was that her own shyness, combined with Fleming's, had for the last year kept locked away among the things that are not said.

Next day, he took her to an auction sale at the charming Tudor village of Lavenham, presented her with a pretty antique vase, and gave her lunch at an old inn. During the meal he asked her about her domestic affairs. She told him about her constantly recurring disappointments. The separation between the Voureka husband and wife which, in spite of their very real affection for each other, had been going on for fifteen years, was now to be legalized. When tea-time came, he sat reading the paper without addressing a word to her. From this she concluded that she had bored him with her personal concerns, that Alice Marshall had a romantic imagination ... and that so had she! On their way back to Barton Mills he drove her a long way round so as to show her some enchanting thatched houses. In the course of the drive he spoke about a book in which the gods came alive and behaved like young men. 'Even the gods,' he said, 'have human feelings.' She deliberately refused to understand these enigmatic words and, a week later, returned to London.

He followed her on September 3rd. On the 17th, Dr Voureka was to read a paper to the Microbiological Society at Manchester. Fleming was to make the journey by road and offered to take her in the car with him. On the evening before they were to start, he invited her to dine in Chelsea with his son Robert and a nephew. He had just received his horoscope which Marlene Dietrich (whom he had met several times, and who now regarded him as one of her heroes) had had cast for him in Hollywood. Of course, Fleming would not have taken it seriously, but opening the document at a certain page, he asked her to read it. She had read only a few words when dinner was announced. Amalia abandoned the horoscope and Fleming never mentioned it again.

Much later, after his death, when she was turning over many memories in her mind, she recollected this episode and wondered what the contents of the page had been which he had wanted her to read. Here is what the horoscope had said:

> Your emotional responses are rooted in your need for security and a home, and this makes your love a very loyal, dependable and devoted thing. You are emotionally very sensitive, since so much is at stake, and are likely to hide this side of yourself until you have found somebody whom you feel to be worthy of your love ...

That, obviously, was what he had hoped to make her understand, but a tiny incident may change everything. Dinner had been announced, and Amalia had read only the first few words.

On the drive to Manchester, he asked her whether she intended to marry again. She replied ('stupidly', she says) that she *was* married. He became more silent than ever. At Manchester, while he was attending a committee-meeting, another doctor did a little gentle pulling of her leg, saying: 'Where is your god this evening?' At this moment Fleming came into the room, and she replied: 'Here is God in person.' After their return to London he took her to lunch in an hotel near Windsor, and then to the Zoo, where he photographed her in front of one of the lion cages. He kept this photograph in his study and called it 'She and the Lion'.

At the Private View of the Academy she much admired a portrait of Fleming by the painter, John Wheatley. He said nothing, but wrote to Wheatley:

Nov. 27. 51

Dear Wheatley,

In the last Academy show you had a small picture of me. Have you still got it? If so, are you prepared to sell it to me, and at what price? I admired it but I am not enamoured of myself but someone who is important to me also admired it and if it is not too expensive I would like to acquire it for him.

He later sent this picture to Athens as a farewell present.

Amalia was due to leave for Greece on December 15th. He asked her to dine with him on the 14th. He gave her a photograph of the little laboratory at Barton Mills under the snow. 'I want you to take this with you,' he said. 'You mustn't forget the little laboratory.' On the print he had written: 'The little lab. which you liked so much, and which liked you as the only person who had ever kept it clean.'

For this last dinner, he took her to his Scottish club, the Caledonian. He gave her champagne, spoke of the five years just past and of the work she was going to do in Greece. Then he took her to the Morning Room where they had coffee by the fire. At first he sat in an armchair beside her, but after a short while he got up and sat down again facing her. 'I want to have a good look at you, to remember you by.' For some seconds he stared at her in silence, and then said: 'What a pity these years are over! ...' Later, he drove her home.

When she reached Athens, she found a telegram from Fleming waiting for her. Good wishes and remembrances. Two or three days later she got a letter which said: 'There is a gap in lab. No. 2. We know why. We miss you.' Then a second letter: 'We still miss you. No. 2 is no longer the same.' A third letter: 'I cross the park alone now: no one to talk to me. We miss you all the time.' But the end of the month brought a more resigned letter: 'We still miss you, but we shall get used to it.'

CHAPTER EIGHTEEN

THE DELPHIC ORACLE

Ὁ δὲ τοῦ ἤθους χρηστοῦ ὄντος ἐραστὴς διὰ βίου μένει, ἅτε μονίμῳ συντακείς.

Πλάτων, Συμπόσιον, X, 183 E

But the lover of a noble nature remains its lover for life, because the thing to which he cleaves is constant.

PLATO, Symposium X, 183 E, Hamilton's translation

AFTER the departure of his Greek pupil, Fleming gave the impression of being lost. He confided in nobody, but he did, which was most unusual with him, express regret in a vague and general way. One of his friends, D. J. Fyffe, describes him at this time, as follows:

One evening my wife and I met Fleming at the Royal Academy Soirée. It was duller than usual, and there seemed to be nothing to drink. He was wandering about in the crowd, and, much to our pleasure, joined us.

'This is a rotten party,' he said, 'I'm going home.'

I suggested that he should come back to our flat, where we could have a party on our own. He drove us home. I found some champagne; my wife cooked bacon and eggs, and we sat down to supper. I think he was always at his ease with us, probably because we all came from Scotland. Anyway, we sat round the table and talked for a long time. He was unusually expansive. He spoke of his early life and of the strange fortune that had been so active in his career. I remember that he was wearing some rare Papal order, and that we twitted him on his collection of cosmopolitan decorations. He suddenly became serious.

He said that all this grandeur had come to him far too late in life, that he could not enjoy it as he should. Had it come earlier it would have given him time in which to cultivate the social graces in which he was deficient. He would have 'learned his manners'. As it was, he said, he didn't know how to behave. He regretted this very much, and was certainly sincere in what he said. He knew that his rather brusque

246

ways had often offended, and wished that he had had a longer social experience.

He talked about all this rather wistfully, but, being a clear-headed, practical man, he accepted the fact as something inevitable in his intensely hard-working life ...

Official journeys shook him out of this kind of brooding. He had been made a member of the UNESCO commission charged with the duty of organizing medical conferences, the Commission of International Scientific Conferences (C.I.S.C.). He was only too glad to go to Paris for its meetings. He got on very well with his colleagues from other countries.

He rarely spoke on these occasions. 'They attach a great deal too much importance to what I say, so it behoves me to be cautious.' He had a very shrewd eye when it came to summing up others: 'A ... says little, but is listened to. B ... talks a lot, but nobody takes him seriously. X ... young and energetic, wants to see results. Z ... pleasant enough, but without ideas: very ordinary.'

Fleming's diary, session of 1951, Thursday, September 27th, 1951: Hôtel Napoléon. Went for a walk along Champs Élysées and had a vermouth at Le Select – no particular reason, but I wanted to sit down and have a drink. Inside, they were serving meals, so I thought I might as well dine there as anywhere. Had a very good meal, but the proprietor and the head-waiter came along and accused me of being the discoverer of penicillin. On the strength of it I got an Alsace liqueur made from raspberries – very good and very potent. What a difference from anything in London! Lights everywhere, and shop windows all lit up ... Lots of English spoken by people in the street. Back in hotel before 10 p.m. ...

On October 30th, 1951, at St Mary's he was attending a session of the School Council, when he was called to the telephone. It was a telegram: 'Would you accept nomination as Rector Edinburgh University. Reply at once.'

The Scottish students themselves elect their Rectors. The post is an honorary one and does not involve residence. Nevertheless, the Rector does actually preside over the University Court, which is the highest authority in matters of administration and finance. Thus the students of Edinburgh in fact enjoy the privilege of electing what amounts to a Patron. They use it for the purpose of paying homage to those eminent men whom, for one reason or another, they admire. One group will choose a politician, another a writer, a scholar or a famous actor. The electoral battle, which is enthusiastic and amusing, quickly turns into a farcical epic.

Each candidate has to have the support of a group consisting of at least twenty students who conduct a vigorous campaign in his favour by means of posters, slogans and even pitched battles, because nightly combats occur between rival bands of bill-stickers. The Fleming faction was at first principally made up of medical students who are very powerful in Edinburgh, a city with an ancient and glorious medical tradition. Nothing could have given more pleasure to the Scottish youth who was still alive in the famous man.

Fleming's diary: Replied 'yes', and when I rejoined Lord McGowan in the Council, he expressed his approval of my decision emphatically. Next morning one of the students [Ian Sullivan] came to ask my acceptance in writing. Was at Drapers' Company Dinner that night, and when I got home, Harold [Montgomery, a nephew] told me they had rung up from Edinburgh for a second signature as they feared their messenger might be kidnapped. It was too late, but apparently messenger got through, and I was duly nominated.

His most dangerous rival (out of eight candidates) was the Aga Khan, P.C., G.C.S.I., G.C.I.E., an enormously rich, powerful and clever man. The Aga Khan faction had hatched a plot to kidnap the messenger of the Fleming group at the Waverley Station. The Flemingites, informed of this, cut the ground from under their enemies' feet by themselves snatching their emissary from the train at London and taking him back to Edinburgh by car.

The most successful poster of the campaign was one carrying the single word 'FLEMING'. It did its job, and it was cheap. Sir Alexander polled 1,096 votes to the Aga Khan's 660. The other candidates were left far behind. Fleming was pleased at having been elected with so big a majority. He had to go to Edinburgh to be installed. Harold Stewart, who made the journey with him, described it as follows: 'We had a very pleasant journey. He said "Hullo!" at King's Cross. We got into the same compartment. He said "Goodbye" at Edinburgh.' *Rectoria brevitas.*

He had to deliver the Rectorial Address which, according to long-hallowed tradition, the students interrupted with shouting, singing, and every variety of noise.

Sir Alexander Fleming to John McKeen, President of Pfizer, Inc., New York: It was a very exciting experience and after 70 you don't want too much excitement. I can remember when I first read a paper to a society, in 1907. My knees shook, but they were concealed behind the lecturer's desk, and apparently my face did not give me away so all was well. My knees have not shaken since until I got up to deliver my address in Edinburgh, amidst a babel of noise. I found them shaking again. This time, though, I had on a long gown, and nobody noticed. I soon got used to the clamour, and when it was so loud that I could not be heard, I amused myself by thinking which bit I could cut without spoiling the story. All went well.

He was determined to make himself heard, and he succeeded. His address, which was excellent, deserved a hearing. He had chosen 'Success' as his subject:

What is success? It might be defined as the achievement of one's ambitions. If we accept this simple definition then everyone is in some way successful, and no one is completely successful. You have all achieved one ambition, to be students of the great University of Edinburgh. But you will have other ambitions, because ambition once achieved leads on to others.

Then he described what he held to be the most successful careers in history — those of Pasteur and Lister — and pointed out that success involved the conjunction of luck and genius.

The success of Louis Pasteur was phenomenal. How did it come about? The answer is, I think, simple — by hard work, careful observation, clear thinking, enthusiasm and a spot of luck. Plenty of people work hard and some of them make

249

careful observations, but without the clear thinking which puts these observations in proper perspective, they get nowhere.

Speaking of his own career, he reminded his listeners, as it was his habit to do, that he had chosen St Mary's because that hospital happened to possess a very active swimming club. About the same time, the greatest of English bacteriologists, Almroth Wright, had gone there because he had quarrelled with the military authorities. But for that double piece of luck — his own love of swimming and Wright's rupture with the War Office — he might have been drawn into some other branch of medicine, and would not have discovered penicillin.

As to that discovery, he would be the first to attribute it to luck. A mould of penicillium had drifted in through a window. It had dissolved bacteria. He had taken notice of this, had continued his researches, and had found a substance possessed of extraordinary properties. What a variety of luck had been needed for him to get that far! Out of thousands of known moulds one, and one only, produced penicillin, and out of the millions of bacteria in the world, only some are affected by penicillin. If some other mould had come in contact with the same bacteria, nothing would have happened; if the right mould had come in contact with some other culture, nothing would have happened. If the right mould had come in contact with the right bacteria at the wrong moment, there would have been nothing to observe. Further, if, at that precise moment, his mind had been occupied with other things, he would have lost his chance. If he had been in a bad mood, he might well have thrown away the contaminated culture.

Had I done that I would not be here giving the Rectorial Address, so your selection of me as Rector really depended on my being in a good temper on a morning in September 1928 — before a lot of you were born. However, Fate ordained that everything happened right and penicillin appeared.

He spoke — also as his custom was — about team-work. There is, he said, great value in a team. For lack of a team he had not, while at St Mary's, been able to purify penicillin, and this had been done, only much later, by the team at Oxford. But there was much, too, to be said in favour of lonely research.

It is the lone worker who makes the first advance in a subject: the details may be worked out by a team, but the prime idea is due to the enterprise, thought and perception of an individual ... If, when penicillin began in my laboratory by an accidental occurrence, I had been a member of a team working on a specific problem, it is likely that I would have had to play for the team and so neglect this chance occurrence which had nothing whatever to do with the problems in hand. But, fortunately, I was not then one of a team, and, though there was nothing tangible to show that this chance occurrence was important, I was able to turn aside into the path which had been opened to me.

When he had finished, the students made a concerted rush at him, lifted him off his feet, and, to the accompaniment of an ear-splitting din of shouts, singing, drum-beating, mouth-organs and trombones, carried him shoulder-high to the Students' Union, where everybody took tea. It was the general opinion that he had come through this by no means gentle ordeal with courage and good-humour. He was a very popular Rector.

The merry-go-round of glory continued to revolve. In 1952 he went to Switzerland for a meeting of the World Health Organization. It took place in Geneva, but on his way there he stopped at Lausanne for a few days of rest and relaxation. On top of the hill at Gruyère he had a lunch consisting only of cheese — 'one of the best meals I ever had.' At Geneva he learned that the World Medical Association was to meet in Athens during October, and that a member of the C.I.S.C. would be expected to attend. He said that he would very much like to be chosen, because he had 'interests in Athens'. UNESCO was only too glad for him to travel to Greece as its delegate. He returned from Switzerland by car via the Jura, and stopped at Dôle where he drank *vin d'Arbois* to the memory of Pasteur.

On October 6th he flew to Athens where he arrived thirty-six hours late, at three in the morning, feeling somewhat uneasy because he did not even know at what hotel he would be staying. When the door of the aeroplane was opened, he saw Amalia waiting for him in a group of friends. Much relieved, he shut his eyes — a peculiarity of his — and stood for several seconds upright and motionless in the doorway, making it impossible for the other passengers to get out. He need worry no longer. The programme of his stay had been drawn up with care and affection. The University of Athens had asked Dr Vourcka to organize every-thing — lectures, receptions, visits and excursions. She was delighted to act as Fleming's guide and interpreter. She was proud of him, and proud, too, to show him her country. Greece fascinated him. On the first morning, he noted in his diary:

> The sun was shining. My bedroom had a wide balcony. It was warm, so without dressing I walked out ... There, in front of me, was the Acropolis, my first joy after waking in Athens ... something never to be forgotten.

Not only did Greece attract him, as it attracts all the peoples of the Western world, but his interest had been stimulated by the description of the beauties of her country which Amalia had given him in the course of the last few years.

> She had told me of the wonderful blue skies and the blue sea, of the sunshine and the fascinating changes of colour on the mountains. After all that I had been expecting a great deal, and although I arrived only in October, I have found that she had not exaggerated the beauty and charm of Greece.

His visit was one of friendship and triumph. He gave his first lecture in the *aula* of the University. So great was the crowd that many official persons could not get in. The Archbishop was present, the Prime Minister, a host of distinguished scientists, and old women in their picturesque headdresses. When these women were politely told that they would not be able to understand what he said because he would be speaking in English, they replied that they had come from their villages to *see* him.

He found an immense pleasure in letting his friend and collaborator do the honours of her country. They took their meals beside the sea. At night the coast looked like a necklace of dia-monds. She flew with him to Salonica. When she told him that he would have to leave a card on the Archbishop, he had to confess that he had not brought any visiting-cards with him, but asked for a blank card on which he wrote his name in letters so perfectly formed that they might have been engraved.

A car had been put at his disposal for a trip to the north of Greece. A royal escort of motor cyclists surrounded him in the wild and beautiful mountains. At Kastoria he lodged with an eminent citizen and, in accordance with the Greek laws of hospitality, was given a cup of coffee, a spoonful of jam, a glass of water and some of the potent local drink, *tsipouro*. Then, all the notabilities — the mayor, the bishop, the chief of police, the senior doctor — came to pay their respects to him. As each new visitor arrived, the tray of coffee, jam and *tsipouro* were brought in, and the hostess courteously offered it to Fleming on each separate occasion. Thinking it to be a ritual obligation, he partook of everything each time the tray was brought to him. Then he had to pay a visit to the bishop and drink still more *tsipouro*. On the way back, his legs were far from steady.

But he revelled in everything like a child; fished in the lakes and was taken to the spot where the frontiers of Greece, Jugoslavia and Albania meet. Sometimes when they passed near a town where no stop had been arranged, the inhabitants stood on the road watching for the car, and carried off the 'man who had found penicillin' to feast and be made much of. At last he returned to Athens where he was to be received into the Academy. He had scarcely time to write his speech, which Dr Voureka had to translate in the car on their way to the ceremony.

It was a great moment for me when I was received into the Academy of the city which had given learning to the world at a time when the inhabitants of my own country were barbarians and savages. Still more was I thrilled when I was presented with an olive branch cut from the tree under which Plato had taught his pupils. This is one of my great treasures.

Then he resumed his travels. He saw Corinth, the Theatre at Epidaurus, the Temple of Aesculapius, Argos and Mycenae, Olympia and Delphi, which, with its six thousand years of legend and history, its temples and its oracle and its glorious olive wood, filled him with wonder. But in his diary, he merely wrote:

Visited temple … marvellous situation … saw ruin where oracle originally sat and position she occupied later in temple.

Visited fountain ... in which people washed before consulting the oracle. Sat there with a pot of beer ... Went over temple again. Much better second time.

In front of the stone on which the oracle sat, he had the way in which she made her utterances explained to him. He began to say 'The Delphic oracle ...' but his companion interrupted him to point out a ray of sunlight which, darting from a cloud, illuminated the olive trees in the valley: 'Look how beautiful it is!' Then, remembering that she had interrupted him: 'You were going to say something?' 'No, nothing,' he replied.

He admitted later that the Delphic oracle had counselled him to marry his travelling-companion. 'An old woman, seated on a stone, and pretending to be wise! She got a lot of people into trouble in the old days and she is still at it.'

On his return to Athens he carried out in the laboratory of the Evangelismos Hospital (the very one of which Dr Voureka was in charge) a series of demonstrations having to do with phagocytosis and the opsonic index. He had long scientific conversations with Professor Ioakimoglou, and a talk, no less serious, with the Professor's niece, Nora, on the subject of her dolls. In the note-book in which he jotted down the outstanding incidents of every day, he wrote: 'Mairoula is afraid of me', and, two days later: 'Mairoula now friendly.' Mairoula, Amalia's niece, was two years old.

He lunched privately with the King and Queen.

Fleming's diary: Drove out to Summer Palace at 1.30. Received by Queen Frederica — a young and attractive woman. Very vivacious — and talked away. King came in soon. Had a drink and then went to lunch. Just the four of us. Dr Voureka, King, Queen, Self. Good General conversation ... Stayed till 3.45. Gave Queen penicillium culture. She seemed very pleased.

At last, after a few days' rest at Rhodes, he was given the Freedom of Athens and the City Medal at a solemn ceremony in the City Hall, the walls of which were hung with alternate English and Greek flags. This occasion marked the end of a marvellous journey. He had witnessed the adoration of the ordinary people; he had had honours showered upon him. He had been deeply touched by the devotion of his young companion. It was thanks to her that his visit had been so pleasant and so perfect. But he was due to leave on November 10th.

On the evening of the 9th, he went to her house to write his letters of thanks and farewell, to collect his papers and arrange his notes. She was sad and tired. All of a sudden, after a month of unceasing effort, she felt overcome with exhaustion. She thought that perhaps she would never see her master again, and was conscious of a sense of painful solitude. They had a last, quiet, melancholy dinner together. Just as he was about to say goodbye, he muttered some unintelligible words which she failed to hear. After a moment, he said: 'You have not answered me.'

'Did you say anything?'

'I asked you to marry me.'

She looked at him without wholly taking in his words. Then her brain started to function again. The meaning of what he had said dawned on her. 'Yes,' she replied.

In Fleming's diary, under the date November 9th, 1952, there are a few technical notes, and then, on a line by itself, the one word 'Yes'.

He left Athens on the 10th, without having had another chance to speak with the woman whom a single word had made his affianced bride. He had to spend all that last morning in receiving the visits of doctors and students who came to say goodbye.

From the aeroplane he wrote his first letter to Amalia as his future wife, and in the next nine days he wrote her nine letters. They were letters full of anxiety, for he was without news of her: disturbed by his laconic proposal, she had decided to wait until she was sure of his feelings, before writing herself. But at last he received two letters by the same post, containing many expressions of exuberant happiness. His anxiety now relieved, he sent her a very matter-of-fact one in reply, realistic and sensible, in which he explained that he could not take her to India with him, and did not want the marriage to be performed before he left on that journey. 'It would be a mistake to marry you and then vanish for two months.' He suggested that the ceremony should take place after he got back from Cuba and the United States, in the second fortnight of June 1953. 'After all, we are launching out on a long-term voyage.' He seemed, she thought, to see life in terms of eternity.

Fleming to Professor and Mrs Roger Lee, January 6th, 1953

My Dear Friends,

Thank you ever so much for your Christmas greetings ...
I am due to give a lecture in Boston on May 20th next, and
I was hoping to stay for one or two days.

It may be that I shall be able to introduce you to a new
wife but please do not say anything about this to anyone. It
seems late in life to marry again but I think it is worth it ...

He left for India at the beginning of 1953 with a number of
doctors, among them a Frenchman, Professor Georges Portmann
of Bordeaux, with whom he struck up a friendship. He very soon
became popular among his companions. They liked his simplicity,
his 'good Scotch fun', his dry humour. They were amazed at his
youthfulness. They called him 'Flem'. They were surprised, and
he no less, at the adoration shown him by the Indian crowds in
Bombay and later in Madras. When he spoke, the halls were not
large enough to hold all those who wanted to hear him, and he
was wildly applauded wherever he went. He said that he felt
like a Hollywood film-star, 'but from the way he said it, one could
see that he really quite liked being a star.'

He insisted on taking his share in all the fatigues of the trip,
and was not at all pleased when four bearers attempted to carry
him up an immensely long staircase which led to one of the
temples. He liked to show how young and virile he was. When he
spoke on medical education, he advised his Indian listeners to
beware of the 'flim-flam' (a favourite expression of his) of public
lectures. He dwelt on the importance of small groups of pupils,
and on individual research-work. Fundamentally, his ideal was
the old Inoculation Department. In the evenings at their hotel
he liked gathering his friends together for what he called a 'frig',
because he kept his whisky in a refrigerator.

Aneurin Bevan, the English Labour M.P., who was a great
orator and happened to be attending another congress in India,
delivered a fine speech on the subject of Social Medicine. He was
surprised to see Fleming in the front row, knowing, as he did, how
hostile he was to all State intervention. Later on, Fleming said
that he hesitated to address the company after they had heard
another Britisher who was so much better a speaker. 'On the

other hand,' he added, 'when I speak, I give you the facts; Bevan has to draw upon his imagination.' After saying this, he told the story of penicillin and pointed out what, to his mind, were the true principles of research. After so much repetition, he had become, where these matters were concerned, almost eloquent. At the conclusion of his speech, the students gave him an ovation and besieged him with requests for his autograph.

He looked at temples and grottoes, ceremonies and dances with the same interest that he showed in all new and beautiful things, and a pleasure which nothing could blunt. He took thousands of photographs. He wanted to examine everything, understand everything, but also, as always, not to be taken in.

Throughout the trip, he was constantly buying *saris*, scarves and other feminine adornments. He chose them with so much love and care that the others began to question him. He replied that they were all for his sister. No one believed this, but it was impossible to get anything else out of him. Personal feelings were, for him, too sacred to be expressed in words. All the same, in spite of his self-control, his emotion when he was buying these things was clearly visible.

He took part in a leopard-hunt and a walking-race. Of all these things he sent long descriptions to his future wife:

> I seem to have written for a whole half-hour which is more than your ration. You are being spoilt. At 6.30 it is just getting light and thousands of sparrows are chattering in a tree outside the window.

Ever since leaving Greece he had taken to writing letters to her every day, and sometimes twice a day.

By the time the trip was over, his companions had grown sincerely attached to him, and decided that, 'in his own quiet, reserved and imperturbable way, he displayed the finest qualities of the human character.' The American, Dr Leo Rigler (from Duarte, California), who was one of his fellow travellers, writes: 'I shall always remember the cigarette drooping from his mouth, and the modest, natural way in which he accepted so much adulation.'

He arrived back in London on March 31st. It had been arranged that Amalia should come as soon as Fleming reached home, that they should get married at once and set off together for Cuba and the United States. She had succeeded in gaining two months on the original time-table.

When she got out of the aeroplane which brought her to England on Good Friday, April 3rd, she looked for him, but in vain. When he had travelled to Greece, she had asked for, and obtained, permission to await his arrival on the airfield. But Fleming always had scruples about asking for favours, no matter how small. He had kept in the background to avoid publicity. She found him, at last, at the exit from the Customs shed, in the very back row of those who had come to meet passengers. Brimming with happiness she ran to him, and was appalled to see confronting her a face like a stone wall. Beside him, looking gloomy, was Elizabeth, Sareen's twin sister. Amalia, frozen and wretched, looked at these two seemingly hostile persons without in the least understanding what was happening. Later on, when she had learned to interpret the least quiver of her husband's face and to divine the secret springs of his otherwise unintelligible behaviour, she came to understand the intensity of emotion denoted by this complete immobility of his features. She knew by then what a struggle between opposed feelings and duties was sometimes going on behind that impenetrable face.

Later, too, she realized that only his immense kindliness had led him to bring his sister-in-law with him to the airport. He had wanted to give the old and ailing woman a feeling that nothing would be changed where she was concerned. The most precious virtues have often a counter-balance of scruples which, in their turn, can inflict profound and unnecessary suffering on the beloved. Fleming had the defects of his qualities. Such a value did he set on loyalty that he tried to be loyal to everybody at one and the same time. Oversensitive, he sought refuge in an excessive reserve. He was too wise, too patient, and extreme patience is sometimes a dangerous virtue. Naturally modest, he found it difficult to believe that anyone should love him. There were no limits to his fair-mindedness, with the result that his efforts to achieve impartiality sometimes made him unfair to himself and to those he loved.

Next morning, Saturday, he went with his future wife to the Chelsea Registry Office to get a marriage-licence. The Registrar took down his name and address with a completely impassive expression. One could have sworn that he had never heard of Sir Alexander Fleming. But when he had finished writing, he said, in the same official tone and not raising his eyes: 'I presume, sir, that you would wish to avoid all publicity. I will post the necessary notice as late as possible. The Press will know nothing about it until the office reopens on Tuesday.' Fleming said 'Thank you.' Both men had observed the maximum degree of reserve and discretion. The Registrar had almost 'outfleminged' Fleming.

On the following Tuesday and Wednesday the newspapers, now in possession of the information, pursued both of them in an attempt to discover the time and place of the ceremony. At 6 p.m. on Thursday, Fleming went as usual to the Chelsea Arts Club for his game of snooker. He said nothing to his friends about his marriage, but on the way out grunted something to the effect that 'I probably shan't be here tomorrow: I may have to make a change in my habits.'

His stockbroker, A. M. Ritchie, who was also his friend, had received from him that day a note in which he spoke of 'important business, which you will probably see something about in the papers'. Ritchie telephoned to ask what the important business was. Fleming was evasive and merely said: 'Come and see me after dinner.'

'Apparently', says Ritchie, 'his marriage had been announced in the late editions of the evening papers, but not in the one I had read, so that, when I went to see him, I knew nothing about it. That, at first, was the cause of some small embarrassment, because I put some questions to him, and he, believing that I already knew, thought I was having fun with him. Finally the misunderstanding was cleared up, and we had a delightful monosyllabic tête-à-tête over whiskies and sodas and cigarettes. He was obviously a happy and satisfied man, which he had not been for several years.'

On Thursday, April 9th, at 11 a.m. the civil marriage took place at the Chelsea Registry Office, in the presence of only two witnesses. The religious ceremony followed at midday, at the Greek Church of St Sophia, in Moscow Road, before a few friends and relations. Finally, there was a small party at Claridge's, where the newly married couple were to spend the week before they left for Cuba.

CHAPTER NINETEEN

TOO SHORT A HAPPINESS

Τεκόντι δὲ ἀρετὴν ἀληθῆ καὶ θρεψαμένῳ ὑπάρχει θεοφιλεῖ γενέσθαι, καὶ εἴπερ τῳ ἄλλῳ ἀνθρώπων ἀθανάτῳ καὶ ἐκείνῳ.

Πλάτων, Συμπόσιον, XXIX, 212 A

And having brought forth and nourished true excellence, the love of the gods will be his, and he, himself – if ever a man can – will be immortal.

PLATO, *The Banquet*, XXIX, 212 A

Fortune has, in many ways, been kind to me, and I have tried to repay Fortune by doing a good job of work. FLEMING

FLEMING's friends approved of his marriage. Ben May wrote from America: 'Dr Voureka has *character* in the sense of courage, sincerity and kindness. She has a fine brain and a good training ...'

She had admired Fleming long before she married him, and their life together served to confirm and deepen her admiration. He was human, but his humanity was of a more than usually high quality. He had copied out in his own handwriting Kipling's poem 'If', and there can have been few men to whom each verse of it is so applicable. Who knew better how to 'meet with Triumph and Disaster, and treat those two impostors just the same'? The delighted surprise and, at the same time, the sincere detachment with which he accepted the honours which had so suddenly invaded his simple life; the fact that at the topmost summit of worldly fame he was still as modest, still as shy as before — gave the man's true measure.

His only defect was the difficulty he experienced in expressing himself, so that his strongest feeling remained unuttered. At first his wife suffered a good deal from this excessive reserve until a day came when an affectionate and spontaneous reply to something he had said took him completely by surprise, and she saw upon his face a sudden glow of radiant happiness. This rare disturbance of his features had revealed emotions so sincere and so strong that she felt herself rewarded for the silences which for so long she had found distressing and disturbing.

On April 16th they set off together for Cuba. At the Havana airport they were met by the usual official personages and also by a young girl, Margarita Tamargo, who had worked at the Wright-Fleming Institute as the holder of a British Council bursary. She was there to act for them as guide and interpreter, the part played by Amalia herself in Greece. Spontaneous, exuberant, authoritative, but radiating kindness, she ordered everybody about and everybody loved her.

In the days when she was working at the Institute, she had been one of Fleming's most ardent admirers. Once, when she was dining with Dr Voureka and other Institute friends, the future Lady Fleming had said that she was translating one of Fleming's lectures into French. Margarita Tamargo had clasped her hands in an ecstasy and exclaimed: 'Oh! if only he would give me something to translate for him into Spanish! ... I would do *anything* for him, yes, *anything* until midnight!' That '*anything*', and the time-limit, had brought her a deal of teasing.

Margarita Tamargo, happy in the good fortune of her friends, surrounded them with attentions and affection. The British Ambassador had reserved rooms for them at the Country Club, which was close to the golf-links, because it was the most English hotel in Havana. Sir Alexander, always ready to accept without a word any arrangement made for him by the authorities, would have remained there. But the Country Club was far from the sea, and the heat was stifling. Lady Fleming and Margarita at once began to hatch a plot to get him moved. They 'did' three hotels in two hours, reduced the Embassy staff to a state of complete bewilderment because nobody knew where Fleming was to be found, and finally discovered a suite with a superb view over the ocean. Meanwhile, mail, flowers and dignitaries were being sent on from one hotel to another. Fleming, astonished and startled, between the exuberant Margarita and the impetuous Amalia, but not a little amused by their audacity, expressed his indignation at their lack of respect for the official planning. Nevertheless, he bloomed in this atmosphere of youth and gaiety which suited him a great deal better than that in which men of his age usually live.

The Cuba visit was an immense success. He delivered a number of excellent lectures at the University, often improvising them at short notice. He spoke not only of what he had done, but of what he hoped to do, and of the research-work which he looked forward to seeing carried out by others. The students were completely carried away by his simplicity. He instructed them in technical matters and answered their questions as though he had been their contemporary. He visited the hospitals and was taken to see the hut where Walter Reed and Finlay had exposed themselves to mosquito bites in order to study yellow fever — one of the 'holy places' of bacteriology.

'He had no vanity,' says Margarita Tamargo, 'and there was something very special about him which I can find no word to describe. He was pleased with what people did for him, with the things they said to him, with the homage they gave to him ... and, above all, with the affection which showed in their eyes. One evening we took him to the Tropicana (a night club) ... He was terribly embarrassed when his presence was announced and everybody applauded.'

At the end of their stay they spent three days at Veradero, in a villa belonging to Alberto Sanchy del Monte and his wife, Margarita's uncle and aunt. Fleming swam, dived and fished. He was given a large straw hat, and a *guayabera*, a shirt worn by the Cubans. He was shown the grottoes full of stalactites and stalagmites where, as formerly in the temples of India, his hosts had the greatest difficulty in preventing him from climbing without a halt an immense flight of steps. He wanted to show that the young women got tired more quickly than he did. He enjoyed himself so much that Margarita suggested a lengthening of their stay. To this he said: 'But, Margarita, I have to work for my living' — which was true.

The Flemings left on April 30th for New York, weighed down by the cigars they had been given. Fleming had never smoked anything but cigarettes, but he disliked all forms of waste and, having been presented with these lovely cigars, he duly smoked them.

In the United States his programme, as usual, was very exhausting — lectures, radio, television, interviews. Here is one example of how his time was filled. He left Duluth in the morning by car, arrived at Saint-Paul where a great luncheon had been arranged, left again, as soon as it was over, for Rochester where he wanted to see his friend Keith (who had been with him at

Boulogne-sur-Mer), visited the Mayo Clinic where he had several long scientific talks, and then, after dining with the Keiths, drove back, after dark, to Saint-Paul. Lady Fleming was worn out. He, however, seemed as fresh as though he had never left his armchair.

It was a great pleasure for him to introduce his young wife to his American friends, and especially to Roger Lee, the Harvard professor. 'Alec would sit down and sigh at times and explain that he was not a desk-man, nor a travelling man; he was a laboratory man who would like to get back to the bench. I never knew how he *did* the travelling, the speeches, etc. He was always accommodating, and everyone loved him. Over the years I have had many communications from Alec, practically all of them short and brief. It is to be noted that he wrote longer letters to Mrs Lee than he did to me, and also that his letters were longer when he was discussing Amalia.'

She came more and more to wonder at his extraordinary capacity for work, at his charming manners and splendid character. He never complained. As an attraction he was promised three days' rest during which he could fish in a wonderful lake. Though experience had taught him how empty such promises were, he kept on believing them. No sooner had he arrived than he was asked to give a dozen lectures during this period of 'rest' (they would be so useful to the students), to visit a number of hospitals (the patients would be so delighted), and to talk on the radio. So his whole time was filled with engagements and tasks which he accepted from sheer goodness of heart, 'to give a little pleasure'.

As a result of being continuously at his side during this trip, she discovered that, when abroad, he was very much less shy than usual. In England an excess of reserve seemed to be imposed upon him by the reactions of others, at which he guessed and which he dreaded. But in America the radiant smile which she had noticed since she had first met him scarcely ever left his lips.

This angelic mood was rarely overcast. But there were certain things he could not put up with. Though modest to the point of humility, he would not permit any lack of respect, even when it showed in matters of omission. He never said anything on such occasions, but would flush slightly, and an icy look, a glint of deep and irrevocable contempt, would show in his eyes.

They returned to England in the *Queen Elizabeth*, both of them delighted at the prospect of getting back to work. His administrative duties at the Institute continued to pose a number of difficult problems. At the time of the passing into law of the National Health Service, it had become necessary for the Wright-Fleming Institute to merge either with the Medical School or with the new Service. Like Wright before him, Fleming had feared that such a merger would mean a loss of autonomy for the Institute. His tenacity, his insistence on maintaining some degree of independence, had irritated the authorities at St Mary's. But he had been sure that he was right, and had stuck to his point so doggedly that a compromise had finally been arrived at: the Institute was linked up with the Medical School, but retained considerable autonomy. As time went on, however, this autonomy — which Fleming considered so important for the scientific spirit of the Institute — had come to be in danger of being destroyed; and to Fleming, the great advocate of 'freedom in research', this was a cause of great distress.

They settled down in London at the house in Danvers Street which Amalia had to some extent rearranged. In the morning he drove her to the Institute where both of them were working. In the evening, he took her home, then went to the club, which was near by, for his game of snooker, even when he had to dress for a dinner. 'There's plenty of time,' he would say, and continue with his game until ten minutes to seven. He reminded his wife, as though he were making an enormous concession: 'In the old days I never got home till half-past.' The extra forty minutes were his tribute to her.

They went out almost every evening or entertained friends at home. When, by chance, they were alone together, he sat in his armchair and she on a stool at his feet. At those moments she felt herself filled with a surge of happiness, of delirious joy and peace. It was good to feel him there so close in mind and heart, so steadfast and so reliable. To have no more fears and doubts: to know that life would no longer hold unsolved puzzles, just because he was there. It was good to have at her disposal so much kindliness, so much knowledge, so much wisdom and to know, and to repeat to herself, that it would be with her for a long time, for ever. For, otherwise, what meaning could there be in all those strange

Lady (Amalia) Fleming

In Rome, September 1953

Sir Alexander Fleming in 1954 in his last laboratory at the Wright-Fleming Institute. A photograph by Douglas Glass

coincidences which had brought together two beings belonging to different generations, different countries, different backgrounds? Fleming had always said that Destiny had played a great part in shaping his life. Could she not now, at last, also trust in Destiny?

He had grown younger and seemed happier than he had ever been since she had known him. 'I shall never be old,' he said, 'until I begin to find life dull.' He certainly had not done that.

In the country, where he and his wife spent the week-ends and the whole of August, his activity shamed his guests, many of them not yet thirty. They had to be for ever on the move, going to see the wonderful strawberries which he had managed to grow in an old tank, watching him building a new greenhouse for the tomatoes, or mending a broken corkscrew with a machine he had set up in the garage which filed, polished and sharpened. If it wasn't any of these things, it was going with him to grub up worms for bait. Of course, he knew exactly where the best worms were to be found, for he had been observing their habits, and went straight to a corner near the strawberry-beds, and stuck a fork into the ground where absolutely perfect worms were wriggling.

'You wouldn't find these anywhere else in the garden,' he would say with pride. 'All the best come from here.'

When he was not carrying off his friends to fish or row on the river, there were games to be played — croquet outside, draughts in. He still took the same childlike pleasure in winning. There certainly was no idling at The Dhoon. 'Let's have a look at the headlines,' said one of his women guests, opening the paper, 'before Sir Alec comes back and drags us off to play some game or other.'

In October 1953 he was due to make a speech at the opening of 'Les Journées Médicales' in Nice. Two days before the appointed date, he woke up with a high fever. He himself diagnosed pneumonia. His doctor confirmed this and immediately gave him an injection of penicillin. His fever abated in the course of the day. The rapidity with which the penicillin had done its work enchanted him. 'I had no idea it was so good!' he said. But any thought of Nice was out of the question. Lady Fleming telephoned the organizers, who not unnaturally protested. They had announced Fleming and Fleming they must have.

'Quite impossible,' she said.

'Then *you* must come instead, madame.'

Her husband insisted on her accepting. 'You can't let me down,' he said. Then, as she stuck to her refusal, he did a most unusual thing: he actually paid her a compliment: 'No other wife could do as much for her husband.'

She took the plane to Nice, read his speech, and returned laden with flowers. The local reporters, however, seeing her there instead of Fleming, had demanded an explanation which she could not avoid giving them. The London papers, having got wind of what had happened, rang up Danvers Street. Fleming answered the call in person: 'Can't a chap be ill in peace?'

Fleming to Mrs Roger Lee: I did get a very sudden and, in the old days, I should think severe, attack of lobar pneumonia. High temperature for perhaps 12 hours, and then, with penicillin, nothing. But the physician would keep me in bed, and nothing would have appeared in the papers if I hadn't been engaged to read a paper at a Congress in Nice ... My illness, though, has had two results which may be good. For six weeks now I have given up smoking — at the moment I think it may be good for the health, but not for the temper. The other is that I have at last appreciated what a difference there is between lobar pneumonia now and when I was a student (especially in an old man).

He kept to his bed for a fortnight, and then got up too soon, since, as Rector of the University of Edinburgh, he had to be present at the installation of the Duke of Edinburgh as Chancellor. It was the Duke, too, who in 1954 presided at a ceremony in Fleming's honour at St Mary's. On May 10th, 1929, the first papers on the subject of penicillin had appeared in the *British Journal of Experimental Pathology*. On May 29th, 1954, to mark the silver jubilee of this event, a memento in the form of two silver soup tureens was presented to Fleming by his colleagues in the library of the School. The Duke said that it was not for him in the presence of so distinguished an audience to recall what Sir Alexander had achieved, but that he knew enough about it to hope that he himself would never have need of that discovery. He added that 'soup tureens were a suitable present to commemorate broth'. Fleming, in his reply, quoted the proverb: 'Tall oaks from little acorns grow.' From a minute spore a mighty industry had developed.

A few moments before the ceremony was timed to begin, his wife noticed that he had forgotten to put the links into his shirt-cuffs. She had hurried round to the local Woolworths and bought him a pair for a few pence. He never enjoyed being the central figure on any public occasion and quite frequently forgot his role. Some time later, the Queen Mother went to St Mary's to lay the foundation-stone of a new wing. She was to place within the marble block a culture of penicillium, a copy of Sir Zachary Cope's book about the hospital, and a stop-watch marking the exact time taken by Roger Bannister (a student at St Mary's) to run the mile. Surrounded on the platform by a group of professors, she rose and delivered a speech in which she did honour to Fleming. Everybody applauded, including Fleming, who was probably sunk in a day-dream and had not heard his own name.

The Flemings spent part of August at Barton Mills in their garden. Sir Alexander had promised to go to Bordeaux in November in response to a request from his friend, Professor Portmann, the Dean of the University. Portmann, who had heard Lady Fleming at Nice, asked her to translate Sir Alexander's address, and to read it in his name.

Fleming's diary, Saturday, November 13th, 1954: ... Met at Bordeaux by Dr and Mrs Portmann. Driven to their house on other side of Bordeaux ... Introduced to family. Young Mrs Portmann very attractive. Mrs Portmann also very attractive with a curious smile. The house was where Benedictine used to be made.

Sunday, November 14th, 1954: Away at 9.30 to St Emilion. Drove through miles of vineyards. There seemed to be quite different autumn colours, some deep bronze and some half green ... The Jurats were all in red robes. The head read a long speech and clothed me in a red gown and pronounced me a Jurat. I said very few words. Then to Pauillac where inaugurated into the order of the Compagnons du Bontemps de Médoc. A ritual. Had to say what a wine was. Completely failed though told by Portmann. Could only say Médoc wine ... Then to Mouton Rothschild for lunch. They had written a year ago about egg-white and lysozyme ... Should resume that research. A wonderful lunch with wines one of which was 1881 (my birthday).

Monday, November 15th: ... To Town Hall for lunch with Mayor. Lunch ended about 4. A very short rest, for at 5 had to go to Theatre to receive degree ... British and French flags. Marseillaise and God Save the Queen. Portmann speech. Rector speech. A. F. in French and then Amalia gave lecture on Search for Antibiotics, in French. Very successful ... Then to University Council dinner ...

He had wanted for a long time to be relieved of his work as Director of the Institute. He was far better suited to free research than to administrative duties. His very qualities stood in his way. 'He detested administration,' says Craxton, the secretary of the Institute, 'so much so that I am strongly of the opinion that if he had been relieved of the administration of the Wright-Fleming Institute at an earlier date he would have been with us now.

'Knowing from experience that administration gave him such a "pain in the mind", I troubled him with such matters as seldom as possible, always made my consultations with him very brief, and always arranged for them to take place as soon as possible after his arrival at the Institute to prevent interrupting his research work.

'I was more often than not greeted with a smiling face that appeared to cover anxiety, and the remark "Good morning, Craxton — no trouble I hope," and when I was able to report a happy state of affairs his face beamed with an expression of relief ... However, one of Sir Alexander's most outstanding gifts was his aptitude for the administration of justice. Never during the whole of my life have I met so just a man, and I have long felt that if he had not taken up Medical Research as a profession, he would have achieved equal fame if he had been a lawyer.'

But he longed to shed the burden of power. In December 1954 Lady Fleming wrote to Ben May:

Alec is very well. I think he has a good wife! He is retiring from his administrative job at the end of the month and will be able to devote more time to research. I am working on a problem which fascinates me but I keep failing to do what I try. Still there is an end even to failures.

In January 1955 he resigned his post of Principal, though he still kept on his laboratory at the Institute. At a small dinner given him at St Mary's, he made a very short speech:

I am not going away. I am not leaving the hospital. This is not goodbye. I shall be here for years, so don't think you are getting rid of me.

Craxton, in the name of the Council and the staff of the Institute, presented him with an album containing all their signatures and said: 'We sincerely wish you a long and happy retirement. We are glad to know that Lady Fleming and you will continue your researches at the Institute. May Providence lead both of you to new and great discoveries.'

On January 15th, 1955, the Society of Microbiology gave a dinner in honour of Sir Alexander on the occasion of his retirement as Principal of the Institute. In his reply to the speeches he said:

I am not retiring to the country to grow cabbages. I would rather grow microbes and I have not given up hope of reading a paper at one of your meetings.

He revelled in his freedom from administrative duties and personal squabbles. He was, however, besieged more than before by visitors. Many of them wanted him to reverse his decision to resign. Others came to ask his advice on private matters. All this tired him out. One day in February, in the course of a discussion on the subject of his resignation, he was taken ill with sudden vomitings and a slight rise in temperature. There was no apparent reason for this. The trouble was diagnosed as gastric flu. On the Sunday he felt rather worse, but refused to have any of his doctor friends disturbed.

'From that moment', says Lady Fleming, 'a change came over him. He seemed to be utterly exhausted.' All the same, he still went every day to the laboratory, and talked about starting on a new piece of work with her, which should bear both their names — A. and A. Fleming. They were due to leave on March 17th for Istanbul, Ankara and Beirut, with a few days in Greece. Amalia hoped that the sun would do her husband good.

March 3rd, 1955: Alec had a rather bad winter, coughing and living in this cold London without any sun. I am trusting Greece to make him regain his beautiful tan colour.

She was wildly happy at the prospect of going back with him to Athens. She knew the itinerary and the dates by heart. He would ask her: 'Where shall we be on the 23rd?' and she would reply with such a wealth of detail that it set him off laughing.

One Saturday, at the beginning of March, when they had gone to Barton Mills for the week-end, the telephone rang at midnight. Fleming answered it. She could hear what he said: 'Oh, they have, have they? ... Many thanks ... I am most grateful ... I shall be back tomorrow.'

His tone was one of polite gratitude. When he rejoined her, he said: 'That was a policeman. He was speaking from the house, from Danvers Street. There has been a burglary.'

'What has been taken?' she asked.

'I don't know,' he answered, 'I didn't inquire.'

They went home next morning. Before leaving The Dhoon they had a last look round. The studio where he had made his little laboratory stood out clearly against the snow between the trees. Amalia thought that the garden was looking exactly like the photograph he had given her when she went back to Greece, saying as he did so: 'You must not forget the little lab.'

There was surface ice on the road. It was snowing. There was a sort of pendent gloom over everything. As they were passing a cemetery, he asked a woman friend who was with them whether she would like to see the crematorium. When she protested, he said in a very low voice: 'I should like to be cremated.' When they reached Chelsea, they learned that a neighbour had raised the alarm just as the burglars, having taken out the safe, had dropped it into the street with a dreadful din. They had then made off, taking with them Lady Fleming's jewellery, a few ornaments and a camera. Reporters arrived. Lady Fleming told them that the most tiresome theft of all was that of the keys to their luggage, which were attached to a valuable seal which had belonged to a woman friend. But seal and keys had vanished. This detail was published in the *Daily Express.* Just about dinner-time Lady

Fleming was called to the telephone. She heard a completely strange, deep, low, unpleasant voice, a 'dirty voice', which said:

'You'd like to have that seal back, wouldn't you?'

Hesitantly, and with a strong feeling of repugnance, she replied: 'Yes.'

'Where can I see you alone?' asked the voice.

'You can't see me alone. Either send the seal back by post, or keep it.'

The voice said again, several times, in a very low tone: 'I'll send it ... I'll send it.'

She hung up the receiver, and reported the conversation to her husband.

'Do you think we ought to tell the police?' she asked him. He was engaged in testing a camera which could project stereoscopic images on to a three-dimensional screen.

'Have a look at this,' he said, 'it really is extraordinary. If one stands a little way off, the flowers seem to come out of the screen and move towards you.'

It was the very latest 'toy' from his Oklahoma friends. He had, as always, shown it to everybody at the lab., and then brought it home with him in the car 'so as to play with it this evening'.

'I have just asked you a serious question,' she said. 'What do you think I ought to do?'

She thought that she could not get him away from his toy. But this was his way of giving himself time to think. They decided finally that if the thief 'did the decent thing' and returned the seal, they mustn't lay a trap for him.

For some days, he had been teasing her about their Middle East journey: 'You want us to go? ... Well, I shall catch typhoid and die.' She begged him to have an anti-typhoid vaccination, but he kept on shilly-shallying.

On the Thursday, Compton told Lady Fleming that he had at last managed to give Sir Alexander the injection. 'Since he wouldn't come down to the clinic, I went and did him in his lab.,' he said with a gay laugh.

Fleming spent all day working at the Institute. He told Freeman how pleased he was at having got rid of his responsibilities, and to be able to do some real work and 'muck about at the bench again'. He seemed well and in a thoroughly good humour, planning all sorts of new research work. After leaving the hospital he went as usual to the Chelsea Arts Club for his game of snooker. His old friend, Dr Breen, thought he was looking remarkably fit and told him so. He replied that he had never felt better and that he was much looking forward to seeing Greece again with his wife.

When he had finished his game, he fetched her and they went on together to a party. After dinner, his son Robert and his fiancée came round, and once more the wonders of the new camera were demonstrated. Amalia was dropping with fatigue. Fleming was in high spirits and enjoyed showing off his marvellous toy. From time to time he scratched his arm which the inoculation had left rather sore.

On Friday morning, March 11th, he awoke in a very gay mood and watched with some amusement the eagerness with which his wife opened the post.

'You're hoping to find your seal, aren't you? You'll never see it again.'

He had a heavy but pleasant day ahead of him: lunch at the Savoy, and dinner with Douglas Fairbanks Junior and Eleanor Roosevelt. He got up, and went to have his bath. When he came back he looked very pale and complained of a feeling of nausea. Amalia felt frightened and went to the telephone to call a doctor. Fleming protested vigorously: 'Don't be ridiculous: don't trouble a doctor for nothing.'

But she had already got through. Dr John Hunt answered her: 'I'll be with you in an hour.' 'Not before that?' she exclaimed anxiously.

Fleming said again that she was being ridiculous, that he'd only been a bit sick. That was perfectly true. If only, she thought, she could learn to take things as calmly as he did, and not start worrying for nothing. Then, remembering the Fairbanks dinner, she wanted to ring up and say that Sir Alexander was too unwell to come.

'Don't do anything about it yet,' he said, 'it may not be necessary.'

He asked for some hot water to drink, then for bicarbonate of soda. He got to his feet and began to walk about the room. His healthy, vigorous body was trying to shake off the unexpected malaise, refusing to accept it. But he had to give in and go back to bed.

Amalia left the room to get dressed, leaving him for a short while with the maid. Dr Hunt, who had been alarmed at the anxiety in Lady Fleming's voice, rang her back. Fleming insisted on taking the call himself.

'Is it urgent? Shall I leave my other cases and come round at once?'

'No urgency whatsoever ... Look after your other patients first.'

His wife came back and found him lying on the bed, perfectly calm and peaceful. The attack, she thought, had passed, and, remembering that he had been inoculated the day before, asked him whether the feeling of sickness might not be a delayed reaction.

'No,' he said. His voice was serious. Then: 'Will you comb my hair?' When she had done this, he said: 'Now I am decent.'

She wanted to take his pulse. His arm was cold. 'Yes,' he said, 'I'm covered in cold sweat. And I don't know why I've got this pain in my chest.'

This time, she felt panic-stricken: 'Are you absolutely sure it's not your heart?'

'It's not the heart,' he said, 'it's going down from the oesophagus to the stomach.'

His voice was still strangely calm and serious. It was as though he were thinking deeply and trying to understand.

Suddenly his head fell forward.

Alexander Fleming was dead.

As the result of a supreme act of self-effacement, a sensitive desire that nobody should be disturbed on his account, a determination not to be in any way a privileged patient, the man who had given to medicine its most effective weapon against disease had died in the very heart of London without medical care. He died as he would have wished to die, in full possession of his strength, in full control of his fine intelligence. He died as he had lived, quietly, stoically, silently.

EPILOGUE

Only in extraordinary circumstances does the name of a scientist reach out beyond the borderline of science and take its place in the annals of humanity.

BALZAC

H E was buried in the crypt of St Paul's, a high honour conferred on only a few illustrious Englishmen. The ushers were drawn from among the students and nurses of St Mary's. Professor Pannett, his friend and companion since the day when they entered the world of medicine together, delivered the funeral oration:

Fifty-one years ago a small group of young men, most of us in our teens, met at St Mary's Hospital Medical School. We were competitors for a scholarship. It was there that I first met Alexander Fleming. He was a little older and more mature than the rest of us, a quiet man with alert, blue, penetrating, resolute eyes ... For the first few years we were rivals but afterwards our paths diverged, yet never was this bond of friendship strained, for Fleming had that steadiness and steadfastness of character that gave the quality of security to a friendship which lasted unsullied until his death. This constancy of his was outstanding and inspired a confidence in his friends and companions which was never misplaced ...

On that early autumn morning how far it was from our thoughts that we were in the presence of one of the greatest men of the century and that, one day, a large crowd would be gathered together in this beautiful cathedral to mourn the death of one acclaimed by the whole world as a scientific genius; and to do homage to his memory.

Tributes to his greatness have poured in from far and wide, for it is generally recognized that by his work he has saved more lives and relieved more suffering than any other living man, perhaps more than any man who has ever lived. This by itself is enough to alter the history of the world. His name will always be cherished as long as this Western culture, so dear to us, exists.

EPILOGUE

I shall not speak of his hopes, his strivings, his disappointments and frustrations ... Every great scientist knows these
and Fleming experienced them in full measure ... but there
is a remarkable aspect of Fleming's life which is not so widely
known. Looking back on his career, we find woven into the
web of his life a number of apparently irrelevant chance events
without one of which it would probably not have reached its
climax. There were so many of these events, and they were all
so purposive that we feel driven to deny their being due to
mere chance ...

His choice of a profession, his selection of a medical school,
his deviation into bacteriology, his meeting with Almroth
Wright, the nature of the work he did with him, the chance
drop of a tear, the chance fall of a mould, all these events
were surely not due to mere chance. We can almost see the
finger of God pointed to the direction his career should take
at every turn.

In the crypt of St Paul's, close to the towering tombs of Welling-
ton and Nelson, the letters 'A. F.' upon a flagstone discreetly mark
the spot wherein his ashes lie, and on the wall near by is a
tablet of Pentelic marble brought from Greece to London. On it
are carved the thistle of Scotland and the lily of St Mary's.
In this way are united three great loves of his life.

The shock of Fleming's death was felt far beyond England. Not
only did official expressions of regret reach his family from the
governments of many countries, but deeply moving tributes from
people in every walk of life. At Barcelona, the flower-sellers
emptied their baskets before the tablet on which his visit to their
city is commemorated. Two little girls of Bologna sent flowers
which they had bought with money saved for their father's
birthday present. Far and wide his name was given to streets and
squares, and subscription lists were opened in many cities for the
erection of monuments in his honour. In Greece the flags were
flown at half-mast. Two motorists driving through that country,
and surprised to see these signs of mourning in every village
through which they passed, asked an old shepherd near Delphi
the reason for this public display of grief. 'Do you not know,'
replied the old man, 'that Fleming is dead?'

275

THE LIFE OF SIR ALEXANDER FLEMING

The following leading article appeared in the *British Medical Journal* of March 19th:

THE DISCOVERY OF PENICILLIN

THE discovery of penicillin introduced a new epoch in the treatment of disease. It has been followed by an intense search for other 'antibiotics', and a whole range of bacterial infections have now come within the effective control of substances produced, for the most part, by moulds, among which *Penicillium notatum* holds pride of place not only historically but also therapeutically. We stand so close to a bewilderingly rapid sequence of discoveries that as yet we probably fail to understand fully the revolution in medicine that has taken and is taking place as a result of Alexander Fleming's discovery. It is natural that the world will acclaim a medical advance 'great' in proportion to the curative benefits it brings, and on this count alone Sir Alexander Fleming has his place among the immortals. And close beside him will be Sir Howard Florey and Dr Ernst Chain, who in a systematic investigation of antibacterial substances ten years later hit upon the technical ways and means of fulfilling the promise Fleming held out for penicillin in 1929. Fleming had the real naturalist's capacity for observation and the scientific imagination to see the implications of the observed fact — a capacity and an imagination which, it is true, only the prepared mind can compass, and which in the great discovery seem invariably to be joined to a mind that is essentially humble. As there have been some popular misconceptions of the part Fleming played in discovering penicillin it may not be inappropriate at this time of his death to recall in his own words some of the observations he summarized in his historical paper in the *British Journal of Experimental Pathology* for June 1929:

> A certain type of penicillium produces in culture a powerful antibacterial substance ...
> The active agent is readily filterable and the name 'penicillin' has been given to filtrates of broth cultures of the mould ...
> The action is very marked on the pyogenic cocci and the diptheria group of bacilli ...

EPILOGUE

Penicillin is non-toxic to animals in enormous doses and is not irritant. It does not interfere with leucocytic function to a greater degree than does ordinary broth ... It is suggested that it may be an efficient antiseptic for application to, or injection into, areas infected with penicillin-sensitive microbes ...

The discovery recorded in Fleming's paper is a milestone in the history of medical progress, and the 'penicillin' he discovered and named has come nearer than any other remedy to Ehrlich's ideal therapia sterilisans magna.

The discovery of penicillin has indeed opened 'a new epoch in the treatment of disease'. The doctor of today can hardly visualize how helpless his elders felt when confronted by certain infections. He has had no experience of that despair which descended upon them when they had to deal with diseases which were then fatal, but can now be cured and even eliminated. Penicillin, and the whole range of antibiotics which its discovery has initiated, has enabled the surgeon to perform operations which in the old days he would never have dared attempt. The average expectation of life has so enormously increased that the whole structure of society has been shaken to its foundations. No man, except Einstein in another field, and before him Pasteur, has had a more profound influence on the contemporary history of the human race. Statesmen act from hand to mouth, but scientists by their discoveries create the conditions in which action is possible.

How was it that this modest, silent research-worker became the beneficiary of the most remarkable piece of good luck to occur to anyone during his lifetime? Because he had patiently prepared himself to recognize and to accept the truth when the moment of its revelation came. 'In science nothing seems easier than what was discovered yesterday; nothing more difficult than to say what will be discovered tomorrow.'[1] Fleming observed much that other men might have observed but did not. The reason for this is that he had a sense of proportion which was all his own.

A flower growing in an unexpected way seemed as important

[1] Biot.

277

to him as the most spectacular of phenomena. The method employed by ants in the building of their nests was to him a miracle at which he peered with close attention. Everything in nature had aroused his interest since those boyhood days he spent upon the Scottish moors. Had he been sent to one of the public schools, he might have been less shy. He might have learned how to express his ideas and demonstrate his facts in a more dramatic fashion. He might have produced a more vivid impression on others. But would he, in that case, have preserved his astonishing freshness of mind?

Of what benefit to a man of profound intelligence are eloquence, self-confidence and brilliance? They may contribute much to his personal happiness, to his prestige, to his material success. But do they have any marked influence upon the importance of such real results as he may obtain? Let us take, for example, these two men, Wright and Fleming. Both had the same devotion to science. But Fleming, having nothing remotely resembling the gift of rhetoric, lacked the power — which Wright possessed in so high a degree — of striking the public imagination. Wright, it is true, had enemies, but even they, when confronted by that massive personality, could not deny him some element of greatness. Everyone knew that to question the value of his work would draw down upon the greatly daring critic a torrent of brilliant and sarcastic argument. What, on the other hand, more tempting than to think oneself superior to the small, shy stoic who would never do anything to dissipate that illusion? Without danger to oneself one could dispute his findings, since not for a moment would he break his formidable silence for, as he regarded it, so trivial a reason.

'The man of genius', writes Lord Beaverbrook, 'is often an egotist. When, as sometimes happens, he is simple and retiring, the world is inclined to underestimate his gifts. Sir Alexander Fleming was a genius of this rare type. Now, to be sure, his fame is universal ... During his lifetime, and in his own country, his merits were sometimes reluctantly admitted.' It may be that justice would have been sooner done to him had he been less reticent, if on occasion he had said something. But what? In spite of his silences, it was he who reached the goal.

The best final judgment on Sir Alexander Fleming is that of Professor Haddow, Director of the Cancer Research Institutes who writes of him:

He was a great natural searcher. He knew the importance of work, and he worked hard for the attainment of great ends, but his real superiority is to be found in his tremendous gift of discernment, in the swiftness with which he could *pounce* upon and grip an unexpected observation the true significance of which would have remained hidden from the ordinary mortal ... in other words, in the power he had to reveal the existence and qualities of fundamental phenomena ... It should never be forgotten that though, for the generality of laymen, it is with penicillin that his name is associated, he contributed other things which, in his eyes, were of no less value, perhaps of even greater value, than penicillin. For this reason alone he would have been a great man, but I think that I would rank higher than anything else in him his tremendous and quiet wisdom, both as regards the world and the nature of research, a wisdom so unruffled and so modest that it escaped most people who knew him only a little. Three things about him struck me most forcibly. This man realized that work mattered, not talk. His real brilliance which consisted in seizing upon the unexpressed and not ignoring it; and, thirdly, his philosophy — hardly expressed and only to be guessed — which amounted to tremendous wisdom about the nature of science and scientific research and, I often think, the world at large and his summing up of other people.

The tribute which would have touched Fleming most deeply was that paid to his memory on October 10th, 1957, in his own county of Ayrshire. On that day a very simple monument was unveiled at the entrance gate to Lochfield farm: a tall block of red granite bearing, as he would have wished, this unemphatic inscription:

SIR ALEXANDER FLEMING

DISCOVERER OF PENICILLIN
WAS BORN HERE AT LOCHFIELD
ON 6TH AUGUST 1881

A few cars had climbed the moorland road from Darvel, and a great crowd had trudged the four miles on foot, as he himself had been used to do as a boy on his way to and from school. When the flags, marked with the St Andrew's Cross, had been pulled aside, the Provost spoke of Alec Fleming's childhood. Here, he had received from those sterling parents, Hugh and Grace Fleming, the instruction which guided him through life. In these valleys, and on these hills, he had learned, at work and play, to know nature and to love it. His wife, looking at the lovely autumn sky, at the vast horizons, and at the gentle undulations of the hills, realized that the lofty indifference to all pettiness of life which she had so dearly loved in her husband had been engendered by those mingled feelings of strength and humility which such solitudes evoke.

Nobody, on that 6th August, 1881 [went on the Provost] dreamed that the tiny, weak and puling scrap of humanity then starting on its life, was to be dedicated to the service of mankind. Fleming himself once wrote: 'We like to think that we control our destinies, but Shakespeare, perhaps, showed greater wisdom when he said:

> There's a divinity that shapes our ends,
> Rough-hew them how we will.'

Each one of us, looking back over his past life, may wonder what would have happened had he done something other than he did do, often for no particular reason. At every moment there are two roads open to us. One we must choose. Where the other might have led we cannot know. It may be that we chose the better, but who can say?

Fleming had chosen the good road, and Destiny, all things considered, had been kind to him.

BIBLIOGRAPHY

ALEXANDER FLEMING'S MANUSCRIPTS

Letters	Talks
Diaries	Laboratory notebooks
Conferences	Student notebooks
Lectures	

Dr S. Craddock's laboratory notebook on penicillin
Dr F. Ridley's laboratory notebook on penicillin

LETTERS OF:

Prof. H. Berry	John E. McKeen
Dr Charles H. Bradford	Ben May
R. Bradford	Sandy Ross
John Cameron	Marion Stirling
Professor C. J. La Touche	Dr Charles Thom
Professor Roger Lee	Dr E. W. Todd

MANUSCRIPT RECOLLECTIONS BY:

Dr V. D. Allison	Mr A. G. Cross
Lord Beaverbrook	Prof. R. Cruickshank
Prof. H. Berry	Sir Henry Dale
Sir Russell Brain	Bebe Daniels (Mrs Ben Lyon)
Dr G. E. Breen	Mrs M. B. Davis
Dr W. D. W. Brooks	Dr H. B. Day
Mrs Helen Buckley	Sir Charles Dodds
H. J. Bunker	Dr Denis Dooley
Prof. G. A. H. Buttle	Prof. Allan W. Downie
John Cameron	Mrs Sheila Doyle
Dr P. N. Cardew	The Rev. Hamilton Dunnett
T. S. Carswell	Dr C. B. Dyson
Prof. E. B. Chain	Dr M. J. Fenton
Sir Weldon Dalrymple Champneys	Bryan E. Figgis
W. Clayden	E. D. H. Firman
Dr H. A. Clegg	Sir Wilfrid Fish
Dr Alvin F. Coburn	Peter Flood
Dr R. D. Coghill	Dr A. W. Frankland
Dr L. Colebrook	Dr John Freeman
Dr A. Compton	Dr R. M. Fry
Sir Zachary Cope	D. J. Fyffe
Dr Stuart Craddock	Dr Hope Gosse
Victor Craxton	Prof. A. Haddow

281

Mr R. M. Handfield-Jones
Dr A. F. Hayden
Dr W. L. A. Harrison
Dr Leslie D. Harrop
Arthur Hayward
Dr W. E. van Heyningen
Dr Gladys Hobley
Dr R. E. B. Hudson
Dr W. H. Hughes
Dr Thomas Hunt
Prof. G. Ioakimoglou
James Jackson
Dr G. W. B. James
L. Jennings
Dr W. Hewitt Jones
Dr Norman Keith
Mrs Hanbury Kelk
Dr Omar Khairat
Dr J. Hugh Laidlow
Prof. C. J. La Touche
Prof. Roger Lee
Dr R. T. Leiper
James Leitch
Dr A. J. Liebmann
Prof. R. Lovell
E. G. Lumley
Sir Alexander McCall
Dr G. L. M. McElligott
Lord McGowan
John E. McKeen
Mrs K. MacKinnon
Mr Douglas MacLeod
Arthur MacMillan
Mrs A. MacMillan
Prof. H. B. Maitland
D. J. Markianos
Dr A. J. May
Ben May
Dr Robert May
Gustavo Gran Mederos
Lady Mellanby
Arthur Mortimer
William Morton
A. Murray

Henry Nash
Prof. W. D. Newcomb
Sir Hazelton Nichols
Dr A. C. F. Ogilvie
Prof. J. W. Orr
Prof. C. A. Pannett
Dr H. J. Parish
Mr Francis I. Peck
Miss Marjory Pegram
Mrs B. Pontremoli
Sir Arthur Porritt
Dr A. B. Porteous
Prof. D. M. Pryce
Dr Roger D. Reid
Dr G. Raymond Rettew
Mrs Elizabeth Reynolds
Prof. Alfred N. Richards
Dr Frederick Ridley
Dr Leo Rigler
A. M. Ritchie
Mrs A. M. Ritchie
Dr K. B. Rogers
Sandy Ross
Miss Agnes Smith
Prof. Wilson Smith
G. Stevenson
Dr G. T. Stewart
Dr K. K. Stokes
Dr E. J. Storer
D. Stratful
Iain Sullivan
Miss Margarita Tamargo
Miss L. Theodoridou
Lady Thomson
Dr H. L. Thornton
Mrs E. W. Todd
Richard Townsend
G. Wackrill
Lord Webb-Johnson
Dr Gerald Willcox
Dr Philip H. A. Willcox
Mr Leslie Williams
J. Willis
Alexander Zaiger

ON THE INDUSTRIAL DEVELOPMENT OF PENICILLIN

Minutes of the Penicillin Committee – England
Reports by Imperial Chemical Industries – England
Reports by Boots Pure Drug Co. Ltd – England
Reports by Glaxo Laboratories Ltd – England
Dr Alfred N. Richards – U.S.A.
Dr R. D. Coghill for Abbott Laboratories – U.S.A.
Charles Pfizer, Inc. – U.S.A.
Dr G. Raymond Rettew for the Chester County Mushroom Laboratories and Wyeth
   Laboratories – U.S.A.
Dr Leslie D. Harrop for the Upjohn Co. – U.S.A.

BIBLIOGRAPHY

ALEXANDER FLEMING'S PUBLICATIONS DISCUSSED IN THIS BOOK

'The accuracy of opsonic estimations' (1908); *Practitioner*, vol. LXXX, No. 5.

'Acute bacterial infections with special reference to the means of investigation of the causal agent and the more recent immunizatory methods of treatment' (1908); manuscript thesis.

'On the etiology of acne vulgaris and its treatment by vaccines' (1909); *Lancet*, vol. I, p. 1035.

'A simple method of serum diagnosis of syphilis' (1909); *Lancet*, vol. I, p. 1512.

'Bacteriology and vaccine treatment of acne vulgaris' (1909); *B.M.J.*, vol. II, p. 533.

'On the use of salvarsan in the treatment of syphilis' (1911); *Lancet*, vol. I, p. 1631. (In collaboration with L. Colebrook.)

'Recent work on vaccine' (1913); *Practitioner*, vol. XC, pp. 591-7.

'On the bacteriology of septic wounds' (1915); *Lancet*, vol. II, p. 538.

'Some notes on the bacteriology of gas-gangrene' (1915); *Lancet*, vol. II, p. 376.

'Fashions in wound treatment' (1916); *St Mary's Hosp. Gaz.*, vol. XXII, pp. 60-3.

'Studies in wound infections. On the question of bacterial symbiosis in wound infections' (1917); *Lancet*, vol. I, p. 604. (In collaboration with S. R. Douglas and L. Colebrook.)

'The physiological and antiseptic action of flavine, with some observations on the testing of antiseptics' (1917); *Lancet*, vol. II, p. 341.

'Studies in wound infections. On the growth of anaerobic bacilli in fluid media under apparently anaerobic conditions' (1917); *Lancet*, vol. II, p. 530. (In collaboration with S. R. Douglas and L. Colebrook.)

'Further observations on acidaemia in gas-gangrene, and on conditions which favour the growth of its infective agent in the blood fluids' (1918); *Lancet*, vol. I, p. 205. (In collaboration with A. E. Wright.)

'The conditions under which the sterilization of wounds by physiological agency can be obtained' (1918); *Lancet*, vol. I, p. 831. (In collaboration with A. E. Wright and L. Colebrook.)

'On some simply prepared culture media for B. influenza' (1919); *Lancet*, vol. I, p. 136.

'The anaerobic infections of war wounds'; *M.R.C. Anaerobic Committee Report*, No. 39, Section 7, p. 70.

'The influence of the aerobic on the anaerobic infection in wounds'; *M.R.C. Anaerobic Committee Report*, No. 39, Section 8, p. 84.

'Blood transfusion by the citrate method' (1919); *Lancet*, vol. I, p. 973. (In collaboration with A. B. Porteous.)

'On streptococcal infections of septic wounds at a base hospital' (1919); *Lancet*, vol. II, p. 49. (In collaboration with A. B. Porteous.)

'An experimental research into the specificity of the agglutinus produced by Pfeiffer's bacillus' (1919); *Lancet*, vol. II, p. 869. (In collaboration with F. J. Clemenger.)

'The action of chemical and physiological antiseptics in a septic wound' (1919, the Hunterian Lecture); *Brit. J. Sur.*, vol. VII, No. 25, p. 99.

'Vaccine therapy in regard to general practice' (1921); *B.M.J.*, vol. I, pp. 255-69.

'On a remarkable bacteriolytic element found in tissues and secretions' (1922); *Proc. Roy. Soc.*, B, vol. XCIII, p. 306.

'Further observations on a bacteriolytic element found in tissues and secretions' (1922); *Proc. Roy. Soc.*, B, vol. XCIV, p. 142. (In collaboration with V. D. Allison.)

'Observations on a bacteriolytic substance – lysozyme – found in secretions and tissues' (1922); *Brit. J. Exp. Path.*, vol. III, No. 5, p. 252. (In collaboration with V. D. Allison.)

'A comparison of the activities of antiseptics on bacteria and on leucocytes' (1924); *Proc. Roy. Soc.*, B, vol. XCVI, p. 171.

'On the antibacterial power of egg-white' (1924); *Lancet*, vol. I, p. 1303. (In collaboration with V. D. Allison.)

'On the specificity of the protein of human tears' (1925); *Brit. J. Exp. Path.*, vol. VI, p. 87. (In collaboration with V. D. Allison.)

'On the effect of variations of the salt content of blood on its bactericidal power *in vitro* and *in vivo*' (1926); *Brit. J. Exp. Path.*, vol. VII, p. 274.

'A simple method of removing leucocytes from blood' (1926); *Brit. J. Exp. Path.*, vol. VII, p. 281.

'On the development of strains of bacteria resistant to lysozyme action and the relation of lysozyme action to intracellular digestion' (1927); *Brit. J. Exp. Path.*, vol. VIII, p. 214. (In collaboration with V. D. Allison.)

'The bactericidal power of human blood and some methods of altering it' (1928); *Proc. R. Soc. Med.*, vol. XXI, p. 839.

'On the antibacterial action of cultures of a penicillium with special reference to their use in the isolation of B. influenzae' (1929); *Brit. J. Exp. Path.*, vol. X, pp. 226-36.

'A bacteriolytic ferment found normally in tissues and secretions' (1929, Arris and Gale Lecture on Lysozyme); *Lancet*, vol. I, p. 217.

'On the occurrence of influenza bacilli in the mouth of normal people' (1930); *Brit. J. Exp. Path.*, vol. XI, p. 127. (In collaboration with Ian H. Maclean.)

'The intravenous use of germicides' (1931); *Proc. R. Soc. Med.*, vol. XXIV, p. 46.

'Some problems in the use of antiseptics' (1931); *Brit. Dent. J.*, vol. LII, p. 105.

'Lysozyme' (1932, President's Address); *Proc. R. Soc. Med.*, vol. XXVI, pp. 1-15.

'On the specific antibacterial properties of penicillin and potassium tellurite. Incorporating a method of demonstrating some bacterial antagonisms' (1932); *J. Path. Bact.*, vol. XXXV, p. 831.

'Selective bacteriostasis' (1936); *Proc. Second International Cong. for Microbiology*, pp. 33-4.

'The growth of micro-organisms on paper' (1936); *Proc. Second International Cong. for Microbiology*, pp. 552-3.

'The antibacterial action *in vitro* of 2-(p-aminobenzenesulphonamido) pyridine on pneumococci and streptococci' (1938); *Lancet*, vol. II, p. 74.

'The antibacterial power of the blood of patients receiving 2-(aminobenzene-sulphonamido) pyridine' (1938); *Lancet*, vol. II, p. 564.

'M and B 693 and pneumococci' (1939); *Lancet*, vol. I, p. 562. (In collaboration with Ian H. Maclean and K. B. Rogers.)

'Sulphanilamide; its use and misuse' (1939); *Tr. M. Soc. Lond.*, vol. LXII, pp. 19-43.

'Serum and vaccine therapy in combination with sulphanilamide or M and B 693' (1939); *Proc. R. Soc. Med.*, vol. XXXII, p. 911.

'Antiseptic and chemotherapy' (1939); *Proc. R. Soc. Med.*, vol. XXXIII, p. 127.

'Observations on the bacteriostatic action of sulphanilamide and M and B 693 and on the influence thereon of bacteria and peptone' (1940); *J. Path. Bact.*, vol. L, No. 1, p. 69.

'Chemotherapy and wound infection' (1941); *Proc. R. Soc. Med.*, vol. XXXIV, p. 342.

'Penicillin' (1941); *B.M.J.*, vol. II, p. 386.

'A simple method of using penicillin, potassium tellurite and gentian violet for differential culture' (1942); *B.M.J.*, vol. I, p. 547.

'*In vitro* tests of penicillin potency' (1942); *Lancet*, vol. I, p. 732.

'Streptococcal meningitis treated with penicillin' (1943); *Lancet*, vol. II, p. 434.

'The use of paper and cellophane discs for the preparation of museum specimens of mould culture' (1943); *Proc. of the Linnaean Soc. of London*, Session 155.

'The discovery of penicillin' (1944); *Brit. Med. Bull.*, vol. II, No. 1, p. 4.

'Penicillin for selective culture and for demonstrating bacterial inhibitions' (1944); *Brit. Med. Bull.*, vol. II, No. 1, p. 7.

'Some methods for the study of moulds' (1944); *Trans. of Br. Mycol. Soc.*, vol. XXVII, p. 13. (In collaboration with G. Smith.)

'Penicillin' (1944, the Robert Campbell Oration); *Ulster Med. J.*, Nov. 1944.

'Micromethods of estimating penicillin in blood serum' (1944); *Lancet*, vol. II, p. 620.

'Penicillin content of blood serum after various doses of penicillin by various routes' (1944); *Lancet*, vol. II, p. 621. (In collaboration with M. Y. Young, J. Suchet and A. J. E. Rowe.)

'Micro-methods of estimating penicillin in blood serum and other body fluids' (1945); *Amer. J. Clin. Path.*, vol. XV, No. 1.

BIBLIOGRAPHY

'Antiseptics' (1945, Lister Memorial Lecture); *Chem. and Ind.*, No. 3, pp. 18-23.
'Penicillin; its discovery, development and uses in the field of medicine and surgery' (1944, the Harben Lectures); *J. Roy. Inst. Public Health and Hygiene*, 1945.
'Penicillin', Nobel Lecture, Stockholm, Dec. 1945.
'Chemotherapy yesterday, today and tomorrow' (1946, the Linacre Lecture, Cambridge).
'The assay of penicillin in the days before it was concentrated' (1945-6); *Bull. Health Org. L. of N.*, vol. XII, Extract No. 7.
'Uses and limitations of penicillin' (1946); *Tr. M. Soc. Lond.*, vol. LXIV, pp. 142-9.
'Estimation of penicillin in serum. Use of glucose, phenol red and serum water' (1947); *Lancet*, vol. I, p. 401. (In collaboration with C. Smith.)
'Louis Pasteur' (1947); *B.M.J.*, vol. I, p. 517.
'Some problems in the titration of streptomycin' (1947); *B.M.J.*, vol. I, p. 627. (In collaboration with J. R. May and A. E. Voureka.)
'The morphology and motility of Proteus Vulgaris and other organisms cultured in the presence of penicillin' (1950); *J. Gen. Microb.*, vol. IV, No. 2, p. 257. (In collaboration with A. Voureka, I. R. H. Kramer and W. H. Hughes.)
'Further observations on the motility of Proteus Vulgaris grown on penicillin agar' (1950); *J. Gen. Microb.*, vol. IV, No. 3, p. 457.
'Motilité et cils de Proteus Vulgaris' (Nov. 1950); *Ann. Inst. Pasteur*, T. 79, p. 604.
'Hommage à Jules Bordet au nom des savants étrangers' (Nov. 1950); *Ann. Inst. Pasteur*, T. 79, p. 495.
'The action of penicillin on the morphology and character of bacteria' (1952); *Proceedings of the Academy of Athens*.
'Success' (1952, Rectorial Address, Edinburgh); *Student*, vol. XLVII, No. 8.
'Recent progress in antibiotics' (1953); *The Scientific Basis of Medicine*, vol. II, pp. 29-45, Athlone Press, 1954.
'Twentieth-century changes in the treatment of septic infections' (1953); *New Engl. J. Med.*, vol. CCXLVIII, pp. 1037-45.
Antibiotics; The Royal Inst. of Great Britain, Nov. 27th, 1953.
'La thérapeutique par les antibiotiques' (1954); *Gazette des Hôpitaux*, No. 6, p. 95.
'A test to show the relative toxicity of a chemical to bacteria and to human leucocytes' (1954); *Int. Arch. Allergy*, vol. V, No. 2 (Paul Ehrlich Memorial Number).
'The Wright-Fleming Institute of Microbiology' (1954); *St Mary's Hosp. Gaz.*, vol. LX, No. 8.

OTHER PAPERS AND PUBLICATIONS

A. E. Wright (*v.* Bernard Shaw): 'The medical aspect of women's suffrage' (1910); *St Mary's Hosp. Gaz.*, vol. XVI, 1910, p. 7.
Col. Sir Almroth E. Wright: 'The question as to how septic war wounds should be treated' (reply to polemical criticism published by Sir W. Watson Cheyne in the *Brit. J. Sur.*) (1916); *Lancet*, vol. II, p. 503.
P. W. Clutterbuck and R. Lovell: 'The formation by P. chrysogenum Thom of a pigment, an alkali-soluble protein and penicillin (Fleming's antibacterial substance) in a synthetic medium' (1931); *J. Soc. Chem. Ind. Transactions*, vol. L, p. 1045.
Percival Walter Clutterbuck, Reginald Lovell and Harold Raistrick: 'The formation from glucose by members of the Penicillium chrysogenum series of a pigment, an alkali-soluble protein and penicillin – the antibacterial substance of Fleming' (1932); *The Biochemical Journal*, vol. XXVI, No. 6.
Dr Roger Reid: 'Some properties of a bacterial inhibitory substance produced by a mould' (1935); *J. Bact.*, vol. XXIX, p. 215.
E. Chain, H. W. Florey, A. D. Gardner, N. G. Heatley, M. A. Jennings, J. Orr-Ewing, A. G. Sanders: 'Penicillin as a chemotherapeutic agent' (1940); *Lancet*, vol. II, p. 226.
Dr Robert D. Coghill: 'Penicillin – Science's Cinderella. The background of penicillin production' (1944); *Chemical and Engineering News*, vol. XXII, pp. 588-93.
R. D. Coghill and Roy S. Koch: 'Penicillin – A wartime accomplishment' (1945); *Chemical and Engineering News*, vol. XXIII, p. 2310.

THE LIFE OF SIR ALEXANDER FLEMING

Sir Almroth Wright: *The History and Development of the Inoculation Department* (1945).
Sir Alexander Fleming: *Sir Almroth Wright*.
J. Freeman: *Almroth Wright*.
Mayo Foundation House Proceedings, July 16th, 1945.
Annals of the Royal College of Surgeons of England, vol. VI, Feb. 1950.
London Scottish Regimental Gazette: 1944, No. 583, vol. XLIX, p. 132; 1947, April, p. 59; 1954, No. 698, vol. LIX, p. 42.
St Mary's Hospital Gazette: vol. LX, No. 5, 1954; vol. LXI, No. 3, 1955.

BOOKS

The Medical Research Club: The First Sixty Years, 1891-1951.
A. E. Wright: *Technique of the Teat and Capillary Glass Tube and its Application in Medicine and Bacteriology*, Constable, 1912 (and 2nd edition, 1921, with the collaboration of L. Colebrook).
A. E. Wright: *The Unexpurgated Case against Woman Suffrage*, Constable, 1913.
A System of Bacteriology, His Majesty's Stationery Office, 1931.
A. E. Wright: *Prolegomena to the Logic which Searches for Truth*, Heinemann, 1941.
A. E. Wright: *Pathology and Treatment of War Wounds*, Heinemann, 1942.
Alexander Fleming: *Penicillin*, Butterworth Medical Publications, 1946 (1950).
Florey, Chain, Heatley, Jennings, Sanders, Abraham: *Antibiotics*, Oxford Medica Publications, 1949.
M. E. Florey: *The Clinical Applications of Antibiotics* (Penicillin), Oxford Medical Publications, 1952.
G. W. S. Andrews and J. Miller: *Penicillin and Other Antibiotics*, Todd Publishing Group, 1949.
Paul de Kruif: *Life Among the Doctors*, Harcourt Brace, 1949.
David Masters: *Miracle Drug*, Eyre & Spottiswoode, 1946.
L. J. Ludovici: *Fleming, Discoverer of Penicillin*, Andrew Dakers, 1952.
Leonard Colebrook: *Almroth Wright*, Heinemann, 1954.
Sir Zachary Cope: *The History of St Mary's Hospital Medical School*, Heinemann, 1954.
Sir Cecil Weir: *Civil Assignment*, Methuen, 1953.
A. E. Wright: *Alethetropic Logic; A Posthumous Work*, Heinemann, 1953.
Robert Fleming: 'Alec Fleming of Lochfield' (manuscript).

OBITUARY NOTICES AND ADDRESSES ON ALEXANDER FLEMING

Dr V. D. Allison
Prof. Léon Binet (Paris)
Prof. F. Bustinza (Madrid)
Dr L. Colebrook
Mr A. G. Cross
Prof. R. Cruickshank
Dr John Freeman

Mr R. M. Handfield-Jones
Prof. G. Ioakimoglou (Greece)
Dr G. L. M. McElligott
Prof. W. D. Newcomb
Prof. C. A. Pannett
Sir Arthur Porritt

Note: All documents referred to in this bibliography, or copies of them, have been deposited with the Sir Alexander Fleming Museum in the Wright-Fleming Institute.

INDEX

INDEX

ABRAHAM, DR, 160, 169
Aga Khan, H.H. the, 248
Aird, Martha, 22
Alba, Duke of, 231
Albert, Prince Consort, 31
Alivisatos, Prof., 222
Allison, Dr V. D., 104-5, 109-10, 116-17, 119, 178-9
Almroth, Prof. Nils, 40
Argenlieu, Adml d', 228
Athens, Archbishop of, 252-3
Aureomycin, 233

BALFOUR, A. J. (LORD), 40, 51, 55, 61, 92
Barker, H. Granville, 51
Barnes, J., 164
Baron (sculptor), 228-9
Bayer company (Germany), 145-6
Bayet, A., 208
B.B.C., 200
Beaverbrook, Lord, 106, 143, 278
Behring, 44-5, 81
Benda, J., 208
Bernard, C., 209
Berry, Prof. H., 153
Bevan, A., M.P., 256-7
Billoux, 208
Biot, Jean Baptiste, 277n
Bliss, R. W., 94
Boer War, 27-8, 47
Bogomoletz, 229
Bonn, Sir M., 61
Boots Pure Drug Co. Ltd, 184, 207
Bordet, Prof. J., 78-9, 122, 138, 198-9, 238
Boswell, James, 18
Bovet, 146
Breen, Dr G. E., 146, 149, 213, 272
Brinton, 71
British Council, 221, 226, 261
British Drug Houses Ltd, 184
British Medical Journal tribute, 276
Broch, Major, 206
Brooks, Dr W. D. W., 216
Buckley, Mrs H., 183, 193-4, 216-17
Budapest Congress (1894), 45
Bulloch, W., 40
Burns, John, 51
Burroughs Wellcome & Co., 184
Bustinza, Prof. F., 229, 231

CALVÉ, J., 94
Cameron, J., 201-3, 205, 211-12
Carrel, 88

Chain, Prof. E. B., 135, 139, 160-7, 169, 179, 188, 204, 211-12, 276
Chantemesse, 44, 46
Chelsea Arts Club, 77-8, 102, 131, 149, 213, 231, 234, 238, 259, 272
Cheyne, Sir W. Watson, 40, 89-91
Chloromycetin, 233
Churchill, Sir W., 32, 210-11
Clayden, W., 94-5, 193, 196, 198
Clegg, Dr H. A., 199-200
Clutterbuck, P. W., 138-9
Coburn, Dr A. F., 158
Coghill, Dr R. D., 173, 191-2, 201
Colebrook, Dr L., 40n, 50, 70, 71, 79, 84, 92, 94, 147, 154
Compton, Dr A., 141, 191, 271
Conant, Dr, 203
Cooper, A. Duff (Lord Norwich), 208
Cope, Sir Z., 36, 63, 106, 197-8, 213, 267
Coutsouris-Voureka, Dr A., *see* Voureka, Dr A. Coutsouris-
Craddock, Dr S., 131-6, 156-8, 167
Craxton, V., 105, 197, 214, 215, 216, 268, 269
Cruickshank, Prof. R., 12, 65, 219
Cushing, H., 93-4

DAKIN, 88
Dale, Sir H., 116, 136, 154, 185
Daniels, Bebe (Mrs Ben Lyon), 200-1
Darvel school, 23
Davaine, Dr, 42
Davis, Mrs Richard, 76, 78, 209
Debré, Prof. R., 54, 209
Delaunay, Dr A., 12, 147
Derby, Lord, 92
Detrez, Monseigneur, 228
Doctor's Dilemma, The, 51-3, 194
Domagk, 145
Douglas, Capt. S., 48-9, 49-50, 84
Dowden, Prof. E., 41
Downie, Mrs A. W., 176
Downie, Prof. A. W., 176
Dreyer, 163
Dubos, Dr, 43-4, 139, 155, 158
Duchesne, Dr, 129
Duhamel, G., 208
Duncan, Sir A., 183
Duval, Prof. P., 94
Dyers, Worshipful Company of, 238
Dyson, Dr C. B., 104, 117, 156

EDINBURGH, DUKE OF, 266
Edinburgh University, 247-51

T   289

Ehrlich, P., 51, 62, 66-8, 71, 81, 108, 130, 145, 146, 148, 149, 277
Einstein, 277
Elisabeth, Queen of the Belgians, 211, 238
Elizabeth, Queen, the Queen Mother, 143, 267
Éluard, P., 208
Epstein (Rhodes Scholar), 161
Evangelismos Hospital, Athens, 239, 241, 254

FAIRBANKS, DOUGLAS, JUN., 272
Finlay, 262
First World War, 83-98
Fleming, Lady (Amalia), 11-12, 260-73, see also Voureka, Dr A. Coutsouris-
Fleming, Lady (Sarah M.), 98-103, 133, 158, 176, 177, 191, 196, 212, 219, 227, 229, 230, 231, 233-4, 235
Fleming, Elizabeth (sister-in-law), 98, 99, 177, 234, 258
Fleming, Grace (mother), 19, 25, 28, 280
Fleming, Grace (sister), 20, 26
Fleming, Hugh (father), 19-20, 280
Fleming, Hugh (grandfather), 19
Fleming, Hugh (stepbrother), 19, 20, 24, 25, 26, 28
Fleming, John (brother), 20, 21, 22, 24-5, 26, 27, 99, 144-5, 233, 234
Fleming, John (uncle), 28
Fleming, Mary (grandmother), 19
Fleming, Mary (stepsister), 19, 25, 26
Fleming, Robert (brother), 12, 20-1, 25, 26, 27, 28, 33, 35, 99, 178, 212, 214, 234
Fleming, Robert (son), 100-1, 177, 191, 212, 219, 234, 272
Fleming, Sir Alexander,
birth and upbringing, 17-22
schooling, 22-6
first employment, 26-9
in London Scottish, 27-8, 35, 71, 74
enters St Mary's, 30ff
London Matriculation, 31
methods of study and successes, 31-3
becomes F.R.C.S., 34, 63
joins Sir A. Wright, 36-8
methods and record there, 54ff
relations with Sir A. Wright, 55-65
scientific style, 60
Gold Medal (London) and Cheadle Medal (St Mary's), 63
injects self with staphylococci, 64
successes with salvarsan, 68-71
view of psychology, 69-70
diagnostic accuracy, 71-2
social interests, 74-8
modifies Wasserman Reaction, 78
in France with R.A.M.C., 84-97
first marriage, 98ff
Suffolk home ('The Dhoon'), 100ff
and house in Chelsea, 102
delivers Hunterian Lecture (1919), 107-8
investigates lysozyme, 110-22
experiments with 'moulds', 124ff
discovery of pencillin, 131-42
and sulphonamides, 146-58
death of brother John, 144-5
perfection and negotiations for mass-production of penicillin, 159-75
Regional Pathologist (Harefield), 176ff
bombs on Chelsea house, 177-8
Sir A. Wright's letter to The Times, 182
F.R.S., 189-91
huge demands for penicillin, 192
activities in 1944 blitz, 193-4
knighted (1944), 196-8
Freedoms of London and Darvel, 199
President of Society of General Microbiology, 199
visits U.S.A., 201-5
Harvard Doctorate, 203
acclaimed in France, Belgium and Sweden, 206-12
appointed Commander of the Legion of Honour, 208
Pasteur Medal, 208
three honorary degrees in Belgium, 210-11
with Chain and Florey, awarded Nobel Prize (1945), 211-12
Gold Medal of Royal College of Surgeons, 213
succeeds Sir A. Wright as Principal, 213-14
member of Académie Septentrionale, 228
acclaim and honours in Spain, 229-31
Freedom of Chelsea, 231
member of Pontifical Academy of Sciences, audience with the Pope, 231
visits U.S.A., 232-3
death of first wife, 233-4
significant observations (with Dr Amalia Voureka) on proteus vulgaris, 235-6
visits Dublin, Leeds (for Addingham Medal), U.S.A., Milan, Brazil, Rome, Brussels (to honour Prof. Jules Bordet), Stockholm (Nobel Institute), and Pakistan (UNESCO congress), 237-40
member of Commission of International Scientific Conferences, 247

INDEX

Rector of Edinburgh University, 247-51
visits Switzerland (for World Health Organization), 251
and Athens (for C.I.S.C.), 251-5
explores Greece with Dr Amalia Voureka, 251-5
Freedom of Athens, 254
proposes to Dr Voureka, 255
acclaimed in India, 256-7
marriage to Dr Amalia Voureka, 258-9
visits Cuba, 261-2
and U.S.A., 262-3
views on the National Health Service, 264
sudden illness prevents visit to Nice (Lady Fleming attends in his place), 265-6
at installation of the Duke of Edinburgh as Chancellor of Edinburgh University, 266-7
visits France, 267
resigns as Principal of Wright-Fleming Institute, 268-9
plans new work and visit to Middle East, 269-70, 271-2
burglary at Chelsea house, 270-1
death, 272-3
burial and tributes, 274-80
Fleming, Tom (stepbrother), 19, 20, 24, 25-6, 28
Flood, P., 156
Florey, Dr Ethel (Lady), 159, 188
Florey, Sir H., 139, 159-75, 179, 181, 183-5, 188, 204, 211-12, 276
Foch, Marshal F., 97
Fonbrune, Dr de, 236-7
Fourneau, Prof., 147
Frederika, Queen of Greece, 254
Freeman, Dr J., 36-7, 40, 50, 51, 54, 58, 62, 71, 72-3, 78-9, 80, 82, 84, 88-9, 94, 103-4
Fry, Dr R. M., 72, 105
Fyffe, D. J., 246-7

Gardner, A. D., 161n, 167
Gaulle, Gen. Charles de, 207, 208
George, King of Greece, 254
George V, King, 143
George VI, King, 196
Glaxo Laboratories Ltd, 184, 207
Gratia, Prof., 103
Gray, Ronald, 75-8, 190
Greece, Prime Minister of, 252
Greene, Prof. Clayton, 33
Gruber, 45-6

Guedalla, P., 194
Guëll, Vizconde de, 229

Haddow, Prof. A., 278-9
Haffkine, 46
Haldane, Lord, 51
Hammersley, Mrs, 75-6
Handfield-Jones, R. M., 189-90
Hayden, Dr, 73
Heatley, N. G., 165, 166, 169, 170, 172, 173, 174
Heyningen, Dr W. E. van, 218-19
Hollis, Dr, 65
Holt, Dr, 141-2, 145
Hopkins, Sir F. Gowland, 160
Horner, Lady, 51, 62
Hudson, Dr R., 176-7
Hughes, Dr W. H., 39, 197, 217, 228, 234
Huisman, G., 228
Hunt, Dr J., 272-3

I.C.I., 184
International Congress of Microbiology
(1930), 122
(1936), 152-3
(1939), 158
Ioakimoglou, Prof. G., 254
Iveagh, Lord, 141, 143

James, Dr G. W. B., 12, 68, 83, 92-3
Jenner, Dr, 43, 44, 60
Jennings, Dr M. A., 167, 228
Jennings, L., 131
Johnson, Dr Samuel, 18, 62
Jones, Dr Carmalt, 33, 34, 50
Joubert, 129

Kaminker, 208
Keith, Dr N., 94, 95-6, 262-3
Kemball, Bishop & Co. Ltd, 184
Kenny, M., 147
Kent (Florey's assistant), 166
Keogh, Sir A., 85
Kilmarnock Academy, 23
Koch, Capt., 206
Koch, Prof., 42, 44
Kolle, 47
Kramer, Dr I. R. H., 234
Kruif, Paul de, 185n

Laidlaw, Dr, 153-4
Laporte, Dr, 209
La Touche, Prof. C. J., 127, 132
Le Corbusier, 208
Lee, Prof. Roger, 93-4, 203, 204, 209, 256, 263
Lee, Mrs Roger, 256, 263, 266

INDEX

Lemierre, 209
Leopold II, King of the Belgians, 212
Lister, Lord, 10, 85, 89-90, 91, 128-9, 142, 147
Loewe, Dr, 185-6
London Hospital, 40
London Scottish Regt, 27-8, 35-6, 71, 74, 83, 240
Loudoun, Earl of, 19, 21
Lovell, Prof. R., 138-40
Lysozyme, 110-22, 145, 157, 158, 159, 160-1, 204

McCall, Sir A., 133-4
McElligott, Dr G. L. M., 149-50
McElroy, Bernard (father-in-law), 98
McElroy, Elizabeth, see Fleming, Elizabeth
McElroy, Sarah M., see Fleming, Lady (Sarah M.)
McGowan, Lord, 248
McKeen, John, 249
Maclean, I. H., 151
MacLeod, D., 148-9, 189
MacMillan, Mrs A., 219, 233-4
Malta fever, 46
'M. and B.', 178
Marie-José, Queen of Italy, 230
Marshall, Mrs A., 234, 243
Martin, Dr R., 147, 208
Martley, 121-2
Mary, Queen, 153
Matthews, 50
Maxwell, Dr, 184
May, Dr A. J., 59
May & Baker Ltd, 184
May, Ben, 226-7, 236-7, 239, 260, 268-9
May, Dr R., 217
Mesnil, 67
Metchnikoff, 46, 48, 51, 113-14
Microbiological Society, 244
Montgomery, Harold (nephew), 234, 248
Montgomery, Lily, 78
Montgomery, Viscount, 210-11
Moore, George, 76, 98
Moran, Lord, 32, 105-6, 143-4
Morgan, C., 208
Morgan, P., 84
Mortimer, A., 184, 185, 187
Moulton, Lord, 61

Neilson, Prof., 204-5
Netchk, Capt., 206
Netley Hospital, 45-7, 48
Newcomb, Prof. W. D., 71-2, 79, 177
Newton, Sir Isaac, 189
Nicolle, M., 67, 79
Nitti, 146
Noon, L., 49-50, 71, 78-9, 80, 104

Ogilvie, Dr A. C. F., 214-15
Oklahoma Foundation, 232-3
Orr-Ewing, J., 167

Page, Dr, 74
Pannett, Prof. C. A., 31, 32-3, 57, 193, 274-5
Paracelsus, 67
Parke, Davis & Co. Ltd, 61
Pasteur Institute, 46, 48, 206, 208, 219, 226, 236
Pasteur, Louis, 10, 42, 44, 60, 81, 123, 129, 204, 208, 218, 219, 232, 249-50, 277
Pegram family, 74-5, 100
Pegram, Marjory, 74-5, 101
Penicillin, 127, 131-42, 145-6, 148, 151, 154, 156, 157, 158, 159, 161, 162, 163-75, 179-92, 205, 206-9, 229, 230, 233, 234-6, 247, 250, 257, 266, 276-9
Penicillin, General Committee of, 185
Pfeiffer, 47
Pfizer, Charles, Inc., 185-6, 202
Pijper, 235
Pollender, Dr, 42
Poole, Major-Gen., 187
Porteous, Dr A. B., 73, 78, 96
Portmann, Prof. G., 256, 267-8
Portmann, Mme, 267
Prontosil, 145-7
Proteus vulgaris, 234-5
Pryce, Prof. D. M., 121-2, 124-5, 156, 177
Pulvertaft, Prof., 179-80, 183

Queen Charlotte's Hospital, 147

Raistrick, Prof. H., 138, 140, 141, 142, 164, 184, 185, 207
Ramon, 208
Reed, Ethel, see Florey, Dr Ethel
Reed, Walter, 262
Reid, Dr R. D., 158
Revelstoke, Lord, 106
Rhodes Foundation, 106, 159
Richards, Prof. A. N., 159, 175
Ridley, Dr F., 113, 114, 119, 134, 137, 140, 164
Rigler, Dr L., 257
Ritchie, A. M., 259
Roberts, Dr, 160
Rockefeller Foundation, 159, 162
Rockefeller Institute, 43n, 155
Rogers, Dr K. B., 141, 151
Romansky, Capt., 205
Roosevelt, Mrs E., 272
Roux, 44-5, 81
Royal Academy, 238, 245, 246
Runciman, Steven, 221

INDEX

ST MARY'S CASUALTY DEPT, 33-4
St Mary's Hospital Gazette, 63, 64n, 110
St Mary's Inoculation Service (etc.), 36-8, 39ff, 47-50, 54-65, 68-73, 78-81, 105-6
St Mary's Medical School, 33, 39, 105, 106
St Mary's Rifle Club, 36
Sanchy del Monte, A., 262
Sanders, Dr A. G., 167, 179
Sargent, J. S., 76
Schoental, Mrs, 163
Sédillot, 42
Semmelweiss, Dr, 42
Shaw, G. B., 40, 41, 51-3, 79, 89, 93, 194
Shaw, Mrs Bernard, 62
Shiga, Dr, 67
Sir William Dunn School (Oxford), 160, 163, 164
Sloggett, Sir A., 92
Smith, J. L., 185-6
Society of General Microbiology, 199, 269
Spilsbury, Sir B., 50
Steer, Wilson, 76, 78
Stewart, Dr G. T., 220, 235-6
Stewart, H., 248-9
Stirling, Marion, 22, 210
Stoker, Sir Thornby, 98
Storer, Dr E. J., 78, 117
Stratful, D., 177-8
Suffragette Movement, 62, 80
Sulphonamides, 146-55, 171, 176
Symons, Arthur, 98

TAMARGO, MARGARITA, 261-2
Taylor, Dr J., 154-5
Therapeutic Research Corporation, 184
Thom, Dr C., 127, 172-3
Thomson, 95
Times, The, on penicillin, 181-2

Todd, Dr E. W., 104, 168, 236
Trefouël, Prof. J., 146, 206, 208
Trefouël, Mme, 146, 208
Trias, 229
Trueta, J., 164
Tuffier, Dr, 94

UNIVERSITY COLLEGE HOSPITAL, 71

VALLERY-RADOT, PROF., 206, 208
Voureka, Dr Amalia Coutsouris-, 221-8, 234-5, 236-9, 241-5, 251-9, *then see* Fleming, Lady (Amalia)
Voureka, Manoli, 221
Vuillemin, 128

WAR, *see* First World War
Warren, Dr, 149
Webb-Johnson, Lord, 128n, 213
Weir, Sir C., 184
Wellcome Research Laboratories, 136
Wells, J., 58-9
Wertheimer family, 76
Westling, 127
Wheatley, John, 245
Wheeler, Dr, 51
Widal, 44, 45-6
Willcox, Dr G., 102
Wilson, Dr C. M., *see* Moran, Lord
Wright, Rev. C., 41
Wright, Sir Almroth, 12, 36-8, 39-53, 54-65, 66-8, 70-3, 76, 78-82, 84-5, 89-95, 103-8, 111, 113, 116, 117, 121, 130, 134, 137, 143, 144, 145, 150, 151, 154-5, 176, 182-3, 189, 197, 204, 213-14, 232, 250, 264, 275, 278

YEATS, W. B., 98
Yersin, 44
Young, Dr M. Y., 145, 234

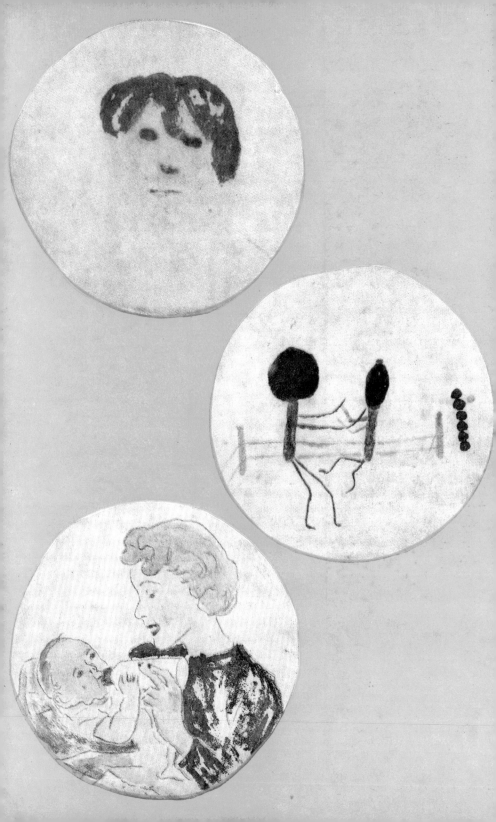